Supporting Learning
and Teaching

Supporting Learning and Teaching

David Fulton Publishers | Edited by Christine Bold

David Fulton Publishers Ltd
The Chiswick Centre, 414 Chiswick High Road, London W4 5TF

www.fultonpublishers.co.uk

First published in Great Britain in 2004 by David Fulton Publishers.
10 9 8 7 6 5 4 3 2 1

Note: The right of the individual contributors to be identified as the authors of this work has been asserted by them in accordance with the Copyright, Designs and Patents Act 1988.

David Fulton Publishers is a division of Granada Learning Limited, part of the Granada plc.

Copyright © Christine Bold and individual contributors 2004

British Library Cataloguing in Publication Data
A catalogue record for this book is available from the British Library.

ISBN 1 84312 127 1

Typeset by Servis Filmsetting Ltd, Manchester
Printed and bound in Great Britain

Contents

Contributors

Alan Barrow is an Associate Tutor at Liverpool Hope University College with particular responsibility for an education seminar group of PGCE students. He teaches about learning styles and literacy to Foundation Degree students. He is a module leader for the new Liverpool Hope University College Foundation Degree 'Supporting Learning and Teaching'. His recent experience as a head teacher makes him an ideal candidate to write a chapter exploring the issues arising from constant change in the system.

Christine Bold is the Foundation Degree Director in the Education Deanery at Liverpool Hope University College. She has published a previous book with David Fulton, *Progression in Primary Design and Technology* (1999). Her primary school experience includes the role of assessment co-ordinator, and she has conducted small-scale research projects on assessing learning and learning processes. She is interested in many educational issues and has extensive experience including secondary primary, ITT, Ofsted and consultancy. Over the past three years, she has been involved in developing and delivering courses for both primary and secondary teaching assistants.

Jean Clarkson has been a Senior Lecturer for 15 years at Liverpool Hope University College and is responsible for the year four BAQTS students and the international exchange programme. She has published articles about books for early years and international issues in *Language and Learning*.

Sue Cronin is a Senior Lecturer in mathematics and is a Module Leader of the new Liverpool Hope University College foundation degree 'Supporting Learning and Teaching'. She has published web-based materials for gifted and talented pupils for John Moores Astronomy Department and Excellence in Liverpool.

Sue Crowley is a Senior Lecturer in Education and ICT. She is curriculum leader for ICT for courses in the Education Deanery at Liverpool Hope University College. Her publications include a handbook for Sefton teachers on the use of overlay keyboards and a Learner Mentors guide for ICT. Her other interests include the use of interactive whiteboards and the Internet in teaching and learning.

Mari Cunliffe is the Study Support Manager for Sefton LEA. She leads a team who train teachers and teaching assistants on all aspects of study support. Her work includes the development of successful bids for the funding of voluntary learning projects within the LEA.

Gavin Fairbairn is Professor of Education at Liverpool Hope University College. He is qualified in primary and special education, has research interests in applied ethics and moral education, special needs, and the development of academic literacy in students and academic staff, and has published widely on these and other topics. His publications include *Reading at University: A Guide for Students* (Buckingham, Open University Press, 2001, with Susan Fairbairn).

Susan Fairbairn works part-time as a teacher at Acacias Primary School in Manchester, as part of Manchester's Diversity and Inclusion team (Ethnic Minority Achievement). She has published in social and environmental psychology and in medical and nurse education, and with Gavin Fairbairn, in addition to co-authoring *Reading at University*, she has edited three books on professional ethics.

Melanie Griffin is a Project Manager at Bury Curriculum and Language Access Service. She manages a team of bilingual support assistants. Her work and research interests are in the education of children learning English as an additional language.

Wendy Hall has been at Liverpool Hope University College for 13 years as Senior Lecturer with main interests in teaching of English and special needs. She is also the Link Tutor for students with disabilities. She has recently contributed a chapter on teaching adult dyslexics to teaching material issued by Hornsby International Dyslexia.

Pat Hughes is a Senior Lecturer at Liverpool Hope University College. She has published widely with Fulton, Scholastic, Oxford University Press, Heinemann, Nelson, Hopscotch, Folens, Multi-lingual Matters and Paul Chapman.

Shirley Potts is a Senior Lecturer at Liverpool Hope University College contributing her expertise in counselling to a range of courses. She is leader of the Special Needs BA pathway in the modular programme. She has two recent publications on counselling issues in Linchpin.

Mike Richardson is a Senior Lecturer at Liverpool Hope University College. His main area of work is in ICT and he is responsible for Year 1 of the initial teacher training for BA/QTS students. He previously taught in secondary and primary schools and was involved in the Merseyside Primary Step project. His research interests include e-Learning, innovation, and ICT and CPD in primary schools. He is actively involved in the European Teacher Exchange Network.

Roger Stevenson is a Senior Lecturer at Liverpool Hope University College and a Module Leader for Language and Literacy in 'Supporting Learning and Teaching'. He has significant experience working with and delivering courses to teaching assistants. At school level, he has both primary and secondary experience, including co-ordination of science. He has also taught science to ITT students. His research interests are teaching pupils with English as an additional language motivation modification, and the psychology of behaviour management.

Preface

Christine Bold

Overview of the Book

This book is devoted to providing the reader with an understanding of practical workplace issues in relation to relevant academic knowledge. Its aim is to encourage the reader to reflect upon his or her own practice, to analyse situations more critically and to apply knowledge from beyond the immediate workplace setting. Each chapter raises issues for further discussion. There is not space to discuss all these issues in depth here but it is hoped that the chapters will direct thoughts and provoke further interest. The book has a number of special features.

Pen Portraits

Each chapter is written with a specific person in mind whom the reader will 'meet' at the beginning of each chapter. Each represents a person working in a school supporting teaching and learning, but each one has a different role, different training and different needs. Our aim is to attempt to represent the nature and variety of adult support in educational settings, and introduce those who engage in study on Foundation Degree courses or other similar pursuits. The chapters explore some of the issues that the pen portraits raise, and provide a range of different perspectives on educational settings. There are references to all Key Stages, including the Foundation Stage where appropriate, but the authors did not necessarily intend to provide the reader with curriculum guidance or ideas for the classroom, wishing rather to explore the issues and encourage the reader to do the same in whatever their educational setting. However, some chapters such as Chapter 6, 'Connections, Questions and Resources: a Recipe for Success' by Sue Cronin do provide some useful pointers for developing classroom activities and suggestions for organisation and management as in Chapter 4, 'Raising the Bar: Improving Children's Performance through Information and Communications Technology' by Sue Crowley and Mike Richardson.

Discussion Starters

The 'discussion starters' are a pedagogical feature for tutors on courses such as foundation degrees to use with their students, or for students to develop their own supportive discussion groups. The aim of these is to encourage students to develop and debate their own ideas based on their own experiences and be confident in expressing their own views supported by experiential evidence from the workplace. This theme is present very strongly in Chapter 13 by Gavin and Susan Fairbairn who encourage students to use their stories from the workplace to inform their writing and to develop their personal thoughts and opinions about issues and not just regurgitate the thoughts of others. Each chapter raises different issues that can transcend age range, setting and the varying nature of student experiences, thus enabling participants on courses to gain a broader picture of the educational scene. In my own experience, students often find common ground, even though one might work with three-year-olds and another with sixteen-year-olds.

Reflecting on Practice

In this section, each author suggests at least one activity for students to undertake in their workplace setting and to stimulate reflection on that activity. The development of reflective practice is the theme of Chapter 1 in which I propose that we reflect at different levels, sometimes in tandem, and that each of these levels has an impact on our work in different ways. I also invite the reader to disagree with my ideas because they are simply that – ideas. However, I formulated my ideas through drawing on my own and others' experiences, and engaging in various academic pursuits. Hopefully, readers will glean from this that in the study of educational settings we should reflect on practice in relation to academic thinking about that practice, with the *intention* to change practice in some way but not necessarily making changes.

Websites

Website addresses are included with brief notes of their content to help students find information that will further support their studies. In these days of electronic media, more and more information is becoming freely available world-wide, which releases us from always having to rely on finding a particular book in under-resourced academic libraries. Having said that, we must say a word of warning about the use of electronic sources as we ourselves found the content of some sites rather dubious in relation to educational theory, and referencing sites can become rather intrusive when written in the text because of their length. In terms of content, readers must ensure that they are clear about the nature of the content. They might ask questions such as:

- Who 'owns' the site?

- Is the site related to an educational organisation, or other type of organisation?

- Does it consist of the writer's own opinion?

- Does it contain some evidence to support the writer's ideas?

- Is the information based on research or other evidence?

The reason for asking such questions is to ensure clarity about where information is coming from, and that when we relate these ideas to someone else, we represent them accurately. Readers will note in Chapter 1 and Chapter 11, 'Informing Practice: Assessing Learning' that I write about teachers' perspectives and educational judgements being influenced by their values and beliefs. When looking at a website, the reader ought to consider the site authors' values and beliefs. Because of the overlong nature of some specific web-page addresses, the website references in the text, in the reference lists and the Website sections have all been reduced to an accessible size, so that the reader can find either the home page or similar and explore further links from there. Website addresses are continually changing and although some home addresses remain relatively stable, others don't. If a website fails, then the reader should explore the words within the website address by performing a search and this will usually bring up the required reference, e.g. in www.nfer.ac.uk, a search for 'nfer' will find the desired website. By their very nature, some websites are easier to navigate than others.

References

Each chapter has its own reference list, some long and some short. Each, in addition to providing support for some of our assertions, provides a useful source of further reading should readers wish to pursue a particular line of interest. Readers will note that Gavin and Susan Fairbairn suggest in Chapter 13, 'Investigating Educational Settings: Weaving the Threads' that too many students look for lots of references in order to impress their tutors in assignments and indeed some tutors perpetuate the myth that more references mean a better depth of understanding. The two do not necessarily go hand in hand, and I would agree with Gavin and Susan that students are better to aim for quality understanding of a couple of key texts than a weak understanding of many. Some of our chapters do have many references, to illustrate the range of relevant texts and websites available for further investigation, but they are not given in order to impress the reader.

Common Strands

Gavin and Susan Fairbairn suggest that story telling can be an investigative tool within the educational setting and that stories are a valuable starting point for writing. This idea features more strongly in some chapters than in others; each author to a greater or lesser extent tells stories or includes anecdotes about practice and relates these to his or her aca-demic understandings. One aim of the book is to present different ways of using stories from our own and others' experiences in our writing.

On reading through the chapters, some ideas repeat themselves in relation to different areas of learning. For example, in Chapter 3, 'Learning and Teaching: What's Your Style?' by Pat Hughes, Figure 3.2 shows Vygotsky's (1978) 'zone of proximal development' (ZPD). The idea recurs in Chapters 5, 'Language and Literacy for Learning', Chapter 6, 'Connections, Questions and Resources: A Recipe for Success' and Chapter 8, 'Bilingual Learners: Inclusive Practice' where the authors relate the ZPD to children's learning. This is an interesting unplanned phenomenon but it demonstrates the strength of ideas that developed because of research undertaken long ago. Vygotsky was not an educationalist, but a Soviet psychologist from a very different culture to that in the UK today. His interests lay in the processes of learning, language acquisition and the relationship between language and thought. His research did not influence education in this country until it was translated, and since then almost everyone in education knows about and appreciates the idea of the ZPD. In addition, the theme of learning styles also appears in several chapters highlighting the importance of working with children in many different ways to ensure their maximum learning potential.

Another recurrent theme is that of the need for those who support teachers to work closely with teachers in a collaborative partnership for the benefit of children. This is particu-larly strong in Chapter 8 when considering bilingual learners, also in Chapter 11 when considering the importance of an assistant becoming involved in formative assessment. Not only are collaborative partnerships encouraged but the development of a broader team within the setting is necessary, e.g. when setting up and organising an out-of-school club as in Chapter 12, 'Study Support: Opening Minds with Out-of-Hours Learning' by Mari Cunliffe. Linked to this is the need for an even broader perspective about the relationships with other teams further afield on whose expertise you might draw as explained by Shirley Potts in Chapter 9, 'Counselling and Guidance in Education'. All adults who support learn-ing and teaching in educational settings are part of several teams or groupings and hold several positions within those teams. This sounds rather complicated, but most educational organisations are because we have to work in teams who cut across each other for different purposes. Here are a few examples of teams to which one assistant might belong:

- a collaborative partnership – with the teacher or other assistants;
- a leader – when working with children, or taking responsibility for a project in school;
- a team member of the overall hierarchical staff team within the school;
- a team member in the SENCO's team;
- a Key Stage 1 team member.

More and more teaching assistants are taking on their own responsibilities for aspects of school life and areas of the curriculum. I have met one who was solely responsible for the subject ICT in the school, including writing the policy and providing in-service training for the teachers. Mari Cunliffe knows several who run Study Support activities. The government is encouraging teaching assistants to take on more responsibility by introducing a new pay structure with a Higher Level Teaching Assistant grade and new training courses for those who aspire to this level and who wish to take on additional whole-class responsibilities.

Individual Perspectives

Although each chapter has a common structure in terms of the pedagogical features, the chapters are also an opportunity for the authors to express their writing in their own style, or in a style to match the subject of the chapter. Certain chapters are quite distinctive for different reasons. In Chapter 2, 'The Changing Educational Scene', Alan Barrow takes the opportunity to present a personal view of the changes during his career as a primary head teacher. It makes interesting reading and a good antidote to the usual dry overviews of the various government reports on education. In Chapter 7, Roger Stevenson takes us on 'Abbas' Journey' through the scientific process. It is a short but well-presented chapter relating theory to practice which is essentially the purpose of this book. Wendy Hall in Chapter 10, 'Inclusion: Special Needs' provides us with a clear and comprehensive overview of the main characteristics of conditions affecting children's learning in school, and some practical suggestions for supporting these children. A distinctive feature of this book is that it contains a chapter on voluntary learning, 'Study Support: Opening Minds with Out-of-Hours Learning', Chapter 12, by Mari Cunliffe. Mari shares her expertise in planning and setting up voluntary learning activities as a valuable part of the curriculum to engage disaffected young people.

In Summary

Editing this book has been an interesting but challenging experience. It has required endless checks of websites and book references; checking consistency in factual content; presenting pedagogical features and opportunities for retaining individuality in approach in order to make it interesting to the reader. I hope that in the role of editor any changes I made for the sake of accuracy or clarity have not altered the message that the authors wished to make as experts in their own fields. Most of all, I hope that readers find the book stimulating and useful in their studies when trying to make sense of the academic ideas about everyday practice.

1

The Reflective Practitioner

Christine Bold

Meet Geoff

Hi! I am a part-time learning support assistant (behaviour) in a secondary school where I work every morning, supporting a specific group of children in different lessons and through withdrawing individuals and groups. My role in supporting learning is to motivate the group of children and encourage them to join in with every aspect of the lesson. During whole-class activities, I encourage my group to watch and listen. I use the whiteboard to copy the teacher's writing. This means they can focus on the words more easily. I provide reinforcement charts for good work, or good behaviour. I make sure each child understands the task.

The children I support have short attention spans and an inability to focus on the requirements of the task. They have bursts of aggressive behaviour towards other children in the group. Although I attended LEA Behaviour Management training in 2002 I need help with coping with outbursts of challenging behaviour during group work. I do not have a problem during whole-class activities because they behave well for the teacher with my support. When I work with individuals, they are sometimes unresponsive but not aggressive.

Introduction

Reflection on practice is at the core of professional development. Education professionals attend courses and they accept different responsibilities in their constantly changing roles, but these developmental activities do not necessarily demonstrate the type of reflection in which they engage. Geoff, who supports children with challenging behaviour, has obviously engaged in some reflection and recognised that he has some difficulty in managing behaviour when the teacher is not present. His reflection might be very superficial, or it might be in great depth. The person involved might have considered some different solutions; tried and evaluated some alternative approaches; he might have sought help from others. The fact that the teaching assistant has communicated a problem does not necessarily convey the level of reflection in which he has engaged. In this chapter, I will describe some aspects of my own development as a reflective practitioner and provide some examples of reflective events from a range of professional situations to raise awareness of some specific issues related to behaviour management. I will also discuss the nature of reflexivity and its relationship to reflective practice and clarify the meaning of these important terms.

In educational training, particularly in initial teacher training, we promote reflective practice as an important concept, although the word 'training' implies that such reflective activity is unnecessary. We might describe reflection very simply as 'looking at oneself', although it is more than that when applied to the educational organisation as a workplace because reflection has to involve looking at oneself in relation to the impact one has on others. As an observer of one's own practice, a person makes judgements about that practice based upon previous knowledge and understanding of the situation. According to Siraj-Blatchford and Siraj-Blatchford (1999), making judgements about observations based upon our previous understandings is a reflexive process. We 'refer back', and compare our new experiences with the previous ones, trying to accommodate these experiences within our current understanding. Each person who observes the same incident might see exactly the same thing, but will interpret the event differently according to his or her previous understanding. Each individual involved in the situation ought to recognise that others will interpret the situation differently and should be able to represent the differing views in constructing a holistic account to present to others. The concept of reflexivity is therefore important when considering the nature of reflection and, in particular, reflection on classroom events because the teacher, teaching assistant and children will hold different views about the same event. We all know of situations where a child has gone home to tell parents an account of a particular event that is not quite accurate in the eyes of the adults involved in the situation. When parents contact the school, teachers often accuse the child of manipulating the story or telling untruths to suit his or her own circumstances, but often the child believes the account to be true. Based on the child's current knowledge and understanding of the situation, it is true. Unless everyone in the situation understands the notion of reflexivity, that people can have different understandings of the same event, the prospect of a suitable resolution is bleak. Too often, in such situations, the child becomes the scapegoat for everybody's wrath. Although Siraj-Blatchford and Siraj-Blatchford (1999) discuss reflexivity in relation to research processes and not specifically in relation to teaching, reflexivity holds an important place within the reflective process in which effective practitioners engage. A colleague recently suggested that we should refer to *reflexive* practice rather than *reflective* practice when working with trainees. The idea presented was that use of the term 'reflexive practice' emphasised that reflection is about the development of new knowledge and understanding of a situation based on previous knowledge and understanding, and taking into account other people's perspectives on the situation. The implication was that reflection might be very superficial if reflexive thinking is not involved.

We cannot ignore the relationship between reflexivity and reflection and I believe that reflection occurs at different levels. I aim to identify these levels and provide a broad model for analysis of reflective practice. I will continue to use the term 'reflective practice' rather than 'reflective teaching', a term used by Pollard (1997). Pollard's ideas stem from those of Dewey (1916, 1933, in Pollard 1996: 4–5). Dewey wrote about reflective experience in an event as passing through these steps:

1 A perplexing and confusing event occurs.

2 A tentative interpretation of the event is made.

3 A careful analysis of the event defines the problem.

4 The original hypothesis is modified based on the analysis.

5 A plan of action is applied to the situation and evaluated.

This is very like the scientific process, or a problem-solving process. Dewey was suggesting that a reflective experience had to result in some action or response to the situation and a continued state of doubt about the responses made. Stages 3, 4 and 5 are crucial in identifying the experience as reflective and moving beyond trial and error. In applying this sequence to the classroom situation, reflection might result in a change in practice, potentially for the better. Better or more effective practice means different things to different people. This chapter is not the place to debate the meaning of effective practice, but to emphasise that reflection on practice must necessarily involve practitioners in judgements about effectiveness, whatever their view may be. Dewey's description of the process seems rather rigid and time-consuming when considering the day-to-day classroom situation where adults working with children have to 'think on their feet' and continually face variants of previously understood events. Donald Schön (1983, in Pollard 1996: 5–7) describes the reflective practitioner as one who engages in 'reflection-in-action', reflecting on practice while events are unfolding and not just after the event. Both of these aspects of reflective practice are important, but they still do not illuminate the nature of the events on which reflection should take place, or the criteria by which we make judgements in order to make changes. In the educational climate at the beginning of the twenty-first century, such reflection inevitably relates to children's levels of attainment and not necessarily to the quality of learning. In many people's minds 'levels of attainment' and 'quality' are always synonymous, but I disagree with this, having had personal experience of children's results being inflated through revision practices that enabled success in the short term at the expense of secure conceptual learning. Again, this is not the place to debate the nature of quality, but to highlight that different interpretations exist that will have an impact on the type of reflective activity occurring in classrooms.

As a focus, the chapter will present some specific aspects in my own and others' development in learning how to manage pupil behaviour, and will try to identify key issues in a complex and interrelated set of concepts. The focus on managing pupil behaviour enables readers to engage in the reflective process by making comparisons with their own workplace experiences. With such a focus, it seems that other important aspects that have an impact on the education system are ignored, e.g. race, ethnicity, religion or sexuality, to name a few. The focus on managing behaviour allows access to reflective thinking by the majority of readers who will most likely have experienced some situations with children and young people in which behaviour management has been an issue. Some of the other issues have a more localised impact, in a particular school or a particular Local Education Authority (LEA). This makes reflection on these issues more difficult as not all readers will have personal experiences to make comparisons with. However, I must stress that a broad range of issues affect educational establishments and all require some reflective thought, even when we do not think they have a direct impact on our current situation.

Here are the three proposed levels of reflective activity:

1 Classroom reflection.

2 Workplace reflection.

3 Extended reflection.

Reflective Practice Analysed

1. Classroom reflection

This is reflection at a very personal level relating to satisfaction about one's own performance in a specific situation. It relates to the 'feel good' factor. Typically, a teacher will come out of a lesson feeling good about the way it went and thinking that it went well and the children enjoyed it. This is a very common level of reflection that we all engage in, but perhaps more so early on in a teaching career than later. During my first year of teaching science in a secondary school, I taught many classes containing children exhibiting challenging behaviours. If everyone behaved and experiments were successfully completed, my evaluation was that the lesson was a 'good' one. Reflexive behaviours developed as I responded to the 'signs' warning me that behaviour might deteriorate. This was mainly 'reflection in action' as described by Schön (Pollard 1996) and I describe my behaviour as reflexive in the sense that working knowledge of previous similar situations in my own classroom where the child's view of the situation was different, informed my practice. This was mainly on an *ad hoc* trial and error basis with little real consideration for the development of long-term strategies to manage the children's behaviour. Good lesson pacing led to minimal disruption. These were important developments as timing and the ability to make rapid judgements are both strategies for reducing the complexity of the classroom situation to prevent behaviour deterioration (Doyle 1977, in Pollard 1996: 210–12). Through all of my first year of teaching, I rarely thought about whether the children had effectively learned the lesson objectives. In relation to children's learning, my reflection on practice was almost non-existent. However, I made significant achievements in my ability to manage the behaviour of the children, and consequently to improve the learning potential within the lesson. It was easier during this first year to focus on managing behaviour rather than on the effectiveness of learning.

In my experience, the absence of the feel good factor stimulates more depth of reflection because if a reflective teacher does not feel good about an activity, the result is often a dissection of the lesson events to discover what was wrong, with the aim of improving it. My own early teaching experience shows that the feel good factor might prevent us from examining some elements of our practice more closely. In my first year of teaching, I failed to examine closely whether the children were actually learning anything. I relied on responses to homework and examination results, rather than any on-going knowledge of the learning processes in my classroom. The feel good factor can therefore limit depth of reflection, as is often witnessed in trainees, who feel good because they have survived the lesson, and the children have enjoyed it, whether they have achieved the objectives or not. In today's climate of accountability and pressure to achieve the highest results possible in tests, many people involved in children's learning have lost the feel good factor in relation to the more general events in the classroom, but instead focus on whether the children have shown any improvement on previous standards over a period of time. The feel good factor is still there, but it relates to results rather than children's learning. If the result of reflection is action or change, then classroom-level reflection provides an immediate impact on the situation providing the feel good factor does not get in the way.

2. Workplace reflection

At the workplace level, the reflective process relates the immediate teaching and learning situation to other professionals within the school and the whole-school objectives. In many of today's classrooms from Key Stage 1 and beyond, the focus of reflection is comparative measures of recorded achievements rather than the examination of teaching and learning practices for conceptual understanding. The influence of the Office for Standards in Education (Ofsted) and in particular the publication of results has led to an over-emphasis on such measures. We could regard this as looking beyond the immediate situation but such reflection seems very limited as it relies on test results rather than qualitative measures. Such reflective practices can also be divisive within an educational setting as each teacher compares the progress of the class in relation to the progress made with another teacher. Comparisons made in this way are not always valid because children do not make consistent progress along the learning curve, and because the instruments measuring attainment are often not comparable from year to year. If reflexive practice is that which teachers develop in response to reflecting on significant classroom events such as the learners' responses to activities, then a focus on comparative measures limits the development of reflexive practice. For practitioners to develop reflexive practice, they must engage in reflection upon qualitative issues and consider different people's perspectives on events rather than quantitative measures. The current focus on the latter, I believe, is detrimental to the development of informed reflexive practice. Elliott (1991, in Pollard 1996: 18–21) identified a new professionalism with reflection on real practical situations as the core. Elliott claimed that the teacher is not the infallible expert that society envisages and one only has to read the newspapers today to realise there are tensions between the expectations of society in general and the nature of true professional development. Reflexive practice develops over time, as new ideas become actual classroom events that are effective for the teacher and for the children's learning. Unfortunately, the British government strategy is to provide a cascade model of training for new initiatives that many perceive as the prescription for success, following the models blindly for quick success (improvement in national test results) without reflection on the real educational impact in the long term.

In relation to my own development with regard to managing behaviour, workplace reflection occurred when comparing the impact of a behaviour management strategy for a particular child from one lesson to the next, or in comparing the strategies used with different children in different situations. It also occurred when comparing my practice with that of another teacher in the school, and in trying to copy effective strategies witnessed in other classrooms, e.g. waiting for silence. Quite often, those effective strategies did not work for me, which was quite frustrating. The fact that they did not work stimulated recognition of the need to find behaviour management strategies that suited my teaching style and my personality. In particular, the strategy of waiting for silence never worked for me at the beginning of my career. The children were used to me being noisy, enthused, excited and openly challenging about their learning. They were not used to me being quiet and imposing my persona in a mild-mannered way. Many myths about being a 'good teacher' exist. For example, in two of my primary schools a quiet classroom was the main indicator of being a good practitioner, and as mine was often 'noisy', other teachers interpreted this as 'losing control' when in fact the children were learning a lot, but in a different way. It is a myth that good teachers do not have discipline problems, and that the ability to exert quiet power over children leads to good learning (Olsen and Cooper 2001).

3. Extended reflection

Extended reflection goes beyond the immediate school situation and compares it with practice witnessed in other schools, read about in popular journals or evidenced in international research. In relation to managing pupil behaviour, it occurs when:

- changing jobs, as a teacher compares practices in the new school with the old, e.g. a teacher is in a new situation with children from a different social background, or a different culture;

- outside agencies come into the school to help the teachers and assistants address children's difficult behaviour and develop effective behaviour management strategies;

- people attend in-service courses of a professional and/or academic nature.

Ofsted inspectors also make qualitative judgements about teaching based on whether they can observe learning taking place in the classroom. For example, from observations made in schools placed under Special Measures the inspectors noted that disruptive behaviour resulted from weak teaching, poor school management, inconsistent approaches to discipline by staff and lack of knowledge about behaviour management (Ofsted 1999). The inspection process is potentially a step towards reflexive thinking for the teacher, with weaknesses identified by the inspectors leading to the formulation of an action plan for the whole school. Unfortunately, a significant number of early inspections in the early 1990s created a negative culture towards the inspection process, hence the strong move towards school self-evaluation that began in 2000. Attendance on an LEA course and particularly on a Higher Education postgraduate course should prompt reflection at this level where time away from the classroom can promote a more distant kind of reflection. A course often provides an opportunity to look back over a particular period and consider progress in knowledge, skills and understanding about the issues. It also offers opportunities to meet with colleagues from other schools and compare experiences, thus learning from each other.

In my experience, reflection at the extended level has been the most challenging and the most revealing. LEA courses and involvement in local initiatives with teachers from other schools had a significant impact on my practice. Advisory teacher demonstration lessons in school, for dance, music and drama, and taught sessions on behaviour management had a strong immediate impact. They provided a clear role model, a set of effective actions that I could put into place. Only on leaving my original education authority did I recognise the localised nature of its professional development programme. Reflection at this level altered my practice to the greatest extent, especially in relation to teaching strategies for particular aspects of the curriculum and in managing specific behaviour patterns. For example, I learned that setting tasks as short, time-limited or quantified activities improved both productivity and learning potential for many children in a particularly disruptive class. Simple solutions often produced the most effective results. This soon became a reflexive process, modifying and adapting tasks according to children's responses to a particular activity or situation.

In particular, attendance on taught courses away from school and requiring assessments focusing on analysing practice encouraged me to question values, beliefs and assumptions about education in general and moved me away from thinking only about my immediate teaching and learning setting or the workplace, into making comparisons with other educational situations world-wide. My truly reflexive thinking was something that developed over a longer period due to the complex nature of some of the issues that I explored in preparing for assignments. I could argue that for extended reflection to be effectively established and meaningful, then teachers must engage in courses requiring some focused classroom research and assessment of their thinking in relation to practice elsewhere. However, in relation to classroom practice in general, postgraduate award-bearing courses can sometimes focus a teacher on specific aspects of the curriculum in depth to the detriment of others, while a teacher attending a broad spectrum of locally based courses might derive a more generalist reflective approach that has a valuable and immediate impact on practice.

Another interesting phenomenon is the transferability of reflective experiences. When studying physical education (PE) as a main subject in college, I was very impressed by the philosophical stance taken in the department. We were all encouraged to compete with ourselves, and not to compare our performance with others during lessons. At the same time, we also learned to become good competitors in a healthy and realistic competitive environment. That philosophy works in any teaching and learning situation, not just in PE lessons, encouraging the children to take the opportunity during lessons to improve their own skills, knowledge and understanding and not to compare themselves continually with others. It benefits the children once they recognise the sense of achievement they gain by working in this way. Thus, the philosophical ideal promoted in a PE department in college was transferable to a variety of learning situations, with learners of all ages. The idea of competing against oneself is a very powerful motivator. In a recent article, mathematics teacher Becky Silvester (2003) relates similar transferable experiences as a learner on a Mountain Leadership course.

She identifies clearly her difficulty with some of the learning situations and that this made her aware of issues about learning in the classroom. For example, she became more aware that knowledge was not something the teacher owns to pass on to the pupils but something to share and generate together. She transferred this awareness to her own teaching.

Quite often when faced with course materials that challenge current practice teachers and teaching assistants can feel threatened and extremely negative towards the ideas and even the person presenting them. My own experience is that my feelings of negativity often prompt me to try out the new proposal and to make final judgements in practice. Most often, my negative feelings subside as I begin to realise that presenters make suggestions based on knowledge and understandings of a range of educational situations beyond my own, and that I can usually change my own practice for the better, or at least add to my repertoire of alternative approaches. The purpose of many courses, and a chapter such as this, is to challenge individual thinking and to broaden awareness of other perspectives, i.e. to encourage reflexivity.

Further Examples of Reflective Experiences

In this section, I invite you to consider the type of reflection in which the teaching assistants and other adults have engaged. You may or may not agree with the different levels of reflective activity that I identified, but you might recognise different types of reflective activity in the examples. My aim is to invite readers to reflect on their own practice through recognition of similar situations and through identifying similarities and differences. Four core issues related to behaviour management are discussed in order to promote reflexive thinking. The Elton Report in 1989 identified the behaviour of the teacher (in today's context, this includes the teaching assistant) as the single most important factor in determining students' behaviour (Gilbert 2002). The Elton Report findings echo those of research undertaken in the 1970s that classified teachers as 'provocative' or 'insulative' with regard to disruptive pupils. A teacher who believes that deviant pupils have no interest in school will generally provoke such pupils into continuing or worsening their deviant behaviour (provocative) (Hargreaves *et al.* 1975, in Pollard 1996: 226–7). In contrast, a teacher who believes that such pupils really do want to join in will change the learning conditions to suit the pupil and reduce the deviant behaviour (insulative). Some of the examples below show some of the features of these two extremes.

Example 1: Earning respect

Nursery nurse Ann experienced few behaviour problems during her ten years working in Key Stage 1 in a small infant school. The children generally respected the teachers and completed all their work. There was a very positive ethos in the school. After a career break of six years, she decided to accept work as a teaching assistant at her children's school with Key Stage 2 children. One class was almost impossible to teach and several children in other classes exhibited challenging behaviour patterns. During small-group activities, Ann found that some children initially exhibited extremes of behaviour that she was unused to coping with e.g. refusing to do any work. Ann noticed that the children behaved well for her when she 'didn't keep criticising and cared about us' (one child's comment). It seemed that she gradually earned their respect, and subsequent improvements in behaviour, by caring about them as individuals and spending some time talking about issues that mattered to them. Mutual respect was the way forward.

Example 2: Changing curriculum and organisation

During the 1980s a northern secondary school in Britain had a policy of 'mixed ability' teaching during the first year (now Year 7) after which the children were put into sets according to their performance on their mathematics and English end-of-year results. A newly qualified science teacher, Liz, taught a significant number of the second and third year (now Years 8 and 9) lower-attaining groups in which pupils exhibited extremes of behaviour that were intolerable in a science laboratory. The impact was detrimental to the learning potential during these lessons, as she could not provide such groups with the same 'hands-on' practical experiences as the others for health and safety reasons. These children, at the age of 12, had clearly decided that learning in school was not for them. They would ask, 'Don't you know we're thick?' if she gave them any activities that required any thought. On the other hand, her first year mixed ability groups were a joy to teach, although some children obviously had difficulty with understanding the content. All the children enjoyed the lessons, and a significant number appeared to have learned something. The end-of-year examination results shattered any illusions of learning taking place for a significant number of children who received marks of less than 20 per cent, earning them a place in lower-attaining groups for the second year. During the second year, there was a marked alteration of attitude and deterioration of behaviour among those who previously had been interested and alert to the subject. The challenge therefore was that of maintaining a positive ethos and a sense of achievement while the school labelled the children as failures. Without a positive ethos and sense of achievement, behaviour management was a challenge.

The departmental response to concerns raised by Liz was to set the children into broad attainment groups in the first year ensuring that they could teach children a differentiated curriculum. The aim was to give the lower-attaining children a better chance of success. Teaching these groups appeared successful and effective but unfortunately the children all had to sit the same examination at the end of the year and the lower attainers still had poor results with the same devastating effect. The impact of common tests and examinations was divisive. Liz was unsuccessful in establishing agreement for differentiated examinations to allow children success with their differentiated taught curriculum. Liz is now Head of Special Needs in a large inner-city comprehensive and focuses her attention on enabling the children to make the best use of the opportunities on offer through knowledge of their preferred learning styles.

Example 3: Differing philosophies

Differing educational philosophies and teaching strategies play an important part in behaviour management problems at all educational levels. Before the introduction of the National

Curriculum, Bob, a primary school teacher with several years' experience, believed that children should be independent learners, and that his role was to provide learning situations that would encourage independence of thought. The children thought differently. Previous teachers spoon-fed the children a specific curriculum diet. Parents and children measured success by the number of workbooks the children managed to complete. Children learned how to do long multiplication, for example, with little understanding of how it worked. Bob had recently gained an Advanced Diploma in Mathematical Education and he recognised the importance of children understanding their mathematics. He encouraged the use of apparatus; he slowed down the pace that some children worked at because they were racing through books with little real development of knowledge and understanding. Bob's ways of working were unusual for the children and their parents. He expected independent qualities that the children did not yet have, and consequently became frustrated with the situation. This resulted in some children responding with negative behaviours and subsequent criticism of Bob from other members of staff and parents. On the other hand, he noticed that other children, who had previously shown challenging behaviour patterns in other classes, would flourish in his class when freed from the constraints of the workbook, and provided with opportunities to extend their own ideas. This gave him the impetus to continue developing appropriate strategies to develop children as independent learners. Bob is now a head teacher of a successful primary school and he still believes that developing independent learners is important, while at the same time recognising that changing philosophies requires a slower pace. He works hard to have a consistently applied philosophy within the school as a key to good behaviour management, in addition to developing independent learning skills. He draws on the national strategy materials and recommendations to provide the most effective learning situations for the pupils while still maintaining that sense of independence. Bob has a common-sense approach to whole-class teaching and suggests that even in a whole-class lesson children learn independently. Nobody else can learn for them, they have to do that for themselves!

Example 4: Intrinsic and extrinsic rewards

An intrinsic reward might be the satisfaction of having learned something new, while an extrinsic reward might be a tick, a smiley face, open verbal praise or a house point. Jenny, a learning support assistant in Year 2 since 2000, works in a school where the philosophy is that effective learning only takes place when children earn intrinsic rewards. This placed great pressures on the teacher and the teaching assistant to provide educational opportunities to which all children will respond positively and gain some internal satisfaction of having succeeded. The notion of intrinsic reward is a sophisticated one and in the current social climate in Britain it is not a popular one. Many people complete activities in their daily lives for some extrinsic reward in the first instance. The intrinsic satisfaction of completing an activity well is often a by-product. For a school to adopt a policy of not providing extrinsic rewards of any kind is to ride against much of the experiences of the children outside school. Jenny was used to giving children smiley faces to place on a class chart in her previous post and this helped to maintain discipline. In Jenny's first class a significant number of children had disruptive behaviour patterns, that a 'good behaviour' chart or giving 'stars' or other extrinsic rewards (not sweets for health and safety reasons) might help to address. The senior management team of the school would not allow the use of such charts. Jenny and her class teacher now have a range of different strategies, most of which are related to ensuring the correct pitch of work, effective management of classroom activities through working as a team and motivation strategies. If children are motivated to learn, then they will behave well. Jenny relates motivation to the intrinsic satisfaction children gain from an activity. Her thoughts about this seem similar to those of Gilbert (2002) who claims that motivation comes from within. He says that teachers should ask themselves how they could get the children to motivate themselves. Motivation is essentially an emotion and is not something we can measure externally. Jenny now accepts that an extrinsic reward might motivate children to want to repeat the pleasure of gaining another reward, but an intrinsic reward of pleasure in learning will motivate children to learn for its own sake, rather than an external prize. Sustaining such an approach each year without extrinsic rewards is proving a challenge, but attendance on courses has provided Jenny with a range of effective strategies.

Reflecting on Behaviour Management Issues

The above examples highlight some fundamental issues that face all of us involved in education and which we cannot always address as individuals. Management of disruptive pupil behaviour has always been an issue in schools and teacher behaviour is usually the important factor. Deviant behaviour is a result of many social issues, but in schools the issues of respect, appropriate curriculum and curriculum organisation, personal expectations, school philosophy and reward systems are strong influences on whether behaviour (a) deteriorates or (b) is manageable in school.

Most behaviour problems manifest themselves because of the situations in which children find themselves at school. I agree with the findings reported by Hargreaves *et al.* (1975, in Pollard 1996: 226–7) that some teachers provoke further deviant behaviour because their philosophy of education is such that they hold no respect for the pupils exhibiting such behaviour and do not really wish to teach them. I recognise that this statement is contentious, and deliberately so. However, I also recognise that in the short term any adult working with children has to develop strategies appropriate to the situation so that he or she manages behaviour and children's learning potential is maximised.

In conclusion, I hope that the reader has identified different levels of reflection occurring in the examples. In any case, the examples should provoke a reflexive response in relation to one's own experience. The first example is highly relevant to Geoff who might find that explicitly showing respect for the children, as young people in their own right, will alleviate some of the challenging behaviours. The second shows the importance of continued reflection and, if the systems are resistant to change, then the approach with the children requires modification. For Liz, the result was to help children learn how to work within the system instead of trying to change the system. Bob successfully integrated his own philosophy of independent learning into a whole-school situation, taking into account the demands of national strategy recommendations. In Jenny's case, she learned that motivation from within is the key to effective learning situations and developed new strategies to support this. Each example provides something for each of us to reflect on. Each time we hear someone's story about his or her educational experiences we can ask ourselves, 'Which aspects are similar to my own situation, and which are very different?'

Discussion Starters

1 What constitutes a reflective activity?
2 Does reflection always have to result in action?
3 What is reflexive thinking?

Reflecting on Practice

1 Keep a reflective diary for one month. In this diary, record the daily events that occurred and your reflection on those events. It is helpful to set it out as below, and to use different colours if you return to an event for further reflection after further reading, or discussion.

Left-hand page	Right-hand page
Date	
Record events here.	Write reflective comments here.
	Add further comments based on reading or discussion with others in a different colour of pen.
	Include references to further reading or relevant school documentation.

2 Choose one of the following situations and consider how you might respond to the situation. Draw on your current level of experience, knowledge and understanding of such situations and identify further aspects to explore for your own development:

(a) Situation 1

During one-to-one support activity, a sixteen-year-old girl raises questions about her own sexuality and relationships with other girls.

(b) Situation 2

At playtime, some six-year-old children are teasing a new child about the colour of his skin and his different clothes.

Websites

www.dmu.ac.uk/~jamesa/learning/contents.htm – useful links to learning theories and reflective practice.

www.leeds.ac.uk/educol/ – links to electronic literature on educational research policy and practice.

www.nfer.ac.uk/ – links to research reports on various aspects of education.

www.ofsted.gov.uk/publications/ – search for behaviour.

www.standards.dfes.gov.uk/schoolimprovement/ – links to 'Schools Facing Challenging Circumstances' and 'Schools Causing Concern'.

www.teachernet.gov.uk – useful link to 'Teaching and Learning' that includes behaviour.

References

Gilbert, I. (2002) *Essential Motivation in the Classroom*, London: Routledge Falmer.

Office for Standards in Education (1999) *Lessons Learned from Special Measures: A Report from the Office of Her Majesty's Chief Inspector of Schools*, London: Ofsted Publications.

Olsen, J. and Cooper, P. (2001) *Dealing with Disruptive Students in the Classroom*, London: TES/Kogan Page Limited.

Pollard, A. (ed.) (1996) *Readings for Reflective Teaching in the Primary School*, London: Cassell.

Pollard, A. (1997) *Reflective Teaching in the Primary School: A Handbook for the Classroom*, 3rd edn, London: Cassell.

Silvester, B. (2003) 'Learning about my learning', *Mathematics Teaching*, 183, 34–5.

Siraj-Blatchford, I. and Siraj-Blatchford, J. (1999) 'Reflexivity, social justice and educational research', in Scott, D. (ed.), *Values and Educational Research*, London: Institute of Education, University of London, pp. 93–110.

2

The Changing Educational Scene

Alan Barrow

Meet Rachel

Hello, I am a part-time teaching assistant in an infant school supporting the Reception class and English in Year 1, in particular Early Literacy Support (ELS). In Reception I ensure the children stay on task and that they know what to do. In Year 1, I use many of the ELS strategies for supporting the children in all aspects of their English work.

Initially, I gained an NNEB qualification and more recently, I attended LEA National Literacy Strategy training. I work with children in Reception identified as needing one-to-one support. In Year 1, I work with children identified as 'vulnerable' – with a reading age well below their chronological age, difficulties in composing writing, handwriting and spelling. I need help with my changing role. I need an insight into the ways that children learn and I need teaching strategies for multi-sensory learning. I want to understand the reasons for changing the ways we approach teaching and learning with younger children. In particular, I would like to become more involved in working with parents in addressing their children's learning needs.

Introduction: School Life pre-1988

This chapter aims to provide Rachel and others like her with a historical overview of the changes in education and the reasons for them. It presents for reflection and discussion a perspective on those changes that have transformed the education service in this country from 1988 to the present day. In order for readers to accept, at least in part, the veracity of the statements made in the following paragraphs, it is important they know the writer's perspective. I was head teacher of a smaller primary school from 1982 until 1988 and was accustomed to running a school pre-National Curriculum. Then, in 1988, the year the National Curriculum entered the statute books, I became head teacher of a larger primary school. Until my retirement in 2002, I oversaw a continual flow of changes that affected every facet of school life. My experiences provide the main substance of this chapter.

Pre-1988 and the advent of the National Curriculum, the educational establishment in

England and Wales had escaped without too much interference from government ministers for several decades. Schools immediately before 1988 were mainly autonomous institutions. Head teachers largely decided the content taught in their schools and, sometimes, the teaching method as well. Cunningham (1990: 4) writes that the Education Act of 1944 did no more than define primary education as 'that suitable for the requirements of junior pupils'. Successive governments had failed to define a primary curriculum more clearly than that. Within a school, although there might be schemes of work in core subjects that teachers were expected to follow, class teachers had a great deal of freedom to determine how they were to teach and the amount of emphasis they placed on any subject. There was no entitlement to a nationally determined education as parents might expect for their children.

Before 1988, children would encounter very different approaches from individual teachers in their local primary school. Teachers acquired reputations for subjects in which they excelled and children would know that when they reached a particular class they would encounter geography, art, physical education or music taught with excitement and enthusiasm. In some ways, this richness was good for the children, who experienced an inspirational and creative approach from a teacher free from the constraints of a closely controlled syllabus. However, children would also encounter teachers who would deliver only the very rudiments of wisdom in subjects they did not like or might omit these subjects entirely from their plans. Moreover, educational fashions sometimes came and went. The teaching in some schools reflected the influential views of local authority advisers promoting their very individual philosophies to teachers and heads. In fairness, some of these were exceptionally gifted educationists who enhanced the teaching in their schools.

One charismatic adviser actively promoted Her Majesty's Inspector Robin Tanner's view that all teachers should learn 'how to make the least promising classroom good to look at, shipshape and easy to work in' (Tanner 1987: 142). He considered the study of poetry, music, book-making, calligraphy and nature as essential for children's development. Along with Tanner, he saw the use of a wide range of beautiful artefacts, sensitively displayed in a classroom, as starting points a teacher could use to inspire children's creativity in many different art forms. Unfortunately, Tanner's ideas, and those of the adviser, demanded a great deal of insight and a generous quantity of natural talent on the part of teachers for them to translate into effective teaching methods. I have seen these ideas, in the worst instances, translated into repetitive and superficial activities, catering for only a few talented children in a very narrow context.

The Snowball of Educational Reform

The report *Children and Their Primary Schools* (Plowden 1967) was an insightful and balanced review of schools at that time. It made many excellent recommendations but right-wing politicians disparaged it as being woolly and ineffective. They used it as a weapon in their demands for a rigorous reform of the English education system (Kemball-Cook 1972). The Schools Council, formed in 1964, had the remit to unite teachers, Local Education Authorities

(LEAs) and the government in developing curriculum, improving teachers' effectiveness and devising improvements for other areas of education. Throughout the country teachers' centres developed and many excellent initiatives were set in place by teachers for teachers. However, there was little co-ordination of ideas between these centres and the government perceived the Schools Council to be ineffective. It had, perhaps, been too subtle, not sufficiently clear in communicating its intentions. As Thomas (1990) suggests in his discussion of the Schools Council's work, it set out to 'fine-tune' the existing situation whereas the mood beginning to build within government was for broad and radical change. The government disbanded the Council in 1982.

In the late 1980s, teacher unions remained unable or unwilling to embrace changes to the status quo, despite warnings that the Conservative Government was intent on radical reform of the public sector. It would be fair to say that the government saw the vast majority of schools as closed communities, not accountable, unclear in their objectives, subscribing, in the main, to vague ideologies. This self-determining model of education was never likely to appeal to a government intent on strengthening its control over the public sector and over LEAs.

In the run-up to the passing of the 1988 Education Reform Act, the Conservatives were mindful that a previous Labour government had launched the great educational debate as far back as 1976. In that year, James Callaghan, Prime Minister of the Labour Government, gave his Ruskin College speech. Using agricultural and horticultural analogy, he argued that the school curriculum should no longer be a *secret garden*, that there were no *holy cows* in education and no areas, therefore, that 'profane hands were not allowed to touch' (Brooks 1991: 6). In essence, he asserted the right of central government to have a controlling interest in education and established the notion that government should be able to determine whether the education services were delivering value for money.

The Conservative Government of 1988 received input from many and varied contributors – Her Majesty's Inspectors of Schools, for example. It acknowledged the difficulties in determining exactly what should be included in a National Curriculum and how best to do this (Thomas 1990). Conservative Secretaries of State for Education including Keith Joseph, Mark Carlisle and Kenneth Baker had presided over a decade of educational debate. The government was not prepared to put off indefinitely grasping the nettle of educational reform and published *The National Curriculum – 5–16: A Consultative Document* in July 1987. After a short period of consultation, with very little change, it became law through the Education Reform Act (ERA) of 1988. It precipitated a continual programme of change, imposed from the top down with little consultation of or contribution from teachers. Teachers had no control over the pace of the reforms heading the way of their profession and their school.

The Impact of the National Curriculum

The 1988 Education Reform Act created the first true National Curriculum as a statutory requirement. It established the subjects all teachers in all schools would teach. It stipulated levels of attainment all children would aim to achieve. It devised national tests (to begin in 1991) that all children would sit and proposed publication of results to which all parents had access. A universally acknowledged, minimum entitlement for all children was born. In addition, the concept of public accountability in education was recognised. The Act established an inspection process with quality control the job of an independent body, the Office for Standards in Education – Ofsted.

Pre-National Curriculum, there might have been little notion of quality control but there had been a lot of thought given to child development and the growth of children's intellect and understanding. As far back as 1926, the Report of the Hadow Committee recommended that a primary curriculum 'be thought of . . . in terms of activity and experience rather than knowledge to be acquired and facts to be stored' (Brooks 1991: 89). The child was at the centre of a learning situation and the best teachers used their understanding of how children learned to inform their teaching. Discovery learning, practical activity and group work replaced a didactic model of learning. Teachers used an approach that sought to give all learning a purpose by making links between subject areas and placing a theme or topic at the centre of their planning. They taught the core subjects with rigour but also with purpose, enabling children to apply their mathematical and language skills to problem solving and communication across the curriculum. To their dismay, they found the subjects of the new National Curriculum written as separate entities, not as coherent parts of a whole. The government showed some sensitivity in its approach by introducing the three core subjects and, later, the seven foundation subjects over a phased period – two years in total. This did not really help matters, however. Schools assimilated the requirements for mathematics, English and science reasonably successfully within their existing long-term planning but found that, in making provision for the content within the programmes of study for those subjects, they had allocated insufficient time within the school day for history, geography, art, music, technology, physical education (PE) and religious education when they came on stream. The result was curriculum overload. Something akin to panic was beginning to be felt within staff rooms the length and breadth of England. A subject-based curriculum was not the only model the government might have chosen. Brooks (1991) examines some elegant alternatives. A different approach might well have fitted more easily into the existing primary school environment and resulted in reform with less upheaval.

Rethinking Teaching and Assessment

The new subject-based curriculum schools forced schools to question whether their previously successful approaches could continue. They increasingly perceived subject-specific teaching as the only way to deliver the content. Teachers sought out new ways of planning and began to change how they organised their children. More worrying to teachers was the publication of national test, Standard Assessment Tasks (SATs) results. Teachers became concerned that the public would use the outcomes of these tests as a crude yardstick to measure their schools' performance. They became obsessed with grids for recording every child's encounter with every statement of attainment in every subject. They needed to ensure that their children were on course to achieve the required levels of attainment at the end of each Key Stage. Measuring performance almost became more important than teaching.

Many primary schools did not clearly understand the purposes of testing or assessment in general. In most instances, assessment and testing were not an important aspect of school life. The report of the Task Group on Assessment and Testing (TGAT 1987) was an attempt to respond to those critics who wanted a more accountable school environment with teachers reporting clearly to parents on their children's progress. However, its recommendations were sensitive and balanced. Assessment should be formative. The task group suggested that tests at Key Stages 1 and 2 would integrate with normal school work. There would be selection from a bank of SATs, and the subject matter would be suited to the children. Parents and the LEA should have access to the results of the test. Most importantly, assessment would relate to profile components or clusters of attainment targets in the National Curriculum, not to every target individually. Results from Key Stage 2 onwards should be published in schools' own brochures but not published nationally (Thomas 1990). The government ignored these last two recommendations. It wanted complete public accountability.

Where there is a perceived need, someone will rush in to supply it. Educational publishers furnished schools with assessment charts that became covered in meaningless ticks and crosses in many colours. Many advisers came forward with suggestions on how to make assessment more manageable. After being converted by the views of one particularly convincing 'guru', I, and many others, instigated the compilation of portfolios of concrete evidence in my school to support teachers' assessment. The teachers dutifully complied with this idea and huge plastic wallets containing significant pieces of children's work were stored in stockrooms, occasionally collapsing in avalanches on unsuspecting cleaners and caretakers. Nobody really got to grips with the fundamental purpose of assessment for a long time, despite the fact that LEAs quickly formed their own support centres and charged them with the task of interpreting government requirements in a meaningful way to the teachers in their schools. It was generally felt by teachers that Ofsted inspectors would only be satisfied if schools could prove they were completing continual and detailed assessments on every child. The government vigorously refuted this expectation in the mid-1990s.

All of this suggests that the government had little understanding of the impact of change on those who had to implement it and made no provision for it. In essence, change we cannot control is potentially damaging. We like to feel we have some say in changes that affect us and the way we live. Even when we recognise that change is for the better, we like to feel in control of its pace and its impact. We also want to prepare ourselves. We might have to behave in a different way, learn new skills, a new vocabulary. For example, something as simple as the purchase of a new domestic appliance, if it is very different from the one that went before, can lead to a period where its owner is operating it entirely by the handbook. Schools were operating by the handbook for a long time after the introduction of the National Curriculum and, most distressingly, not always understanding the instructions.

Ofsted inspectors, too, were working to a handbook when they began to arrive in schools in 1994, to judge the quality of teachers' work and pupils' learning. There were guidelines for Registered Inspectors (an interesting mix of LEA advisers, Heads and Deputies, and independent consultants) governing the way in which they inspected schools. Some inspectors interpreted inspection guidelines rather loosely. These inspectors saw their role as one to seek out and expose teachers deemed to be *failing*. The worst inspectors inspected in a negative and aggressive fashion, causing distress and anxiety out of all proportion to the usefulness of their final reports. I knew, personally, several head teachers and class teachers who resigned rather than face the brown envelope containing notification of an inspection for their school. Not all of these people were expendable. Many were a serious loss to the profession. These negative Ofsted inspectors were sometimes encouraged in this by a hostile press and by a Chief Inspector appointed in 1994, Chris Woodhead, who appeared not to trust entirely the profession of which he was ostensibly the head. Woodhead and his colleagues produced a report (Alexander *et al.* 1992) that was heavily critical of child-centred and topic-based curricula. They claimed there was clear evidence that much topic work led to fragmentary and superficial teaching and learning. The report also suggested that 'highly questionable dogmas' hampered pupils' progress in primary schools and the authors were critical of the devaluing of the place of subjects in the curriculum.

Local Management of Schools

An aspect of education reform few people outside the teaching profession understood was Local Management of Schools (LMS). Pre-1988, LEAs had controlled money used to resource schools and pay support staff. The government was determined to break this LEA control. Local authorities devolved funding to schools with the advent of LMS. Schools would pay their own staff, pay for repairs to their premises and pay for resources they used. The money was to be delivered to schools almost entirely through an amount per child – the age-weighted pupil unit (AWPU), i.e. money per capita with greatest weighting for secondary pupils, some weighting in favour of nursery and reception infants, the least weighting for all other primary children.

This was one of the most revolutionary reforms of all. Part of the reasoning behind it was that successful schools (measured largely by the results of public tests) would attract more parents, more children and, therefore, more money. This would link very nicely with the need for schools to strive for excellence. Rewards for good schools would be tangible – the more children they attracted, the more money they received. This proved to be an over-simplistic equation. Additional funding would be delivered through a register of free school meals (denoting deprivation and need) and still more money through other criteria, usually devised by LEAs charged with devising ways and means of apportioning money for heating and lighting, and premises maintenance to individual schools. School governing bodies (composed of unpaid, co-opted citizens) would manage these budgets. The result would be openness not seen before in local government funding. Schools would have greater freedom to manage their money. Everyone would benefit.

The crucial document for everyone with responsibility for LMS was DES Circular 7/88. This offered guidance on the new system of funding. It suggested that funding should be based on *'objective needs rather than simply on historic spending'* (Coopers and Lybrand 1988, my emphasis) but most LEAs chose to ignore this. The government asked local authorities to create a formula to deliver this funding in a very short space of time and not surprisingly, most of them resorted to the use of historical factors that were no longer relevant. Many primary schools thus received a slice of funding inadequate for the management of a modern school. A source of funding statement went to schools by each LEA after LMS to show schools how the LEA calculated individual items of funding for their school. If one were able to scrutinise a typical statement for my school for any year from 1990 to the present day, one would discover some interesting perspectives on the LEA's interpretation of Circular 7/88. For example, they grouped the head teacher with class teachers to establish the pupil–teacher ratio but not for management purposes. The LEA statement would suggest that the school was able to cope with a part-time secretary and a part-time caretaker. In the case of classroom assistants (and this is most significant, given the audience for whom this chapter is largely intended), it would show that there was funding for one, a part-time nursery nurse intended to support my Reception teacher. Until the advent of initiatives such as Additional Literacy Support, I could not contemplate appointing a teaching assistant at Key Stage 2.

In many ways, LMS has been the change schools have found hardest to manage. Right from the start, LEA officers would acknowledge, without any suggestion of irony, that devolved funding would create winners and losers. It did not seem to occur to anyone that this was an unacceptable aspect of the previously unregulated education system – surely, one of the anomalies the 1988 Education Reform Act was designed to remove. Schools with falling pupil rolls cannot pay their staff, adequately resource their curriculum, plan beyond the next school budget. Such schools were caught in a recriminatory crossfire between the government and the LEA, each accusing the other of mismanaging public funds. Over time, it became obvious that schools generally have little control over pupil numbers – even schools that are recognised as excellent by any criteria Ofsted might care to use cannot always attract additional pupils. My personal experience is that the demographics of pupil populations are due to factors beyond a school's control. Today, in an attempt to ensure that children are equally distributed among half-empty school buildings, some education officers are forced to curtail parental choice by limiting school intakes and imposing rigorous admission criteria. Yet, good schools still close!

The present Labour Government has adopted a compensatory approach to LMS. It supplements school budgets with injections of cash direct from central government and usually ring-fenced for specific purposes – ICT, school buildings, etc. While these injections of cash are welcome, they do not allow school governors freedom to direct funds to areas of greatest need, usually shortfalls in staffing. Other initiatives designed to raise standards do not reach all schools – Education Action Zones (EAZs), for example.

The Impact on Schools

At this stage, it would be as well to pause and reflect on what has gone before. There are those in government circles, both local and national, who adhere to the view that in order to change an institution where there is a strong, entrenched resistance to change, it is best to be swift and incisive, to allow no time for opposition to mobilise. There will be some damage, some instability and confusion, perhaps, but out of that will emerge something better. The period from the 1988 Reform Act to the publication of the Dearing Report of 1993 reflected this philosophy (Review of the National Curriculum 1988–1994). It was unrelenting with short time scales; brief consultation periods; and the weight of the law ensuring statutory requirements were met. However, after the initial shock had worn off, those most directly affected by the reforms began to take charge of their own destinies. They began to learn how to manage the imposed changes. Teachers, advisers and LEAs generally went through fire but emerged better at doing many things. They also, it has to be said, were forced to change certain entrenched attitudes, such as relationships with parents, planning and assessment, management structures, professional development, and roles and responsibilities.

Relationships with parents

Pre-1988, it was possible for teachers in some schools not to meet with parents formally at all – no parent evenings and, in some instances, no reports about children's progress. Some schools displayed signs informing parents that their presence in school was not welcome.

Post-National Curriculum, teachers had to recognise that parents were partners in their children's education, something about which Plowden (1967) had previously expressed concern. Parents now had a minimum entitlement to an annual written report but most schools were keen to offer much more. Teachers became inventive at creating home–school links and at making their aims clear. Schools organised workshops to show parents how they taught the new curriculum and evening meetings to explain the administration of national tests and the real implications of attainment levels. More and more teaching assistants like Rachel engage in direct communication with parents as they begin to take responsibility for specific learning programmes or specific children.

Planning and assessment

Pre-1988, teachers' planning and assessment were not usually subject to inspection by an outside agency and many schools did little of either. Post-National Curriculum, after the initial trauma referred to above, teachers began to gain greater insight into the purposes of planning and began to understand the reason for assessment. They began to make assessment manageable and useful.

Management structures

Pre-1988, there was a management structure in place in schools but, in the majority of cases, the head teacher ruled over the school like a (hopefully) benevolent despot. Amazingly, pre-1988, some teachers had rarely attended a staff meeting! Post-National Curriculum, head teachers realised that only by working with their staff as team leaders would they survive the legislation coming their way and be able to deliver the new curriculum. They had to begin to learn new management strategies. Consultation, evaluation, delegation were unfamiliar terms to most head teachers. Now they had to use these terms, understand the implications of them for their school and create staffing structures designed to put them into effect. Schools produced action plans and organised staff meetings with real agenda and real purpose.

Professional development

Pre-1988, teachers did attend courses designed to improve their skills but they did so in a very *ad hoc* fashion. LEA advisers ran many excellent workshops but they were very much projections of their individual philosophy. Teachers often chose to attend because they wanted to experience something for which they already had a great liking, art, poetry, science or mathematics, and sometimes their pupils did reap the benefit of the ideas and inspiration with which they returned. However, such courses rarely supported school priorities and were often an indulgence with few tangible rewards for teacher or children.

Post-National Curriculum, schools began to allocate money for training designed to plug gaps in teachers' knowledge and understanding. Priorities were linked to the needs of the school. In the best schools, a teacher who returned from a course was expected to give an account of it to his or her colleagues and to use new understanding for everyone's benefit. Moreover, advisers began to respond to the needs of teachers and a bottom-up model of in-service training was created in the most supportive LEAs, in place of the top-down one that had gone before. Twenty-day courses targeting specific subject areas were created and teachers were funded from government money to be released from school for extended study periods. Excellent advisory teachers were appointed as an additional tier of support for teachers desperate for help with the delivery of a science or technology curriculum. Higher Education Institutions organised courses in conjunction with schools to broaden teachers' understanding in areas such as technology, ICT and mathematics.

Roles and responsibilities

Pre-1988, the head teacher ordered resources in many schools (who was probably the single person on the staff who knew how much money the school had been allocated for this). This was an ineffective way of operating. The expertise of individual teachers was rarely utilised, nor were resources related to any audit or linked to priorities. Often, there were large underspends that LEAs instantly reclaimed. These, in turn, sent out the wrong messages to those in charge of school funding. Post-National Curriculum, schools began to recognise the value of the subject co-ordinator, whose responsibility for the successful teaching of a particular subject area included resourcing it. Cockcroft (1982) had previously recommended the development of the role of the subject co-ordinator or subject leader in mathematics and other subject areas copied this initiative. Schools acquired excellent resources and made effective use of them, particularly in subjects such as mathematics, science, history, geography and religious education.

Above all, after 1988, schools recognised the need to be accountable and to adopt the notion of *stakeholders*. Not only were parents to become active partners in children's education but so also were school governors and the local community and beyond them, the wider community, particularly as represented by the media. Schools had to learn to communicate their intentions to these different bodies, encourage their interest and solicit their opinion.

The Impact on Education for the Under-Fives

The Reception class in an English primary school had gained world-wide recognition as a model of all that is best in early years' education before the inception of the National Curriculum. Possibly, this unique status safeguarded it from the most rigorous changes delivered to the rest of the education service. A Reception classroom today would retain many discernible features found in a Reception classroom of 1988. Before the introduction of the National Curriculum, the child-centred classrooms that flourished throughout the primary phase reflected good early years' practice. However, the changes wrought by the National Literacy and Numeracy Strategies in particular have seen Reception classes become the last outposts of the holistic approach. I have to admit that in my school, almost immediately a child moved from Reception, learning through play almost ceased to happen. Oral language development began to take second place to formal written language and the child's working day became much more formal.

Nursery and Reception classes were declared to be the Foundation Stage of the primary phase from September 2000. They have a curriculum divided into six broad areas of experience. Children move along 'stepping stones' towards Early Learning Goals (DfEE/QCA 2000). The government has handled early learning practitioners carefully. In return for the above re-structuring and re-labelling, as a sort of public declaration that they really do exist to prepare children for the future rigours of the National Curriculum, they can retain many of the approaches to learning that earned them their enviable reputation. As a head teacher, I would expect to find a Reception classroom with an environment that was stimulating and multi-sensory. The Reception teachers would nurture different learning styles through interactive displays, linking subjects such as art and literature, science and maths and technology. There would be objects to handle, sounds to listen to and scents to smell. Acknowledging the importance of early language development, the displays would have a strong literary bias, with items clearly labelled and opportunities provided for children and their carers to read and discover more about the world in which they live.

Foundation Stage teachers plan using a topic-based approach where possible, believing that young children see their world as a whole and not divided up into subject areas. Class teachers recognise that the best learning takes place through experience, experimentation and discovery and so there are opportunities provided for children to handle a wide variety of materials – all kinds of construction kits and sand and water, clay and paint and dough. These teachers recognise that the best learning takes place when the children's interaction with these materials is in the company of a receptive and perceptive adult who, through careful prompting and listening and responding to the children, acts as a guide to help them discover a wide range of concepts. Oral language development is a priority at this stage. Consequently, I would expect to meet a number of regular adult helpers at the Foundation Stage, engaged in small-group activities with the children and actively encouraging discussion and debate about the tasks in hand.

Both the 1988 teacher and her present-day counterpart would understand the importance of play as a way of learning and for working out ideas or exploring feelings. They would both have established role-play areas where children could take on many different identities and become astronauts or shopkeepers or a character from a favourite story. However, the Reception class teacher today is probably more adept at recording the individual progress of each child and is particularly good at tailoring learning situations to suit each stage of a child's development. Most probably, the teacher recognises more readily the role of the child's parent or carer as a partner in his or her education and builds into each day a time for dialogue about each child. The teacher seeks to establish with these adults the recognition of each child's need to grow and develop in independence and confidence, moving through the same stages of development but at his or her own rate. Today's Reception teacher actively makes contact with those adults who care for the child pre-school, including child minders and nurseries. Where I was head teacher, the Reception teachers ran excellent pre-school sessions with a range of activities so that children and adults got to know each other. We placed a high regard on forging links so that the transition from nursery to school was a seamless one.

Sometimes, Reception teachers carry out home visits. They model approaches they intend to adopt with the children and convey to parents and other carers their expectations. They offer advice and help as to the kind of support parents and other carers can offer the children. When teachers and parents have similar goals, children are likely to feel more secure and achieve more. Teachers' work during pre-school sessions is designed not only to help young children settle more readily into school in September but to exchange information on each child and begin the process of baseline assessment. In 2003, Reception teachers use baseline assessment to establish a starting point not only for themselves and for colleagues throughout the school. Any future progress a child makes will be measured against this early assessment (a 'value added' measure). The responsibility for establishing an accurate baseline of achievement for each child entering Key Stage 1 is one of the most significant changes to impact on early years' teachers. It is not the intention of this chapter to put forward any arguments either for or against the latest Qualifications and Curriculum Authority (QCA) model for baseline assessment – 13 distinct assessment scales with 9 progression points for each (QCA 2003). It simply queries whether this amount of data is necessary. Will it enable the Reception class teacher to do a better job or will it divert his or her energies into measuring the child as opposed to helping that child develop?

The Influence of Information and Communication Technology (ICT)

Keeping pace with all the other changes to the curriculum has been ICT; initially, an unwanted and overlooked addition to the core subjects but now, increasingly, an enabling tool and a vehicle for curriculum enrichment. Computers found their way into schools well before National Curriculum. The government gave every primary school a computer. These were usually slow and uncertain, accessing programs from a tape recorder. With only limited software at their disposal, few teachers could see a role for them in their classrooms. LEAs were equally confused. And courses they ran provided inappropriate instruction in writing computer programs instead of focusing on pedagogy. Many head teachers and teachers regarded the computer as a problem, rather than an educational solution. We often locked computers in cupboards or covered them with drapes in classroom corners, especially when they broke down. Enterprising teachers did use them with their children, seeing their potential as teaching tools. As the technology became more sophisticated and tape recorders gave way to discs, the way forward was not a clear, straight road but a track that wound uphill with many branching paths. For example, not all LEAs bought hardware and software that was compatible with the new personal computers (PCs) and many good educational resources were lost as PCs cornered the educational market. The problems associated with ICT in schools (and it was a National Curriculum foundation subject almost from the very beginning) were:

- different and incompatible systems;
- software that was *either* a useful teaching aid but boring, repetitive and unsophisticated *or* sophisticated but not really tailored to educational use;
- unreliable hardware;
- no effective technical support;
- not enough computers;
- inadequate training.

Not surprisingly, Ofsted inspectors began identifying ICT as a key issue in schools across the country.

Slowly and painfully, ICT is finding its place in the scheme of things since the present government began to direct large amounts of capital towards improving the situation. It recognised the huge potential for education that lies in the Internet and its aim has always been to make ICT a powerful support mechanism in all schools.

Where I was head teacher, progress in ICT happened in the following key areas:

- All the teachers had laptop computers. This enabled the computer-phobics to engage at home with *the beast* in comparative security where they found it to be a powerful and friendly support that could produce labels and worksheets and reports far quicker and far better than any other means.
- Government funding provided better organised and more effective technical support for the school.
- We installed PCs, far faster and more reliable than ever before. Compatibility of educational software was no longer a problem.

■ We purchased well-designed educational software that was targeted towards areas such as special educational needs much more effectively.

Schools have finally plotted a way forward that ensures delivery of most strands of the statutory framework for ICT. They use a combination of computer suites and stand-alone machines in their classrooms. In the suite, they teach skills to a whole class and the classroom machines allow transfer of these skills to all parts of the curriculum. Most LEAs employ advisory teachers, most of whom are very good indeed and have enabled schools to write purposeful action plans and to devise relevant schemes of work. Schools are also linked via machines for administration purposes. LEAs provide a lot of support here and encourage schools to use computer databases and spreadsheets to record pupil progress and make assessment more manageable.

There is a range of technologies available to enhance children's learning. These include interactive whiteboards, tape recorders and digital cameras and VCRs. There are peripherals that can lead even the youngest children into the world of robotics and monitoring and control technology. However, only the tip of the iceberg has been revealed. ICT remains a *bolt-on* area of the primary curriculum. Cameras record children's work and school activities but only a very few schools enable their children to use them as creative tools. Their potential is enormous. When linked with presentation or design programs, they provide children with exciting alternatives to pencil and paper for reporting and creating. Tape recorders can help develop speaking and listening skills but are under-used. As for the interactive whiteboard, it could prove to be one of the most significant developments of all with the capability of bringing any subject to life and giving enormous impact to the way in which teachers communicate ideas to their pupils.

Alongside these developments lies the growth of the Internet, the information highway. Most teachers have recognised its effectiveness, either by encouraging pupils to research topics via websites or by downloading worksheets and articles for their own use. Some schools experiment with video conferencing and links with schools in other countries. Unfortunately, my experience of the Internet as a teaching tool is that of an encounter fraught with frustration and peril. Links failed to connect or broke down at a crucial point. Young children stumbled upon disturbing websites, although providers of Internet links affirmed that they had created safe portals for schools to use. A somewhat bizarre but very real threat is now posed by those who send out a torrent of 'spam' or pop-up messages which have the real potential to create a log jam that will destroy the free flow of e-mails.

ICT is *the* area of curriculum that will need continual government funding of a significant kind. Schools need to be able to commit to investment in training, renewal and expansion of hardware and software and on-site, effective technical support. I could argue that ICT needs to be moved centre-stage. Should not a curriculum for the twenty-first century be organised more effectively around the new technology? At present, it remains an addition to most subjects. Imagine if every child had a notebook PC. Early acquisition of keyboard skills at Key Stage 1 would certainly need much more emphasis than at present. Teacher and pupil would eventually be able to interact in a way not possible currently. The capacity to differentiate one's teaching might finally be realised. Could we fine-tune the National Curriculum so that the different strands of ICT are integral components of and not additions to each subject?

New Labour: New Changes

Somewhere around 1997 would have been an appropriate place to finish this chapter. By then teachers were taking ownership of the National Curriculum. They had become more effective at delivering its requirements and teachers were promised a period of consolidation. However, a New Labour government elected with a huge majority in 1997 declared publicly that education was top of its agenda. It felt that the National Curriculum was still failing children and saw the need for further, immediate change to secure their future. It decided to set national targets in literacy and numeracy – National Curriculum Level 4 in both subjects was the target for all Year 6 children. The government asserted that 85 per cent of all eleven-year-old children would reach Level 4 in English by the summer of 2002. There were to be no more vague aspirations. Instead, schools would set clear school targets linked to national benchmarks and expected to achieve a year-on-year improvement in standards of attainment until they reached the government's objective.

To ensure they did so, they provided training of a very detailed nature. In fact, there was so much detail that the National Literacy and Numeracy Strategies (DfEE 1998, 1999) were destined to become the long-term and medium-term plans for most primary schools in English and mathematics. Few teachers realised that the material contained in National Literacy and Numeracy documentation was non-statutory and did not constitute the whole of National Curriculum English or mathematics. This was due, once again, to the effects of teachers having to assimilate vast quantities of new legislation, relate this to previously acquired knowledge and synthesise both elements into a coherent whole. The intention of the information overload was to compensate for a perceived lack of subject knowledge on the part of teachers and their apparent inability to teach those skills required in core subjects. Unfortunately, instead of enabling teachers to teach better, the amount of prescriptive detail de-skilled them by not allowing them sufficient room to utilise their own creativity.

The result of this over-prescription led to teachers, once again, losing control of their own classrooms. They attempted to become carbon copies of those colleagues whose lessons had been videotaped and used as teaching models in Department for Education and Employment training packs. Many primary schools, faced with Ofsted inspections, adopted the infamous *wheel model* for the literacy hour. This recommended very specific amounts of time for each element of the literacy lesson – shared reading, group activity, plenary, etc. Some teachers were extremely nervous at going beyond these recommended times. Others felt they had to use a *big book* in every lesson. Most distressingly, the pace at which teachers felt obliged to go resulted in children rarely finishing a piece of writing. I discovered in one classroom countless bits of uncompleted pieces of work. Completion of extended writing happened during some other part of the timetable. This had an impact on other subject areas – often the humanities and the arts.

The reader can relate this back to those symptoms that manifested themselves soon after the introduction of the National Curriculum. Experienced professionals were abandoning their own judgement in deference to a script they were afraid to alter to suit their particular situation. The *one-model fits all* philosophy of teaching recommended by the Literacy Strategy (DfEE 1998) had a more traumatic effect on teachers' morale than did that designed for the Numeracy Strategy (DfEE 1999). Perhaps the government felt there was more to alter in the teaching of English. Certainly, the government has continued to send out more and more material to ensure we reach literacy targets. There is an intervention package for almost every year group from Year 1 to Year 6 and beyond for teachers to administrate. These packs are heavily weighted towards phonics-based materials designed to be used with small groups of children who were deemed to be *vulnerable* – not likely to achieve a Level 4 at the end of Year 6. This raft of intervention strategies by the Labour Government, in a sense, is a kind of recognition that schools needed a particular sort of differentiated support for those children for whom National Curriculum targets and formal tests were an uphill struggle.

Significantly, LEAs train teaching assistants like Rachel to deliver many of the intervention strategies the government has devised. As head teacher, I appointed three teaching assistants who worked alongside Key Stage 2 teachers as a vital additional support group in literacy and numeracy lessons. Sometimes they withdrew children to teach specific skills, sometimes they sat in on whole-class sessions to prompt and help vulnerable children to stay on task and actively participate in shared reading and writing, sometimes they helped with assessment and planning. One had almost total responsibility for the delivery of Additional Literacy Support (ALS) and Early Literacy Support (ELS) sessions. The general increase in the numbers of teaching assistants at Key Stage 2 and their new status are largely attributable to the government's drive towards achieving its literacy targets.

Government policy on inclusion is the other reason for schools seeking to appoint highly qualified teaching assistants at all Key Stages. The Warnock Report of 1978 followed by the Education Act of 1981 had established a principle for mainstream schools to make provision for handicapped children. Inclusion, therefore, is not a new concept. Both central government and LEAs expected schools to cater for a broad range of disabilities within their classrooms. Special schools and units attached to mainstream schools have taken in some of the most severely physically and emotionally disabled children but a far larger number have remained the responsibility of the mainstream primary school Special Educational Needs Co-ordinator (SENCO). In most cases, support takes the form of an Individual Education or Behaviour Plan (an IEP or IBP), a programme of intervention tailored to an individual child's needs and delivered by the resources available within that child's school. One of the chief resources, in my experience, is a trained teaching assistant. Working under the guidance of a class teacher and the school SENCO, he or she can deliver small-group sessions or one-to-one tutorials using a different approach and at a different pace from the main lesson. No mainstream school can discharge its responsibilities to those children who have significant difficulties coping with the National Curriculum without trained support staff. I do believe that schools today are better at recognising children with conditions such as autism and dyspraxia and at supporting them in coping with National Curriculum.

It is now almost six years since the introduction of the new initiatives, long enough to reflect on some of the results. On the plus side, shining a spotlight on how reading and writing were taught revealed serious weaknesses in some teachers' understanding and on their lack of subject knowledge and the materials provided by the government did a great deal to put this right. In the very best LEAs, reflective practitioners have devised ways and means of adapting the prescribed models for literacy and numeracy so they became less of a strait-jacket. Advisory teachers have shown colleagues how modelling good reading and writing skills could take children forward and help them achieve excellence. Teaching within the core subjects of English and mathematics, in the best schools, has developed a sharpness and purposefulness that was not so apparent before. Some of the most effective results have been the small innovations that help teachers communicate concepts more clearly and help children to interact with their teachers to work out ideas. I can think of two excellent innovations – the increasing use of number lines in numeracy in creative and varied ways and the individual whiteboards and pens used by children in both literacy and numeracy lessons.

On the minus side, a new collective noun is in our vocabulary – a *proliferation* of worksheets. Many teachers have chosen, unfortunately, to differentiate in their teaching entirely by worksheet. Often in literacy lessons, mundane exercises keep children occupied during group activities (frustratingly, these sometimes follow on from a purposeful and interesting introductory session). An over-emphasis on literacy and numeracy has driven the arts and humanities (and even technology and science, in some schools) to the sidelines. Schools have to make a conscious effort to find room within their timetable for subjects that were once seamlessly integrated and valued. From somewhere, almost imperceptibly, has come a new guiding principle. Only if a subject has a clear vocational purpose and is capable of measurement *quantitatively* is it to be valued. You will not find this guiding principle written anywhere, but in many LEAs, the quantitative factor has led to qualitative experiences almost disappearing from view. Moreover, the LEA provides most training for teachers and is centred very much on government initiatives and delivered via government resources and directives.

We must frame the justification for the inclusion of the arts and the humanities within a primary school curriculum in qualitative terms. The benefits that accrue from a study of the arts are not easily measured. They tend to be long term, of an individual and personal nature and often without immediate material value. There is a tendency in many primary schools to import a quick fix of creativity after national tests are over, sometimes via external arts providers. However, art education is a process. Children develop skills, insights and understanding over many years until they are able to use them with confidence.

There is also a feeling abroad in some quarters that if a topic is not within National Curriculum documentation, it cannot be a valid topic for study. This mindset can lead to teachers going to convoluted lengths to justify that which is clearly worthwhile.

2003 and Beyond

All chapters must have an ending but the rate of change facing primary schools has no discernible end. The government's latest publication *Excellence and Enjoyment* (DfES 2003) contains some good things. These can be categorised as either reassurances or promises or, occasionally, considerations:

- A reassurance would be a signed declaration from the present Education Secretary and the Chief Inspector of Schools intended to clarify the government's expectations regarding teachers' planning.

- One of the many promises is that of continued support for extending the role of teaching assistants, although some aspects of this remain unclear.

- A notable consideration is that of the government finally accepting that children with certain disabilities ought not to have their national test results included in performance tables – albeit, at the moment, this consideration targets a small percentage of children with severe disabilities. However, national tests remain in place, as does the exhortation for all schools to continue with their drive to reach the government's target figure of 85 per cent Level 4s at age 11, although no definite date is now set for this to happen.

The document suggests that there will be government support for school networks and for effective head teachers (to be known as Consultant Leaders) to be enabled to support colleagues in raising standards. It refers to Specialist Schools collaborating with partner primaries and Breakthrough Groups trialling the use of data to track changes in performance. The use of words such as *partnership* and *collaboration* is in itself encouraging. However, the tone throughout promotes a kind of elitism. Schools are encouraged to pursue charter marks and accreditation, to become beacon schools or centres of excellence. Some gain membership of one group, some become part of another. Some do not qualify to be members of any. There is a definite sense of the formation of a hierarchical establishment. I know from experience that this approach can breed resentment. Teachers not recognised or included in the upper echelons can close their minds and become inward-looking. What we need is a forum where all schools are welcomed as equal partners and encouraged to share their ideas and access information in return. There is also a need to return to a study of the child and how he or she learns and this is where a teaching assistant like Rachel can be invaluable. Assistants can provide detailed information about the groups of children with whom they work closely. Moreover, the National Curriculum needs constant scrutiny to ensure it remains the most suitable model for children living in the twenty-first century. We need to ask ourselves questions such as these:

- Shouldn't children be educated on how to cope with the insidious influence of the media from an early age?

- Is there not an argument for a specific area of study for this purpose, given the enormous impact of the media on our lives?

It is noticeable that, throughout this chapter, the prime mover for educational change has been central government. Proctor (1990) makes out a case for this not only being perfectly acceptable but actually desirable. Only government is in a position to balance the interests of all the stakeholders in education and ensure no single body has undue influence. From its vantage point, government can reach an accommodation between what children, schools and teachers can do, and what society offers and requires of its members (Thomas 1990). Government is a facilitator, bringing together expertise, canvassing opinion, acquiring evidence. However, it does not follow on from this that government ministers should make all the major decisions concerning education. I would venture to say that schools today are now much better than when I embarked on my career. Teachers know more. They are more informed. Schools are the most accountable and well-regulated institutions in the public sector. The best are models of economy and give value for money that most industrialists would find hard to emulate. Surely now is the time for government to move from centre-stage to the wings? It would need to retain a light touch. It would need to set in place a mechanism whereby continual monitoring, evaluation and fine-tuning of the system could take place. All identifiable, legitimate stakeholders would be involved in this but arguably, teachers would have a majority interest. Maybe it is time to go back and review the Schools Council and teachers' centres of some 30 years ago. With improved, twenty-first-century communications, might it not be possible to use some sort of network system centred on the General Teaching Council to allow ideas to be shared, ways and means to be trialled, standards to be maintained and reasonable targets to be agreed?

Conclusion

- Change over which we have control is less threatening.
- Change to which we contribute is better understood.
- Change to which there is general agreement is better implemented and more effective.

Dearden (1968) wrote about the need to avoid change brought about as a violent reaction to the status quo, one 'ism' replacing another. This is, as I see it, the pendulum principle. English school education is too narrow and controlled so we swing across to a child-centred, freer model. This proves too broad and unstructured for the control freaks among us so we swing back to accountability and control. This is not a good model to adopt. I would much rather we adopted the model for educational change advocated in Bruner's (1966) spiral curriculum. We circle back over old problems and solutions but at a higher level of understanding. We make things a little better than before until we pass that way again and make further improvements. I really have to believe that we are not moving backwards and forwards but onwards and upwards.

Discussion Starters

1 Why was the National Curriculum introduced in 1988?
2 How has the National Curriculum changed since it was first introduced?
3 What has been the impact of the National Curriculum on educational standards since 1988?
4 Are child-centred theories of learning relevant in a primary school today?
5 What subjects would you include in a core curriculum for secondary school children in the twenty-first century?
6 How effective are intervention strategies in improving learning in the long term?
7 What educational changes would you like to see in your workplace and why?
8 How might the role of the teaching assistant change over the next decade?

Reflecting on Practice

1 Think about your own workplace. How does the way in which ICT is organised relate to the author's view of its development in a specific primary school?
2 What emphasis does your institution place on the importance of assessment results, and what is the impact on children with special educational needs?
3 Reflect on how your role has developed since you began. What impact (if any) have you had in making changes to teaching and learning approaches, assessment systems and organisational procedures? Create a chart of the changes you would like to make and consider the means by which you might make them.

Change	Means of effecting change

Websites

http://education.guardian.co.uk/ – for news features about current issues in education.
www.dfes.gov.uk/foundationstage/ – curriculum guidance for the Foundation Stage.
www.qca.org.uk/ – for links to the National Curriculum and associated publications.
www.standards.dfes.gov.uk/seu/ – for links to various sites connected with raising standards.
www.teachernet.gov.uk – for links to various sites including management of teaching assistants, and teaching and learning issues.

References

Alexander, R., Rose, J. and Woodhead, C. (1992) *Curriculum Organisation and Classroom Practice in Primary Schools*, London: Department of Education and Science.

Brooks, R. (1991) *Contemporary Debates in Education: An Historical Perspective*, New York: Longman Inc.

Bruner, J. (1966) *Toward a Theory of Instruction*, Cambridge, MA: Harvard University Press.

Cockcroft, W.H. (1982) *Mathematics Counts*, London: HMSO.

Coopers and Lybrand (1988) *L.M.S. Report to the Department of Education and Science*, London: HMSO.

Cunningham, P. (1990) 'Primary education – early perspectives', in Proctor, N. (ed.), *The Aims of Primary Education and the National Curriculum*, Bristol: Falmer Press, p. 4.

Dearden, R.F. (1968) *The Philosophy of Primary Education: An Introduction*, London: Routledge and Kegan Paul.

DfEE (1998) *The National Literacy Strategy: Framework for Teaching English YR to Y6*, London: DfEE.

DfEE (1999) *The National Numeracy Strategy Framework for Teaching Mathematics Years R to 6*, Cambridge: Cambridge University Press.

DfEE/QCA (1999) *The National Curriculum for England*, London: HMSO/QCA.

DfEE/QCA (2000) *Curriculum Guidance for the Foundation Stage*, London: HMSO.

DfES (2003) *Excellence and Enjoyment: A Strategy for Primary Schools*, Nottingham: DfES Publications.

Kemball-Cook, B. (1972) 'The Garden of Plowden', in Boyson, R. (ed.), *Education: Threatened Standards*, London: Churchill Press, pp. 50–60.

National Curriculum Council (1989) *Non-Statutory Guidance*, London: HMSO.

Peters, R.S. (ed.) (1969) *Perspectives on Plowden*, London: Routledge and Kegan Paul.

Plowden Report, Department of Education and Science, Central Advisory Council (1967) *Children and Their Primary Schools: A Report of the Central Advisory Council*, London: HMSO.

Proctor, N. (ed.) (1990) *The Aims of Primary Education and the National Curriculum*, Bristol: Falmer Press.

QCA (2003) *The Foundation Stage Profile*, London: QCA.

Tanner, R. (1987) *Double Harness*, London: Impact Books.

Task Group on Assessment and Testing (1987) *National Curriculum: Report of the Task Group on Assessment and Testing*, London: DES.

Thomas, N. (1990) *Primary Education from Plowden to the 1990s*, Bristol: Falmer Press.

Warnock, M. (1978) *Report of Enquiry into the Education of Handicapped Children and Young People*, London: HMSO.

3

Learning and Teaching: What's Your Style?

Pat Hughes

Meet Marjorie

I have 15 years' experience as a full-time teaching assistant in a small primary school working throughout the school giving support to the teachers on a fixed timetable. Most of the teachers are younger than I am and they largely leave me to use my own initiative. Indeed, I often lead in finding or developing resources to make the learning more relevant to the children. Some teachers want all the children to carry out the same task and I may have to extend or adapt these to the needs of particular children, groups of children or occasionally the whole class.

The school has had two very good Ofsted reports and the LEA recognises the work it does in supporting children's needs. Recently, I attended a Support Assistants Training in Mind-Friendly Learning course that was very relevant as many of the children are not very effective at learning within the school setting. I thought I could use a lot of the ideas, but would like to know more about how I can help children to learn more effectively. I would like to know more about the research in this area as well as the practical strategies I could use with my groups.

Introduction

The terms 'learning' and 'teaching' imply two separate activities. The term 'lifelong learning' challenges this separateness. We are all learners, just as we are all teachers. Some people may have a job that gives them the title of teacher, but in their daily work, they are also learning. Learners also teach – themselves and others. 'Teaching' covers a number of activities including presenting, authenticating, directing, leading, training, facilitating, developing, mentoring and coaching (see www.alite.co.uk, accessed August 2003). The stereotyped image of teaching tends to concentrate on the 'presenting' side, but the learning revolution which is taking place means that this traditional view of 'teaching' has been challenged, has been found wanting and is being replaced by a greater variety of 'teaching' strategies than ever before. Marjorie, the teaching assistant, is already adapting activities and resources to suit the children's learning needs, and she recognises that children learn in different ways. This chapter aims to provide her with some more knowledge about the ways children learn, and identify useful sources of information for further study. We will examine some of the research into how people learn and the obvious implications for how to support and develop this learning. As this is such an extensive area, the chapter will also identify other texts and websites where readers can find out more information that has particular relevance for their own work experience.

Starting Points: Ourselves as Learners

What sort of learner are you? It is tempting to think that we all learn in the same way. Indeed, this is the assumption behind the frameworks for literacy (DfEE 1998) and primary mathematics (DFEE 1999) in England. They identified core content for each year and term of a child's primary school career and advised on lesson structure and teaching strategies. This contrasted with the Australian approach to a literacy programme known as First Steps (McDonald 1999). The designers based this on observation of children learning and identified effective teaching strategies to move them forward. In the guidelines that followed, they avoided specific ages, and non-age-related learning continua in reading, writing and spelling developed.

This latter approach fits in much more closely to research evidence about learning. For much of the research in the past 100 years makes it clear that we learn in different ways and at different speeds. For example, you may be reading this, sitting in a comfortable chair with the television on. Someone else might need to sit in silence at a table or desk. Another person might prefer to listen to someone else reading it aloud. You may or may not make notes, create a learning map or devise a diagram to help you remember what you have read. The popularity of professional development audio cassettes, CD-ROMs and interactive media indicates that there is a growing market for different types of presentation. Many of the references in this chapter will refer to e-books, websites and audio tapes.

The Barsch learning style audit in Figure 3.1 provides a useful way to determine your own learning style (DfES 2001, 2002). When completing it, remember no particular style is best and each style makes its own demands on the learning and teaching environment. Many other 'tests' also claim to identify learning styles. The commercial website http://www.accelerated-learning-uk.co.uk offers a free learning profile for adults with generous points! There are also a growing number of such audits for children.

Historical Overview

There is a huge amount of literature on how people learn covering cognition, learning, development, culture and the brain. It also covers the nature of the subject itself. This is sometimes explicit, e.g. Blyth (1990) considers whether five-year-olds are too young to learn history. More often, it is implicit as in the National Literacy and Numeracy Strategy documents, which explain the teaching approaches for the subjects.

Place a check on the appropriate line after each statement. Then score, following the directions after the questionnaire.

Statement: I . . .	Often	Sometimes	Seldom
1. Can remember more about a subject through listening rather than reading.			
2. Follow written directions better than oral instructions.			
3. Like to write things down or take notes for visual review.			
4. Bear down extremely hard with pen or pencil when writing.			
5. Require explanations of diagrams, graphs or visual directions.			
6. Enjoy working with tools.			
7. Am skilful and enjoy developing and making graphs and charts.			
8. Can tell if sounds match when presented with pairs of sounds.			
9. Remember best by writing things down several times.			
10. Can understand and follow directions using maps.			
11. Do better at academic subjects by listening to lectures and tapes.			
12. Play with coins and keys in pockets.			
13. Learn to spell better by repeating the letters out loud than by writing the word on paper.			
14. Can better understand a news article by reading about it in the paper than by listening to the radio.			
15. Chew gum, smoke or snack during studies.			
16. Feel the best way to remember is to picture it in my head.			
17. Learn spelling by 'finger spelling' the words.			
18. Would rather listen to a good lecture or speech than read about the same material in a text book.			
19. Am good at working and solving jigsaw puzzles and mazes.			
20. Grip objects in my hand during learning period.			
21. Prefer listening to the news on radio than reading about it in a newspaper.			
22. Obtain information on an interesting subject by reading relevant materials.			
23. Feel very comfortable touching others, hugging, handshaking, etc.			
24. Follow oral directions better than written ones.			

Scoring procedures:

Place the point value on the line next to its corresponding item number.

Often = 5 POINTS
Sometimes = 3 POINTS
Seldom = 1 POINT

Next sum the values to arrive at your preference scores under each heading.

VISUAL – Number of Points	AUDITORY – Number of Points	TACTILE – Number of Points
2.	1.	4.
3.	5.	6.
7.	8.	9.
10.	11.	12.
14.	13.	15.
16.	18.	17.
19.	21.	20.
22.	24.	23.
Total VPS (Visual Preference)	Total APS (Auditory Preference)	Total TPS (Tactile/ Kinaesthetic Preference)

FIGURE 3.1   The Barsch learning style audit

In the beginning

This research literature has built up over the centuries. In Ancient Greece, philosophers adopted a question and answer approach, which has remained the traditional teaching structure for many years. Greek philosophers and teachers such as Plato and Socrates (see Taylor at http://www.briantaylor.com/Socrates.htm, accessed August 2003) would ask questions for which they would teach their followers the answers. Their followers would in turn transmit their learned knowledge in the same way. The basis of much formal education is this presentation approach with a question and answer technique employed to assess learning.

Early years

It was not until the nineteenth and early twentieth century that people questioned this method of learning. Unsurprisingly this was largely in the area of early years' education, where formal presentations were particularly inappropriate. Educators such as Froebel, Montessori and Steiner looked more closely at the children themselves (Bruce 1987). Such educators and their followers no longer saw children as blank slates. This blank slate approach implies that failures in learning are the child's fault, rather than a closer inspection of other factors that might be relevant. They saw learning as holistic, rather than separated out into subjects. These educators gave relevance to other factors, such as differences between learners in terms of their motivation, self-discipline and individual development. They observed children as they learned and this led to looking at implications for changing designs of formal learning environments such as schools. If we look into any good nursery today, we can see how far the learning environment has changed from the traditional question and answer approach to stimulating and exciting indoor and outdoor play provision. Informed and talented adults support and extend learning. They are also prepared to continue to observe and learn from their children.

Children's learning

Until quite recently, the work and ideas of three psychologists – Jean Piaget, Lev Vygotsky and Jerome Bruner (Whitebread 2002) – have influenced most of the thinking about children's learning in schools. Many educational texts and websites refer to their work, e.g. Alfrey and Durell (2003). I like the websites because they provide photographs, hyperlinks on difficult terminology and, in some cases, spoken extracts. As we have seen from the learning styles audit above, this is more to do with my preferred learning style, than a statement about which is the most effective method of further informing yourself about their work. Here is a brief summary:

- *Piaget*'s work alerted educators to children's active role in their own learning and the importance of mental activity. He emphasised the importance of children interacting with the physical environment and produced a series of age-related stages through which children progressed in an apparently linear fashion.

- *Vygotsky* looked more at the role that language and social interaction played in learning. He argued for a much more central role for the adult that could extend children's 'level

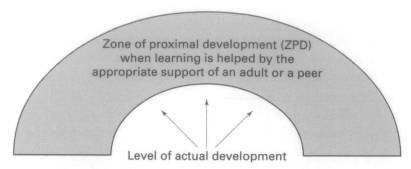

FIGURE 3.2   Vygotsky's zone of proximal development

of actual development' into the 'zone of proximal development' (ZPD). Figure 3.2 provides a visual explanation of this.

- *Bruner* looked at the relationship between language and thought and the need to provide children with a relevant and appropriate vocabulary so that they could use this in thinking, talking and exploring ideas. He also coined the phrase 'the spiral curriculum', and demonstrated the importance of revisiting topics at different levels of understanding. This translates very easily into school curriculum terms, when children learn about a specific thing at one stage, e.g. playing with blocks and learning about the way in which cubes are different from cuboids when building a tower. Later in their school careers, they learn how to make nets of different types of cuboids and cubes and discover additional different properties such as edge sizes. Bruner also used the term 'scaffolder' as a metaphor for how adults should encourage and extend the child's 'own active search for understanding' (Whitebread 2002).

The work of all three provided different views on learning that had an impact on teaching at all levels. Piaget's developmental approach suggested that teachers needed to be facilitators and organisers. Vygotsky and Bruner both gave more importance to language and the adult (and peer) role in teaching. Bruner's 'scaffolding' metaphor is the rationale behind the guided reading and writing parts of the literacy strategy and the 'thinking aloud' element of the mathematics lesson.

Other factors influencing children's learning

Once compulsory education came into force in the UK in the nineteenth century, it became obvious that other factors influenced children's ability to learn. The pyramid diagram in Figure 3.3 summarises these very effectively. This shows Maslow's hierarchy of human needs. The most effective learners are those at the top of the pyramid. Clearly, if you are starving, i.e. at the base of the pyramid, you are unlikely to be able to think of more than how you can fulfil your basic need of hunger. This does not make you an effective learner in a formal situation.

When looking at the pyramid, you might like to think of two different children, or indeed adults, whose particular needs at specific levels hinder effective learning. This initial hier-

FIGURE 3.3 Maslow's hierarchy of human needs

archy is from over 50 years ago, but its importance in identifying basic physical and emotional needs remains. Much of the work on emotional literacy/intelligence stems from Maslow's initial identification of basic needs (Hughes 2002). The growth of breakfast clubs in schools, the role of learning mentors, and policies on bullying and anti-racism demonstrate the practical ways in which many educational institutions are addressing some of these needs for specific children.

Teaching styles

There is less research on teaching styles in the UK than in the USA. The question and answer approach has dominated teaching in educational institutions. Bennett (1976) and his research colleagues set out 13 characteristics of what they termed 'Progressive Teachers' and contrasted these with 'Traditional Teachers'. For example, the progressive teacher would act as a guide to educational experiences, where the traditional teacher was a distributor of knowledge. Pupils had an active role in the progressive teacher's classroom, whereas they had a passive one in the traditional teacher's classroom. The most controversial finding was that children did better when the teacher was a traditional one. This seemed to conflict with other research evidence about children's learning which required interaction such as Bruner described, but it did fit in with the political agenda at the time. Galton (1980) actually went into primary and later secondary classrooms while Bennett had simply gathered his data through questionnaires. Galton found much less 'progressive' teaching than the government had feared and the media had announced! Some years later Bennett revisited his initial data and came forward with different conclusions. However, by this time the damage had been done and his initial findings continued to be used as a rationale for the traditional 'distributor of knowledge' style of teaching, which completely ignored children's different learning needs and styles.

Although there were several other studies on teaching styles in the UK, later studies supported a political agenda of more centralised control, both in the classroom as well as from the centre. For example, Alexander *et al.* (1992), called the 'Three Wise Men' due to its publication at Christmas, in their documentary inquiry on primary education, reaffirmed the need for more 'traditional' presentation-type teaching. In parallel, increased centralised control over the contents of the curriculum and the teaching methods arose as discussed by Alan Barrow in Chapter 2.

Summary

This historical review has noted the work of a few key researchers in the area of children's learning, and has suggested how the findings fit in with a particular view of teaching. It has very briefly reviewed two major studies into teaching styles in the UK that were carried out at a key period, when central government (both Labour and Conservative) determined to take a tighter hold on education in order to make educational institutions more accountable for the money spent. Both the Literacy and Numeracy Strategies for primary and secondary schools gave specific recommendations to increase the use of a whole-class interactive teaching style. Only later (DfEE/QCA 2000) did the Curriculum Guidance for the Foundation Stage release Reception classes from the literacy hour and daily mathematics lesson where so much whole-class teaching is inappropriate.

Fortunately, we are living at a time when global changes are forcing all governments to re-examine their approach to education at all levels. There is a genuine understanding by most key UK policy-makers that we all need educating, whatever our age, to live and cope with such a rapidly changing world. The 'Learning Revolution' – a term used by Dryden and Vos (2001) – is here, fuelled by international changes in communication and revolutionary changes in identifying how people learn. It also challenges four myths of learning that:

- School is the best place to learn.
- Intelligence is fixed.
- Teaching produces learning.
- We all learn in the same way.

The Learning Revolution

Everyone now has to become a self-acting manager of one's own future. However, much education still resembles the declining industrial method of production: a standard assembly-line curriculum divided into subjects, taught in units, arranged by grade, and controlled by standardised tests. This no longer reflects the world we live in. And traditional educational systems can no longer cope with new realities.

(Dryden and Vos 2001: 61)

Dryden and Vos have written a book you will either love or hate. There is no modesty in its blurb; it promises to be a catalyst to change the way you think, live, learn, work, teach and act. Most importantly, it is great fun to read. This is an inspirational text, rather than an academic one, and summarises research in a popular format from a wide range of disciplines. It reports that knowledge is already bringing about revolutionary breakthroughs in learning, education, business and families. It presents current findings crisply and clearly and the layout helps easy reading. You may disagree with some of the evaluations and find the hype off-putting, but it is a book worth reading either as a starting point to challenging conventional views about learning or as a popular review to some of the work being done on translating new ideas about teaching and learning into practice around the world. The book is also available to read on-line at http://www.thelearningweb.net.

There has been a revolution in the study of the mind over the past 40 years resulting in amazing findings about the power of the brain. So far, most of the practical outcomes of this are for business and personal growth. In the past five years, however, the implications of these new ideas have been developed and adapted for education. In both the USA and the UK, much of this work is through commercially based professional development organisations. Their success with practitioners, pupils and students is leading to a change in the approach of central government and a greater awareness of the need to vary teaching styles and encourage creativity in both learning and teaching.

A new science of learning

On a more academic note, a new science of learning is emerging, which has important implications for education. This new theory of learning leads to a very different approach to the design of curriculum, teaching and assessment. It involves a growth of interdisciplinary inquiries and new kinds of scientific collaborations. This integrated approach to research has helped make the path from empirical research to educational practice more visible. In particular, neuroscience is beginning to show how learning changes the physical structure of the brain. This starts at conception and is heavily concentrated in the first four years of life. However, for those of us who are a little older than this, neuroscience provides some useful findings about ways in which the brain fixes itself. There are also strategies to keep the brain sharp as we age.

The American National Research Council (2000) summarised the work of two of its committees linking the findings of research on the science of learning to actual practice in the classroom. They consider the latest research in the field and explore the development of a variety of research approaches and techniques and ways in which evidence from many different branches of science is beginning to converge. Here is their summary:

- Research from cognitive psychology has increased understanding of the nature of competent performance and the principles of knowledge organization that underlie people's abilities to solve problems in a wide variety of areas, including mathematics, science, literature, social studies and history.

- Developmental researchers have shown that young children understand a great deal about basic principles of biology and physical causality, about number, narrative and personal intent, and that these capabilities make it possible to create innovative curricula that introduce important concepts for advanced reasoning at early ages.

- Research on learning and transfer has uncovered important principles for structured learning experiences that enable people to use what they have learnt in new settings.

- Work in social psychology, cognitive psychology and anthropology is making clear that all learning takes place in settings that have particular sets of cultural and social norms and expectations and that these settings influence learning and transfer in powerful ways.

- Neuroscience is beginning to provide evidence for many principles of learning that have emerged from laboratory research, and it is showing how learning changes the physical structure of the brain and with it, the functional organization of the brain.

- Collaborative studies of the design and evaluation of learning environments, among cognitive and developmental psychologists and educators are yielding to new knowledge about the nature of learning and teaching as it takes place in a variety of settings. In addition, researchers are discovering ways to learn from the 'wisdom of practice' that comes from successful teachers who can share their expertise.

- Emerging technologies are leading to the development of many new opportunities to guide and enhance learning that were unimagined even a few years ago.

(National Research Council [NRC] 2000: 4)

In the beginning, these new research findings had little opportunity to develop in the UK, as the National Strategies from Key Stage 1 to Key Stage 3 relied on a delivery input. This teaching style, particularly the literacy lesson format, has permeated into other curriculum areas as well at Key Stages 1 and 2, e.g. history and geography lessons starting with the 'big' book for information and followed up with five ability groups doing short-term tasks.

The National Literacy and Numeracy Strategies from Key Stages 1 to 3 were supported by a vast quantity of central government and commercial publications which set out generic planning for these two subjects. This planning now includes very detailed lesson plans telling the teacher what to do, say and practise. Central Government Standards outlined for the Foundation Degrees and Initial Teacher Training Degrees are similar, in that they encourage writers of texts – such as this – to write for specific standards. The danger is that the standard then has a defined and fixed content, which does not take account of the learning needs of individuals studying the course, the placement situations in which they work and changes in technology which may have occurred in the lapse of time between writing and reading. This is to some extent inevitable, but the important task of both the reader and writer is to acknowledge that this is taking place.

Research into the brain and improving learning

Anything you learned two years ago is old information. Neuro-science is exploding.

(Kotulak 1996, in Dryden and Vos 2001)

The pace of research related to the brain is phenomenal. Methodological advances have been made in the field of developmental psychology and much of what is known about how the mind works comes from the study of how infants learn. For example, it is now possible to use non-nutritive sucking as a means of showing that infants from 5 to 12 weeks old can learn how to control a projector lens, so that the images shown come into focus more clearly (NRC 2000). Clearly, new knowledge about the working of the brain has important implications for learning and teaching if we now have the techniques to see into the learning process of a five-week-old baby.

Dryden and Vos (2001) provide a quick overview of the potential for learning. Your 'magic brain' as they dub it:

- has a trillion brain cells;
- can grow up to 20,000 branches;
- has four distinct brains in one;
- has two sides that work together;
- runs a 'telephone exchange' that shuttles millions of messages a second between the left and right sides;
- has many different intelligence centres;
- operates on at least four separate wavelengths;
- controls a transmission system that flashes chemical-electrical messages instantly;
- holds the key to your own personal revolution.

Popular authors such as Tony Buzan use such findings to provide learning self-help manuals for us all. Buzan and Buzan (2003) have produced many books, audio cassettes and videos on the brain and how to improve memory; Mind Map®; develop thinking and creativity; and speed read. These are easy to follow 'handbooks' about improving the working capability of your own brain. They have produced several for children. Like Dryden and Vos, Buzan and Buzan provide a useful reminder that finding out more about our own learning style informs our knowledge about learning and teaching.

The Educational Kinaesthetics movement looks directly at strategies using simple movements to integrate the whole brain, the senses and the body to prepare people with the physical skills they need to learn more effectively. It originally came from the United States and was the result of research into learning and brain function by Paul Dennison (www. braingym.org, accessed August 2003). Originally, its aim was to help adults and children with learning difficulties such as dyslexia, dyspraxia and Attention Deficit Hyperactivity Disorder (AD/HD). It has now developed into a more generic action programme to improve everyone's life. The benefit claims are extensive and linked closely to the Healthy Schools programme in the UK. The Brain Gym® movements are claimed to help with:

- academic skills – reading, writing, spelling and maths;
- memory, concentration and focus;
- physical co-ordination and balance;
- communication skills and language development;
- self-development and personal stress management;
- the achievement of goals, both professional and personal.

The Brain Gym® philosophy is being used very successfully in many UK schools and practical strategies such as drinking water in classrooms and 'brain breaks' are now quite common in many Local Education Authorities (LEAs). Smith and Call (1999) provide several examples of this and link it closely to their accelerated learning approach. Ginns (2002) provides examples for secondary pupils.

Multiple intelligences

Howard Gardner (1983) suggests that we each have several different types of intelligence, but only two of them are valued in traditional education. He calls the first one *linguistic intelligence* and this covers our ability to read, write and communicate with words. The second one is *logical or mathematical* and this gives us our ability to reason and calculate. If we look back at our own educational experience, we can see that most of assessments we have ever undertaken have focused on these two talents. If we look in schools today, we can see much the same. Gardner says that this gives us a limited view of learning potential and suggests that there are at least six other individual intelligences:

- visual/spatial intelligence;
- musical intelligence;
- bodily/physical intelligence;
- interpersonal intelligence;
- intra-personal or reflective intelligence;
- naturalistic intelligence.

Fuller descriptions of these intelligences are found on the Accelerated Learning website www.accelerated-learning-uk.co.uk (accessed September 2003).

The link between Gardner's work on learning styles and work on visual, auditory and kinaesthetic (VAK) learning styles is simple. Gardner's learning styles are linked with specific intelligences, which he has identified in eight centres of the brain. VAK identifies the main pathways to the brain through which we learn. The VAK process is a summary of the six pathways through which we learn:

- by what we see;

- by what we hear;

- by what we taste;

- by what we touch;

- by what we smell;

- by what we do.

The senses of taste, touch and smell link with the practical activity of 'doing' to make the pre-ferred kinaesthetic learning style. When looking at all these ideas, it is important to remember that just because you identify yourself as having a specific learning style, this does not mean that all your learning must take place in this way. Translated into 'teaching' styles, it means that teachers need to take account of and value different learning styles, while working to extend the opportunities that we all have to develop other styles. Various sup-porting materials from the national strategies promote the use of teaching methods that allow children access to the curriculum using their different learning styles, e.g. Key Stage 3 National Strategy *Learning Styles and Writing* series of guidance documents for different subject areas (DfES 2002, www.standards.dfes.gov.uk/keystage3/publications, accessed September 2003).

Accelerated learning/mind-based learning/brain friendly learning

We use all of these terms to describe the practical strategies for learning and teaching which these new research developments have indicated are necessary. Rose (1985) originally coined the term 'accelerated learning'. Initially, the American management training system used the concept but only recently have its growth and expansion come into the UK education system. This is largely through the work of Alistair Smith, the organisation Alite and the publishing house Network Educational Press. The Alite website www.alite.co.uk (accessed August 2003) contains useful readings, case studies, bulletin boards and courses. It suggests an accelerated learning cycle to aid learning which teachers and learners share. Strategies include:

- work on physiology and learning linked to Maslow's work on 'hierarchy of needs'. These strategies acknowledge that learners have to be in a good physical state for learn-ing which includes learners having:
  - constant access to water to avoid dehydration which can lead to drowsiness, inatten-tion and poor learning;
  - a good diet;
  - a room to work in with the appropriate temperature;
  - physical breaks, also known as 'brain breaks'.

- teaching specific skills such as listening, paying attention, concentrating, good sitting, etc.

- providing a good, secure and purposeful working environment.

The accelerated learning strategies also draw on Goleman's (1996) work. Goleman refines what it 'takes to be smart'. In the UK, it is being used in the Learning Mentor Training to give support to 'under-achieving' and 'non-productive' pupils, and in many schools the term 'Emotional Literacy' is being used to describe in more detail what is meant by a 'good, secure and purposeful learning/working environment'.

The Twenty-First-Century Learning Society

You can expect to have on your wrist tomorrow what you have on your desk today, what filled a room yesterday.

(Negroponte, cited by Dryden and Vos 2001: 42)

This is the age of instant communication, which is changing the shape of the future. Educational institutions are already changing to accommodate this, but they are changing slowly. One of the main features of the learning revolution is that the Internet can change your life and your learning because it is global, personal, interactive, low cost and forever growing and changing. The personal computer (PC) has revolutionised individual learning and provides access to electronic, interactive, multimedia software, which, coupled with the Internet, can provide almost unlimited potential for learning and education.

It is always dangerous to predict what sort of technological changes will take place, which will significantly alter learning and teaching. We might ask how the massive growth of texting and e-mail should alter what is taught in literacy lessons. After all, we no longer teach children to write with quill or fountain pens, so how do we adapt and respond to writing needs in the future? The answers to such questions are unpredictable. What we can be sure of is that such changes will take place and all of us will need to learn to swim in the tide, or otherwise drown.

Conclusion

This chapter reviewed some of the work that has been done on how people, particularly children, learn and how all of us, including babies, are both learners and teachers. It points out that we are now in the challenging position of being part of a learning revolution, which is changing nearly all our assumptions about effective learning and teaching. Marjorie had recognised this and intuitively sought to make changes to her practice. This chapter has identified texts, individuals and groups who have tried and tested different strategies to support people like her – adults who support learning and teaching. Many of these make inspirational reading and will help us all face the challenges ahead.

Discussion Starters

1 What factors make it easier for us to learn?
2 How are nurseries/schools/colleges/universities changing to encourage a more positive working environment for their pupils/students?
3 How is technology changing current practice in teaching and learning?

Reflecting on Practice

1 This chart is adapted from the Learning Mentors Module (DfES 2001, 2002). Suggest at least one strategy which could be used to help the learner and record this in the final column. You might find it useful to identify a specific age group for the learners.

Characteristic displayed	Principle	Suggested action
Learner regularly arrives late to school and is tired and/or hungry	Brain needs adequate food and rest to work effectively	
Children feel tired, seem inattentive during long lessons	Brain needs adequate oxygen supply and water	
Learner is impatient to begin and complete activities. Likely to be among the more restless in the class. Fidgets during teacher input and own work	Learner likely to have a preferred learning style which is kinaesthetic	
Learner forgets verbal instructions	Likely to have a preferred learning style which is visual	

2 Identify five other ways in which you have learned something from reading this chapter, or by using further reading, which will help you in your workplace. Compare your five points with those of a colleague.

Websites

www.accelerated-learning-uk.co.uk – free learning profile for adults based on Howard Gardner's theory of multiple intelligences.

www.alite.co.uk – Alite website.

www.braingym.org – website giving an overview of Paul Dennison's work.

www.briantaylor.com/Socrates.htm – website giving overview of Socrates and his method of teaching.

www.Mind-Map.com – Buzan Centre for details of books, software, audio and video tapes.

www.nwlink.com/~donclark/hrd/styles.html – Don Clark has an on-line lecture on learning styles.

www.skepdic.com/ – The Skeptic's Dictionary website provides some fascinating descriptions and insights into specific theories.

References

Alexander, R., Rose, J. and Woodhead, C. (1992) *Curriculum Organisation and Classroom Practice in Primary Schools*, London: Department of Education and Science.

Alfrey, M.A. and Durell, J.A. (2003) 'How children think and learn', in Alfrey, C. (ed.), *Understanding Children's Learning: A Text for Teaching Assistants*, London: David Fulton, pp. 1–18.

Bennett, N. (1976) *Teaching Styles and Pupil Progress*, London: Open Books.

Blyth, J. (1990) *History in Primary Schools*, Milton Keynes: Open University Press.

Bruce, T. (1987) *Early Childhood Education*, London: Hodder and Stoughton.

Buzan, T. and Buzan, B. (2003) *The Mind Map® Book*, London: BBC Worldwide.

Dennison, P. and Dennison, G. (1986) *Brain Gym*, London: Body Balance Books.

DfEE (1998) *The National Literacy Strategy: Framework for Teaching English YR to Y6*, London: DfEE.

DfEE (1999) *The National Numeracy Strategy: Framework for Teaching Mathematics Years R to 6*, Cambridge: Cambridge University Press.

DfEE/QCA (2000) *Curriculum Guidance for the Foundation Stage*, London: HMSO.

DfES (2001) *Mentor Training Modules 1–4*, Liverpool: DfES and Liverpool Excellence Partnership.

DfES (2002) Key Stage 3 National Strategy Learning Styles and Writing series of guidance documents for different subject areas, at www.standards.dfes.gov.uk/keystage3/publications, accessed September 2003.

Dryden, G. and Vos, J. (2001) *The Learning Revolution*, Stafford: Network Educational Press. Also available on-line (freely) at http://www.thelearningweb.net.

Galton, M. (1980) *Inside Primary Classrooms*, London: Routledge and Kegan Paul.

Gardner, H. (1983) *Frames of Mind: The Theory of Multiple Intelligences*, Oxford: Heinemann. Summary, at http://www.ed.psu.edu/insys/ESD/gardner/menu.html.

Ginns, P. (2002) *The Teacher's Toolkit: Raise Classroom Achievement with Strategies for Every Learner*, London: Crown House Publishing.

Goleman, D. (1996) *Emotional Intelligence*, London: Bloomsbury.

Hughes, P. (2002) *Principles of Primary Education Study Guide*, London: David Fulton.

McDonald, S. (1999) 'First Steps to improving literacy', in *Literacy Today*, 21, accessed on-line at www.literacytrust.org.uk/../Pubs/macdonald.html, September 2003.

National Research Council (2000) *How People Learn: Brain, Mind, Experience, and School*, Washington, DC: National Academic Press, accessed on-line at http://www.nap.edu, August 2003.

Rose, C. (1985) *Accelerated Learning*, New York: Basic Books.

Smith, A. and Call, N. (1999) *The Alps Approach: Accelerated Learning in Primary Schools*, Stafford: Network Educational Press.

Whitebread, D. (ed.) (2002) *Teaching and Learning in the Early Years*, 2nd edn, London: Routledge Falmer.

Audio cassettes

Goleman, D. (1996) *Emotional Intelligence*, Thorsons Audio.

Tracy, B. with Rose, C. (1995) *Accelerated Learning Techniques*, Simon and Schuster Audio.

4

Raising the Bar: Improving Children's Performance through Information and Communication Technology

Sue Crowley and Mike Richardson

Meet Inez

I am so pleased to have just taken up a new post as a teaching assistant (inclusion) in a Year 3 primary classroom that allows me to take a lead role in supporting the inclusion of children using ICT in other subjects/topics. I love using computers and have a lot of confidence with them. So I could help the children, I completed the Parents as Educators course at Level 2 and have used some of the New Opportunities Fund training materials for ICT available in the school.

The children have not had much experience of using ICT independently. They have mostly used self-contained instructional CD-ROMs that were subject-based and they use word-processing to write up work. I will support the children by preparing ICT and other resources to support children with special educational needs and/or showing challenging behaviour in a range of subjects. However, I still need more support in applying my skills in ICT to learning situations and understanding how to help the children make effective use of the resources.

Introduction

Information and Communication Technology (ICT) can be an extra, versatile tool for learning, which sits alongside books, pens, glue and other vital items in the primary and secondary teacher's toolbox. In the past, children were introduced, sometimes reluctantly, to many such tools from slates to slide rules, and Heppell points out in the Foreword to Loveless and Ellis (2001) that they have even had innovations such as the ballpoint pen and mobile phones confiscated. However, it is now time to embrace new technologies and use them to change and improve pedagogy. The desire of the teacher should not be to set a standard that all children must achieve, but rather to enable children to realise that ICT offers practical and fun ways to achieve more. The assistant in the classroom needs to be prepared to reinforce this ethos and Inez is an example of one who exemplifies the need for specialist support in the use of ICT if it is to become firmly established as a quality learning resource in school. We believe our children need to know about the use of ICT in everyday life around them and its potential for the future, but more importantly they deserve opportunities to begin to realise the full potential of ICT as a tool to support and present their developing learning and creativity.

One ultimate goal of the use of ICT in education is that the pupils are able to use the technology independently and appropriately. Moseley *et al*. (1999) found that successful teachers of ICT gave children choices rather than directing them. Teachers who were not confident users of ICT would employ another adult to help and direct the children with ICT and hence not use ICT in any way to change pedagogy. The teaching assistant is not simply someone to sit with the children while they are at the computer, but can prepare specific resources and activities as Inez does. In addition, the assistant will help the children learn how to use ICT for learning. Pupil empowerment is more desirable rather than receiving instruction or completing work from an adult's point of view. Naturally, children need to acquire certain skills, which need teaching. However, once basic skills have been learned, ICT offers a medium that is ripe for experimentation. Children show fewer inhibitions than adults and are more willing to try different icons and menus without fear of damaging the computer. They may not experiment if an over-zealous adult tells them what to do, or presses the keys for them. Having said this, there are great advantages to having assistants in the classroom to support learning with ICT; they may act as teacher, guide, mentor, resource-maker (e.g. Inez) and assessor.

Confidence and Skills

Monteith (2002) suggests that teachers who are skilful in ICT are most likely to develop skilful pupils. It is important that the teacher and the assistant both feel confident that they can support their children with ICT skills and have sufficient knowledge to be able to plan appropriate ICT activities into the curriculum for all children. At secondary level, children will learn many ICT skills in their ICT lessons, before applying them in other curriculum areas, where they may require specific support. This chapter does not include guides to software but we hope that both the teacher and assistant are aware of areas for their own personal development. Remember that nobody needs to know everything about the appropriate software to be effective. It is important to stay open-minded as your learning continues, so that you will be able to support pupils' ICT work appropriately.

The teacher and the assistant should work in partnership to develop ICT capability for themselves and their pupils. If both adults have little experience, then it might be best to take different aspects of ICT to develop personally, then pool and share their knowledge and ideas. If the assistant is new to ICT, and the teacher has some knowledge, then they could spend some concentrated time, i.e. an in-service morning or afternoon going through the core skills in relation to the ICT planned for the term/year. It is better to spend time learning, and teaching each other, away from the busy school day. Ideally, teachers will give the assistant time and opportunities to get to know all the ICT peripherals so that he or she will be able to do what is required with ICT. For example, the children will benefit from the assistant's ability to use a digital camera immediately when a situation arises. Too often, we miss the opportunity of catching children's smiles of satisfaction when they have recognised a significant achievement.

The general principle we are trying to promote here is that teachers and assistants should try, as much as possible, to pre-empt potential causes of frustration. You can promote a positive attitude to the subject by refusing to allow the computer or any ICT equipment to become a 'nuisance in the corner'. When all the adults in the room are prepared to cope with the difficulties and know when to refer difficulties to a technician, the more they will view the computer as a valuable learning and teaching tool. We need to be positive about ICT no matter how we feel! When unsure, we must seek help from a sympathetic technician, friend, colleague or relative and explain that we want to learn how to do things for ourselves (not just be shown). The secret of becoming a confident user of ICT is to use it a little and often at first and be prepared to ask for advice. We practise what we preach; we have been using computers for personal use and in our teaching for nearly 20 years, but we will still come into each other's rooms and say 'How can you do this?' or 'Is there another way to . . .?'

As a confident user of ICT, a teaching assistant can be invaluable to a school as one assistant from Castlefield Infant School, Rastrick (DfES 2003a) stated:

> I advise, I teach ICT in small groups, I keep my own records, run parents and pupils sessions and a lunchtime ICT club, and by fair means or foul have encouraged the other staff to use e-mail. I used the children's enthusiasm for e-mail to influence the teachers.
>
> (www.teachernet.gov.uk, accessed June 2003)

The head teacher from Mission Primary School (DfES 2003b) has also praised his teaching assistant on her knowledge of the use of ICT:

> Julie exemplifies the progressive development of the TAs. In addition to her classroom support duties she has also become expert in training pupils in the use of ICT. Julie has a powerful influence in ICT. In partnership with the designated teacher, she has reviewed the QCA requirements for ICT. She has then selected the most appropriate software to deliver the curriculum. I have tried to promote the idea that each TA develops a specialist expertise such as literacy, numeracy or special needs, and that these skills are then practised across the curriculum. In this way the TAs develop two focuses to their work: one will be class-based but the other is related to the whole school curriculum. Like Julie with ICT, each TA then becomes an important additional resource in a specialist area. The response of the TAs has been overwhelmingly positive.
>
> (www.teachernet.gov.uk, accessed June 2003)

Many primary and secondary schools in the north-west of England are now employing assistants with particular ICT expertise to work in the classroom. This has happened because of a service agreement with an IT company. They have signed up to a level of service that includes a weekly visit from a technical assistant. Teaching assistants often receive training alongside the staff to enable them to function in partnership with the technical support staff from the outside agency. There are many ways to implement these support facilities and this is usually a senior management decision in the school.

One result of the situation outlined above might be the introduction of *peer tutoring* to a school. A school in Birmingham and a number of schools in the Merseyside region have successfully implemented such an initiative. Indeed, it was so successful in improving ICT skills in one class in one Merseyside primary school that the teacher implemented the system for mathematics as well! Peer tutoring is a way of boosting the acquisition of basic computer skills and, as such, is a valuable opportunity to ensure that a school's ethos permeates the delivery of ICT. The main idea is that the classroom teacher or assistant trains the children in mentoring skills. These children pass on ICT skills and knowledge to other children. It is an effective use of support because the teacher or teaching assistant can take the mentors away as a group and demonstrate a new skill or piece of software, usually in a suite or at a bank of computers. The important factor is that no one person becomes the fount of all computer knowledge and children are encouraged to learn to seek help from more than one person. Teaching assistants may play a part in the training of peer tutors. It is important to remember that nobody expects the teaching assistant to be a computer expert, but rather to be prepared to oversee the children and train them in mentoring techniques that are simple and straightforward. These mentoring skills can be learned independently of any computer knowledge and chiefly involve common-sense rules and some areas of 'etiquette' that are covered when training people to use the hardware, such as 'Do not grab the mouse'. All people training individuals on computers would do well to make these rules of etiquette part of their own good practice!

Making Opportunities, Planning and Assessing

Whether it is a whole-staff or departmental approach, the ICT co-ordinator's or the class teacher's plan, the curriculum at all levels should include ICT for the whole year. In this way, ICT opportunities can be broad, balanced and progressive. Planning should start with the big picture: a table of topics in all taught subjects in the year with identified opportunities where ICT can support the subject. Obvious examples might be:

- a Key Stage 3 geographical topic on the local environment, possibly leading to the children producing a leaflet to advertise local amenities;

- a Key Stage 2 mathematical topic on 2-D shapes, involving work with a programmable toy;

- a Foundation Stage topic on the seasons, using an art programme to show what a tree looks like at different times of the year, e.g. a picture could be pre-made by the teacher or assistant of the trunk and branches and the children complete the picture.

Once all the obvious ICT is in place for the year, an audit needs to be made of the types of ICT used to ensure a balance. Auditing is a simple process of gathering information about the delivery of ICT. As teachers are very busy, any lightening of administrative duties that help to inform their teaching is generally welcomed. Hence, the teaching assistant may find that he or she becomes involved in the auditing process. There needs to be some of each aspect of ICT across the curriculum, i.e. communication, information retrieval, information handling in the form of data collection and graphs, presentation, modelling, monitoring and control. If one type of ICT is lacking from the first scrutiny of the year plan, then teachers should seek opportunities to extend the range where it would be appropriate. At times, it may be relevant to plan a discrete ICT project in order that aspects such as control or modelling are taught as part of a specific ICT lesson. In addition to ensuring the ICT curriculum is taught, an audit will look at the resources needed to deliver the lessons. For example, some equipment may need servicing or need the batteries changed. Although the ICT co-ordinator, head of department or technician is the person who has primary responsibility for ensuring these resources are in place and working, he or she will rely heavily on other members of staff at the school to inform them when these maintenance or preparation tasks are required as well as help with suggestions on how to improve provision. A teaching assistant working closely with children using ICT will make a valuable addition to the team.

In making use of resources some software can be used in ways that were not conceived of by the designers. An example of this would be using PowerPoint to provide a mental maths starter using the timing feature to keep the pace at the correct level for the children. Preparing such resources requires investment in development time but, once created, they can be used repeatedly, either in subsequent years or with other classes. We would suggest that repeated use and modification for other classes are essential if you are going to get good returns for the time invested in preparation.

If the school is following the QCA schemes of work, then planning is relatively easy with plenty of guidance available at www.standards.dfes.gov.uk/schemes3/. The site provides examples of adaptations made to ICT schemes of work at Key Stages 1–3 to fit in with the school's curriculum and the children's needs. Short-term planning based on the schemes should include reference to any assistant's role. As stated earlier, this does not necessarily mean that the assistant is sitting by the computer or other ICT peripheral all the time. A variety of support strategies is best. This will allow the teacher and the assistant to enjoy more varied styles and methods of teaching and will give the children an opportunity to experience a variety of teaching and learning styles. Naturally, the teaching assistant can support the teacher with assessment procedures. These will vary slightly from school to school, and different age phases, but will often include the organisation of a portfolio of selected work for each child, either printed or saved into a folder on a hard drive or disc. Advice on assessing children's work is on the DfES website www.ncaction.org.uk/.

Using Individual or Small Groups of Computers

Individual or small groups of computers are often found in both primary and secondary school situations. The primary classroom might have a single stand-alone computer, or one linked to the Internet. In a secondary school, a group of computers is often found within a departmental area as a central resource for the subject. In both primary and secondary schools, there is often one or more dedicated ICT suites. Teachers use these facilities in different ways to suit the curriculum and the situation in the school.

Teaching the skills

Inevitably, computer skills such as inserting and moving images need to be taught to most children at some time in order to carry out planned projects. For example, in making a poster/leaflet to advertise local amenities, in a geography project, the assistant and teacher will have to do the following preparatory work. First, they will need to discuss a list of skills required. These skills will include:

- the ability to use font sizes and colours appropriately;
- the use of text editing features such as centring, <u>underlining</u> and **bold**;
- the insertion, resizing and moving of images;
- the use of digital camera for the more able;
- the use of word art;
- the use of three columns to make a fold-over leaflet.

Prior assessment of the children's knowledge and ability will need to be carried out and a plan of action drawn up as to who needs to be taught what. You should not need to teach the entire class all the skills. If the children are in small groups of similar ability, then the teacher or assistant can teach each small group the skill required for the project; this would move them forward from where they are in their computer knowledge. These small ICT ability groups may not fit in snugly with numeracy and literacy groups in a primary school situation, or in subject groups at secondary school. We suggest that at primary level the assistant can take them out of the subject lesson for 10–15 minutes and teach computer skills related to the planned subject ICT activity. Inez might follow this suggestion. It is quite feasible in many schools, as long as it fits in with the subject expectations. Once the project is underway, the children will learn from each other any particular skill they really want.

When children are learning from one another, some may see this as an opportunity for feeling superior or even carrying out minor bullying. We can prevent such bullying by establishing a good ethos in the school that leads to a clear etiquette for computer use. Peer tutoring principles can help. The key features are the selection of children as tutors, training in mentoring skills and clear expectations given of what was involved. Such a system needs to be a whole-school strategy.

Using the computer as a tool

Once the teacher or assistant has taught the skills of a project, then the children can use the classroom computer/s on a rota system for small groups or as individuals to produce and present their work. Ideally, no other adult should be required for this project; however, ideal situations and computers don't always mix! The children should know that if they have an important query either the teacher or the assistant is available. Therefore, only one of these adults should be working with concentration with a group of children while the other is available to ensure the computer project can progress, allowing the children to work independently. The children need to know who is on 'computer duty'; you could follow the example of a colleague of mine who used to put on an apron with a large cat on the front when she didn't want to be disturbed! A wall display containing 'prompts' is very useful for older children at Key Stages 2 and 3, especially if situated near the computer area. Such a display aids independence, and is something for which Inez might take responsibility.

Some computer activities may require planned intervention in order to encourage thought and reflection. For example, when producing computer graphs from data collected from an investigation, there needs to be the prompt 'What does your graph tell you about your findings?' or when using a modelling program that includes decisions; 'Why did you take that path?' This need not occur often but it is a good opportunity for speaking and listening skills to develop alongside reflective thought. However, the teacher and assistant need to discuss whatever is going on that day and decide on the teaching strategy and who will do what, whether it is teaching, planned intervention or waiting for invitations to help. This kind of approach works well in situations where there is less time pressure on the curriculum. For example, in Sweden where the compulsory element to the curriculum is approximately half that of our own, teaching assistants are able to provide support to children as they engage in independent learning activities.

The Computer Suite

If the teacher and assistant teach skills in the classroom as described earlier, the focus in computer suite time might be project work. However, in the secondary school situation skill teaching most likely occurs in the computer suite, as part of the ICT curriculum. The children will then apply the learned skills in the departmental areas. Having a teacher and an assistant in the suite enables all children to receive support and move on as necessary. Groups of children of similar abilities might be near each other and each adult has allotted groups. There may also be opportunities for mixed ability groups to work together, in which case it is more than likely that the job of adults in the room is to ensure all children participate and that some are not dominating or sitting back. A mixture of these methods may be desirable during a term or year to benefit all children. The pedagogy should match the objective and the children, and all adults in the room should understand their part in the lesson and not interfere with or undermine another's role. The teaching assistant can aid differentiation especially when skill teaching is required as part of the work in the suite. One adult could teach a small group of children while the majority are getting on with work at the computers supervised by the other adult.

If the computer suite is small, or is very large with room for worktables, then one group could use computers while others do similar work off the computer either in the classroom or at the worktables. This work could be a lead-up to computer work, e.g. planning a story or presentation, it may be book research to complement and compare with computer-based research or it may be similar complementary work. A successful Internet site activity could lend itself to the teaching assistant producing similar off-computer activities to reinforce knowledge or understanding.

ICT Supporting Subject Teaching

A good practitioner would always make quality resources available for his or her classroom and to support the children's learning; this also holds true with ICT. The teacher and assistant can prepare resources to motivate learning for research, to reinforce learning and to support the children's learning. Some resources for the computer can be made quickly and some may take a while but the main advantage of computer-made resources is that they can be stored for future use and adaptation. They will not wear out, fade or curl up at the edges! These resources are easy to make once teachers and assistants master simple skills, and it actually takes less time compared with making the same resources from card and felt tips. It is possible to make economical, but professional-looking resources using the computer, a printer and a laminator. Something for Inez to master!

In subjects, ICT is an effective and appropriate resource to teach objectives within the National Curriculum and not the objectives for ICT capability (Tyldesley 2002). ICT may support pupils through all their subjects but not necessarily all the time; the significant factor is the efficiency and effectiveness of the mode of delivery. At present, the first part of many lessons in most schools involves whole-class teaching. Coincidentally, presentation tools such as the digital projector or, even better, the interactive whiteboard have been developed, producing innovative uses of technology to support lessons. These resources actively engage and motivate the pupils. Presentations on various topics are easy to make by copying and pasting illustrations and text from the Internet and then editing the text to suit the particular abilities and needs of the pupils. Such presentations are useful as an introduction to a topic and can then be utilised as a source of information for independent work later. The benefit of these tools to the teacher is enormous. A teacher can model new concepts to the whole class simply and without much technical knowledge. The equipment is becoming easier to set up, and in some classrooms, it will already be present. Its use is very intuitive. That is to say, the interactive whiteboards are merely an extension of what the teacher might use anyway. Some commercial educational IT providers offer many support resources with software for use with this type of equipment. Again, it is not the hardware that provides the solution but its application. During the recent Primary Step project in Liverpool the interactive whiteboard was used to great effect in a Numeracy road show. Children playing a mathematics game using the whiteboard in a game show format were able to develop some very complex mathematical language in a 40-minute period. Interactive whiteboards come with their own software and one can download further software from the Internet to produce pre-made resources. This is generally easy to use and will employ the interactivity of the boards. There are many advantages to using interactive boards in any subject:

- features of programs can be highlighted;
- Internet sites can be viewed collectively;
- notes can be collaboratively produced, saved or printed for future reference;
- they allow learners to absorb information more easily.

However, there may be disadvantages to interactive whiteboards in terms of cost, durability and operation.

ICT enhances the process of shared reading or problem solving in many subjects due to the interactivity and the quality of the text. For example, teachers or children can highlight the text on CDs and Internet sites if necessary to make a point such as text indicating the feelings of a character. Unfortunately, the text will not stay highlighted using these sources but when copied and pasted into a word processing package the highlighting and text colouring features can mark points permanently in the text. The advantage of using such a self-made resource is that of tailoring it to match the ability and interests of the pupils. Talking books can also be self-made – all you need is a microphone, your voice and a bit of know-how! During shared writing, an adult or children can word process the ideas for further editing either as a class, or for group or individual activities.

ICT software gives the teacher and the teaching assistant the tools to make quality versions of games and the ability to include support where needed. Most games break down into well-known types:

- matching games;
- race games (depending on the accumulation of points);
- games to find missing objects or quantities (the basis for algebra!);
- pattern recognition;
- strategy games;
- calculation games.

There are probably many other types but how would you categorise Snap? Some commercial companies have produced games that are full of scenarios that reinforce mathematical development through problem solving. One such CD-ROM is 'The Logical Journey of the "Zoombinis" ', produced by Broderbund. The game consists of a challenge to take a group of little people on a journey to their 'promised land'. The problems solved on the way contribute to their success. Other games may reinforce subject concepts such as a historical timeline. These applications relate strongly to the idea of learning through play that some early years practitioners advocate (Bruce and Meggitt 2002). The assistant can always take a small group on one computer while the teacher takes most of the class.

The advantage of the children working on the computer with these resources is that they are more able to collaborate; they may try different ideas, read their work and edit their work more willingly. The main benefit for the children is that they can clearly see previously written text on the screen. Unfortunately, children do find writing using a keyboard quite difficult and slow. Children often express concern about spelling because they find their writing full of the teacher's alterations. Teachers and assistants can make resources to support children's writing. There are some excellent children's word processors such as Clicker Plus which include the feature of a word bank. The word bank allows the adult to input a selection of words for the pupil. Images can accompany the words for ease of recognition. The pupil then has to click on a desired word to insert it into the word processing page at the cursor. Similarly, an overlay keyboard and relevant software are useful in this situation. An overlay keyboard is a rectangular lightweight board attached to the computer. It has touch sensitive pads, to program with words or phrases, and pictures. Overlay keyboards are useful in all phases of education for a variety of subject-related applications.

In our experience, children gain in confidence in their writing by using word banks or overlay keyboards. The smile on Reception children's faces when they have completed their first sentence is a joy to behold and this support develops their reading as well as their confidence in writing. They read the words with an adult on the word bank, read them again as they go onto the screen in their sentence, read the complete sentence, read it when it is printed out and then go and read it to any child in the class willing to listen. We hope that the reinforcement of this reading will continue when the child takes the printout home. One of us used this method of supporting writing with an older child, Ryan:

> Nine-year-old Ryan was a reluctant writer and deemed himself a failure; yet at a visit to a wildlife sanctuary, he asked interesting and informed questions of our guide, showing that he had intelligence and was very interested in the water birds. I did not want that enthusiasm to wane when we were back at school the next day writing about our experiences so I developed an overlay (BBC computer and concept keyboard) with all the words I thought he might use. Ryan wrote all day! He produced a good piece of work, which had centre place on our display; he was very proud of his achievement and the confidence gained transferred to his ordinary writing with paper and pen.

Writing frames can also support children's writing when appropriate, e.g. a newspaper-style file with headings and sub-headings, a persuasive writing frame with sentence beginnings such as 'The reason most people want a by-pass is . . .' or a ready-made file with relevant images inserted in order that pupils can select, copy and paste those ones appropriate for their writing.

However, there are some questions about supporting children without masking their learning difficulties. For example:

- Isn't the computer going to do calculations for the children and mask their true ability?
- Can't children use the software to get the answers?

This would be true if the computers were teaching machines. We advocate a different approach that allows the children to interact with modelled situations, asking questions of a hypothetical nature and using the elements of computers and software to solve problems. Children need support with the process and the more engaging the process, the more likely a child is to see a problem through to its solution. However, there are times where a computer can make repetitive tasks more challenging and therefore more interesting too. In either case, the computer can only do whatever the child inputs and so it cannot mask their difficulties. In fact, it can help to identify difficulties and provide a means of addressing them.

We have already hinted at some areas where the computer might play a positive role in discussing modelled situations. This is a major role for ICT. Here ICT has some definite advantages in trying to explain events in the world past, present or future. Imagine the difficulty of explaining how the earth revolves around the sun. We cannot observe this from a sufficiently distant viewpoint to get the whole picture, which has led to phrases in our language such as 'the sun rises'. It doesn't. Not in the literal sense such as a child tends to think in at seven years old. So how do we explain the concept? Using darkened rooms, reproduction planets suspended from the ceiling and torches, we can attempt to model the phenomena. Modelling in ICT merely uses the graphical tools on the computer to represent these events. Use of these may inspire one to develop skills in this area and become a real benefit to the children in the class. The National Numeracy Strategy (NNS) (Department for Education and Skills 2000) provides some very good animations to illustrate problems in practical ways, to model the mathematics for the children.

In mathematics, younger children rely on concrete operations to aid the understanding of ideas. A programmable toy moving along a number track, or number line in combinations of steps, will aid the formation of the concepts of addition, subtraction and multiplication. Disguising the repetition of mathematical operations in a game is a long-established technique in supporting mathematical development, but more importantly, the programmable toy is modelling the use of the number line as a precursor to informal written methods. Adding a story to the use of a programmable toy enables children to engage imaginatively. We have seen many students training to be teachers become enthused about the use of ICT in the class when using it to tell the story of *The Very Hungry Caterpillar* (Carle 1970). In particular, they often report on the way the children seemed to become more engaged in the tasks and activities.

In addition, the use of peripheral equipment such as scanners and digital cameras can really liven up lessons in practical ways. For example:

> In the school where one of the authors worked, children went on a 'shape hunt' using the digital camera. They walked around the school capturing images of different tessellations on the camera. The results were then displayed on-screen for the benefit of the whole class.

Use of video and digital photography can also enable children to observe changes that take place over a longer period, e.g. a dish of water near a window as the water evaporates, or a flower as it opens and closes in the sun. These events stimulate discussion and children are naturally curious to be able to explain what has occurred.

A teaching assistant may accompany a group to specific parts of the school or its environs. By making this into a 'treasure hunt', other skills can be included. Clues and rewards for solving problems are one example of extending this activity. Older children can use the camera to capture images of local historical interest. Digital video can also be part of a class presentation at the start of a topic. The images remain on the computer for students to look at and use. All adults working with children benefit from learning how to use the latest technology in order to make effective use of it in the classroom. The ability to pass on what you know is a valuable commodity in the school community. Once you have created a computer model, you have it for all time, to be amended, improved and shared as you wish. Another use of modelling software is the ability to perform tasks on-screen that are difficult or expensive. One such program enables children to model electrical circuits with batteries, light bulbs and buzzers. The program simulates real-life so bulbs blow and batteries run out of power without wasting real resources.

Branching database software allows children to feel supported in the skill of identifying and classifying and fits in well with a social constructivist approach to teaching. Use of such a database out of context is often unsuccessful and it is much better to use it while children are actively engaging with the items for identification. For a database to be of use to primary children, it needs to follow similar rules in presentation that many of the good non-fiction texts employ to engage the reader, such as colourful and attractive layouts; easy to read text with pictures to support reading; ease in navigation; and interactive features that allow the child to interrogate the data. Because they use software specifically designed to enable children to create their own databases, programs such as Junior Pinpoint or First Workshop are often very effective although there are some very good CD-ROMs available containing specific databases on science, geography and history topics.

Many of the points raised here with databases would also apply to spreadsheets. They do not have to look like spreadsheets to make use of the spreadsheet functions. Here the software would support the kinds of 'What if?' activity that is encouraged in the teaching of science. Spreadsheets also have the tools to produce graphs that can quickly aid the identification of a pattern or a trend, suggesting perhaps that a 'rule' is in place. This is how scientists make new discoveries and make predictions to test out their ideas. Being able to predict certain kinds of behaviour is another important area of development in science that teachers wish to encourage. A spreadsheet can model a prediction based on the figures available. Like a database, a spreadsheet is also a tool for sorting a large amount of information very quickly.

The teaching assistant can support foundation subjects by researching the Internet for background information and illustrations for the teacher, and also look for suitable sites for the children to use. Children will more readily learn through real artefacts and visits to historical places but when this is not possible, the Internet can provide some valuable source material. Searching the Internet may also provide relevant trips for the children to take. For example, there is a wealth of information and some interesting virtual tours through Egypt. If the objective of the lesson is to *use* information from the Internet, then it may be easier for an adult to find an appropriate site and bookmark it or make an interactive Word file that links pupils to it rather than children wasting time searching. This file could contain closed and/or open-ended questions related to the site for the pupils to find the answers to and complete on the computer.

In considering how ICT supports subject teaching, we should not leave out the very useful peripheral equipment often connected to a computer such as printers, sensors, scanners, microscopes and other measuring devices. There are relatively low-cost versions of these available today. As with the use of any equipment in the classroom, having an extra pair of hands to assist in its deployment is very welcome. The equipment always takes time to set up and sometimes is quite fragile although children should be actively encouraged to have experience of the equipment under adult supervision. These lessons can really provide the extra motivation some children need to engage with a subject. They soon realise that they are active participants on this voyage of discovery, and can quickly lose interest if they feel they are not included in the practical side of the lesson.

Conclusion

Teaching assistants will need to work alongside teachers in preparing for the use of ICT in lessons by:

- ensuring they understand how to use equipment;
- making resources and assisting with their use;
- supervising computer use and assisting children with their developing ICT skills.

Although some people claim to be techno-phobic, with a little perseverance these technical skills are well within their reach. After all, much of the equipment or in some cases software is designed for use by children. Most problems come because things are done out of sequence due to assumptions made by the user. The best advice is to spend some time with unfamiliar equipment or software so that you are aware of the pitfalls and dangers. All the best users of technical equipment can tell the tale of the time when they came unstuck because they didn't prepare themselves. If you don't like doing it on your own, then find others who will be prepared to join you in a practice session. Finally, children love having people who are prepared to learn with them and good teachers have been doing it for years.

Discussion Starters

1 You are asked to support a child with a lack of motivation in learning – what advantages does ICT have to offer in a National Curriculum subject, e.g. mathematics? What may be the disadvantages of using ICT in this way?

2 What is the benefit of the interactive whiteboard in comparison with other boards (chalk-board, flip-chart, dry-wipe)?

3 Is the amount of money spent on ICT in school justified in relation to the children's learning outcomes?

Reflecting on Practice

From the following, choose an activity that best fits your role:

1 *Supporting children identified as gifted and talented or having special educational needs*: Look at the teacher's medium-term planning and identify elements where ICT could support an individual or small group (this may be used to modify an Individual Education Plan [IEP]).

2 *Supporting small groups and whole-class teaching*:
   (a) Prepare ICT resources to support a specific learning activity.
   (b) Evaluate their use with the children.

3 *Organising peer tutoring*: Devise a programme of four sessions to train peer tutors in the classroom to provide ICT support for a specific project.

4 *ICT support assistant*: Set up a programme of ten sessions for an ICT club before school, at lunch time or after school (see Chapter 12).

Websites

www.becta.org.uk/ – home page of the British Educational Communications and Technology Agency. Foundation Stage to Key Stage 4 and beyond.

www.ncaction.org.uk – the DfES website.

www.standards.dfes.gov.uk/numeracy/publications/ – look for 'Interactive Teaching Programmes' and 'Computer-based resources'.

www.standards.dfes.gov.uk/schemes3 – a site for guidance on the QCA schemes of work.

www.techlearn.ac.uk/ – a site for people working in Further and Higher Education with useful information about the latest technologies.

References

Bruce, T. and Meggitt, C. (2002) *Childcare and Education*, London: Hodder and Stoughton.

Carle, E. (1970) *The Very Hungry Caterpillar*, London: Hamish Hamilton.

DfES (2000) *Using ICT to Support Mathematics in Primary Schools*, London: DfES Publications.

DfES (2003a) ' "Castlefield Infant School": a case study in support for the curriculum', at www.teachernet.gov.uk/management/teachingassistants/Management/casestudies/, accessed June 2003.

DfES (2003b) ' "Mission Primary School": a case study in support for the curriculum', at www.teachernet.gov.uk/management/teachingassistants/Management/casestudies/, accessed June 2003.

Leask, M. and Meadows, J. (2000) *Teaching and Learning with ICT in the Primary School*, London: Routledge Falmer.

Loveless, A. and Ellis, V. (2001) *ICT, Pedagogy and the Curriculum*, London: Routledge Falmer, pp. xv–xix.

Monteith, M. (ed.) (2002) *Teaching Primary Literacy with ICT*, Buckingham: Open University Press, pp. 1–29.

Moseley, D., Higgins, S. and Bramald, R. (1999) *Ways Forward with ICT: Effective Pedagogy Using ICT I Literacy and Numeracy in Primary Schools*, Newcastle upon Tyne: University of Newcastle upon Tyne.

Tyldesley, A. (2002) 'A reflective view of the NLS', in Monteith, M. (ed.), *Teaching Primary Literacy with ICT*, Buckingham: Open University Press, pp. 46–59.

5

Language and Literacy for Learning

Jean Clarkson and Roger Stevenson

Meet Stuart

After I gained my Basic Skills Teaching Certificate I planned to teach adults, but now I am a basic skills support assistant working in two primary schools and one secondary school, supporting English and language development, in addition to bilingual support in a mainstream classroom. The children have difficulties in English speaking, listening, reading and writing. Occasionally I work with children with special language gifts. I use resources to enhance understanding and I have discussions with the children to link spoken language to their reading and writing. I find interesting ways to practise spelling and writing skills, and motivate the children.

I would like to improve my knowledge about the language system and the links between spoken and written language. I also need to know how to adapt resources to suit different ages and competencies with English language, helping children to understand, and making learning more enjoyable and raising self-esteem.

From the Beginning

Communication skills develop in children from birth. Babies hear and recognise their parent's voice before they can clearly focus and interaction is vital for children's survival, so we need to support their innate skills for literacy for them to flourish. This chapter is about learning to nurture children in the classroom and develop their communication skills through literacy. It will examine the procedures used in school to teach children to become literate and explore some of the key factors that can affect their learning of English. Most schools use the recommended documents as appropriate for the age-range:

- *Curriculum Guidance for the Foundation Stage* (DfEE/QCA 2000);
- National Literacy Strategy Frameworks for Key Stages 1–3 (DfEE 1998; DfES 2001).

Language is a crucial element in our life. We need to be skilled communicators to play our rightful role in society, at home and in the workplace. We need communication skills to live in harmony with our fellow beings; we need language to love, to dream and have a sense of well-being. Any person unable to communicate successfully in all of the interrelated language activities of speaking, listening, reading and writing suffers emotionally and socially (Crystal 1987). Therefore, it is imperative to teach children to communicate with others to give them a sense of power and to enable them to take command of their life academically as well as socially. A literate person is a powerful person.

This chapter aims to support Stuart's development by exploring the integrated areas of speaking, listening, reading and writing. It will describe the theoretical underpinning of children's language skills as the framework for the chapter and will discuss the social process of language. We will invite the reader to explore the role literacy plays in concept development in other curriculum areas. Language is the vehicle that carries all other subject knowledge and to be a good scientist or mathematician one requires a good command of language skills, both verbally and in written form. We will discuss the connection between language and thought formation particularly as it relates to discussion opportunities in other subjects in the curriculum. The chapter will offer suggestions how adults can support language development with all children, including those for whom English is an additional language and boys who under-achieve. It will celebrate the pleasure of language and suggest ways that will encourage children to engage with the text and develop their own writing skills, through reading. We will also examine the National Literacy Strategy and the use of systematic reading instruction and schemes to develop reading, including the changing nature of teaching and learning through Information and Communication Technology (ICT).

The Literacy Hour: A Structured Way to Teach Reading

There is a great deal of literature that discusses the acquisition of language before children arrive at school and the importance of an interactive environment to support children's innate ability to communicate, e.g. Crystal (1987); Wells (1987); Wray and Lewis (1997); This section will focus on the development of the language elements developed *after* a child reaches school and how an interactive adult can foster the child's inherited ability to communicate.

Shared reading and writing

Most primary schools in England adhere to the recommendations of the National Literacy Strategy but adapt it to their needs. Most secondary schools choose to audit their current practice against the Key Stage 3 Strategy recommendations, and choose the most effective teaching approaches and content for their situation. Despite the criticisms of the national strategy and the formulaic way it initially operated, there has been an increase in children's achievements as evidenced by the national test results, and most children who have language difficulties are identified at an early stage through baseline assessment and do not 'fall through the net'.

The Literacy Hour is highly structured to include three teaching strategies: whole-class teaching, group work and independent activities. Shared reading and writing are undertaken through whole-class teaching, where the teacher provides a 'role model' for the children to copy and demonstrates how to do both. Writers such as Southgate (Southgate *et al.* 1981) and Holdaway (1979) advocated an 'apprenticeship' approach such as this. The method draws on the work of Clay (1972), who suggested that the sharing of a book as in 'bedtime stories' and collaborative reading and learning through the text could be replicated by teachers in a kind of mass-produced version of parent–child bonding at bedtime. The cosy setting of gathering children around your knee in an intimate style and relaxing to enjoy a book could encourage children to consider books and reading to be a pleasurable activity, thus creating the beginning of a positive engagement with literature sustainable throughout life. In addition, the teacher is providing the opportunity to extend the child's own reading skill level into the 'zone of proximal development' (ZPD) (Vygotsky 1978), as described by Pat Hughes in Chapter 3. Group work and independent activities ensure that children have a variety of ways to learn and practise skills at their own level.

The importance of creating positive attitudes as well as teaching reading skills is a feature of the strategy that teachers sometimes overlook. Teaching reading is the balance of the skills needed to 'decode' (Smith 1973) and understand the text, and the pleasure of the story or information that is gleaned, and should motivate the children to conquer this extraordinary complex task. To be able mentally to process symbols representing sounds and speech into meaning, quickly and fluently, sometimes when a child is but seven, is nothing short of a miracle. The content of the book is always the reward for the effort of processing reading and provides the major motivation for a child wanting to read independently.

The 'big' book

Publishers, delighted at a new marketing initiative, began to manufacture the 'big' book as a convenient way for teachers to use a communal text big enough for all to see during the Literacy Hour. Creative teachers made their own enlarged texts using the names of the children as players in the story or photographs of the children's world as a base for non-fiction. Children were involved in the construction of their own books through word processing and illustration. Some classroom action research had Year 6 children write designer books, based on the adventures of Reception children, for the library (Clarkson 1996). This particularly benefits the children for whom English is an additional language (EAL). The big book is not the only way to share texts, and with older children, in particular, overhead projector transparencies are useful, especially when making comparisons between two different types of reading texts. Even better is the interactive whiteboard. However, let us not forget the use of class texts, from which everyone has the opportunity to read individually and develop debate. We recommend a range of age-appropriate methods, not just the big book.

Learning How to Read

Children learn to read by using their linguistic, cognitive and experiential knowledge of the text. They use their letter and word recognition skills and text level cues such as the context and illustrations to help them comprehend. Here are three main strategies that children use when they decipher text:

- semantic knowledge (including contextual influences);
- sight vocabulary;
- phonics.

Semantic knowledge: the understanding of the text

Semantics is knowledge about meaning, a term often used in relation to the structure of the language, i.e. how words are put together to make meaning, but children most often interpret text using their prior knowledge of the world. In other words, they often take a pragmatic (common-sense) approach to interpreting meaning. Pragmatic knowledge about meaning takes into account the contextual, often non-linguistic, factors such as pictures and the whole setting of the story. A word changes its 'sense' in various contexts (Wertsch 1991), and as children progress through school they need to develop an awareness of this, e.g. 'volume' in the everyday context of the television, and 'volume' in relation to the mathematical concept of three-dimensional space at Key Stage 3.

Children are able to read a book with much more ease if they have experiential knowledge of the content, e.g. if a child has been to the zoo, he or she can read text about the animals in the zoo with greater confidence. The child will read the word 'elephant' without difficulty, especially if the book uses illustrations as visual clues. Knowledge of the content with a good grounding of oral language can allow the child to use 'psycholinguistic' skills to have a good educated guess at the words. Smith (1973) called this a 'psycholinguistic guessing game'. Thus, the semantic structures that determine meaning are understood through the application of contextual clues that help children 'make sense' of the words. Discussion about the book is vital to develop semantics or understanding and meaning. This crucial act links the spoken language to the symbolic form in reading. An assistant like Stuart is an ideal person with whom children can discuss their reading books.

Sight vocabulary

Most children have a good memory of the written word and can recognise the 'picture' of the whole word especially if it has enough 'ascenders' and 'descenders' to make it distinctive. Again, 'elephant' is a good example. This is a distinctive pattern with enough shape to make it instantly recognisable. Key words and high frequency words on card help children take a 'photograph' of the word for their 'mind's eye'. When they see it repeated on the page, they remember it. This applies also to word patterns, words with the same endings or beginnings, suffixes, prefixes. Imagery is a powerful tool when learning to read at any age.

Phonics

Graham and Kelly (2000) state that phonics is the association between symbols, i.e. letters and letter combinations and sound, and how they are represented by the written form. When first teaching children phonics, they learn to listen and distinguish individual vowel and consonant sounds in speech and to identify the written symbols used for these sounds. Knowledge of phonics gives the child an additional support to decode the words. To use the example of 'elephant' again, the 'e' is a good starting point to guess the rest of the word using sight recognition and a knowledge of the context. Research supports the use of phonics in teaching learning and Haigh (1996) discussed classroom research in Tower Hamlets that claimed that children and adults both sound out unknown words phonically.

One of the mainstays in teaching phonics is reading schemes. Campbell (2002) describes reading schemes as a collection of books written with the sole intention of teaching children to read. Teachers who advocate schemes say they offer structure to the teaching of reading because of their graded levels of difficulty. It could be argued that this structure is a weakness too as it does not facilitate adaptation and can be perceived to be too rigid. The key feature of schemes includes a natural increase in vocabulary, with regular repetition and a systematic introduction of letters and letter combinations. The major criticisms of reading schemes are by the children themselves who claim they are boring, especially as children move through the primary years and become more discerning in their tastes. Many children will use the reading scheme books and some schemes remain in schools sometimes for decades. Modern children have interests in contemporary issues and thus some schemes, currently used, are dated and are not sufficiently modern to appeal to the child of the twenty-first century. Most primary schools use a mixture of scheme materials, particularly at Key Stage 2, to provide a range of graded materials with different features and interest levels. At secondary level, some children have difficulty with phonics and there are specially designed schemes for more mature readers with appropriate contextual content, while at the same time providing the necessary phonic development. Hofkins (2003) criticises phonic teaching, claiming that schools teach phonic skills too slowly and that we should teach the letter sounds and digraphs quickly in Reception and leave the complicated decoding and analytical phonic methods until later on when the child is more fluent.

Developing decoding skills with the National Literacy Strategy (NLS)

Phonics, sight recognition, semantics and innate syntactical knowledge, i.e. grammatical knowledge, all contribute to the child's ability to read. Consider the following dialogue. You should be able to identify the different strategies the children are using to decode texts:

TA:	So what strategies do we use when we come across a word we don't understand?
Bilal:	We can go back to the start of the sentence and read again.
Aisha:	We look at the pictures for clues, Miss.

TA:	Yes, good . . . and is there anything else that you do?
Bilal:	I skip the word, Miss, and read to the end of the paragraph and then we can guess the word.
Aisha:	We can sound it out, Miss, by breaking the word down into . . . parts.
TA:	Great – you have remembered all the things we have been practising this term!

FIGURE 5.1   Strategies for decoding text

The NLS addresses each one in different sections:

- text-level work;
- sentence-level work;
- word-level work.

In text-level work, the focus is on semantics and comprehension of the text. Shared reading and writing in the Literacy Hour is text-level work in the first 15 minutes. In the second 15 minutes, word-level work emphasises sight vocabulary, high frequency words and phonics while sentence-level work emphasises punctuation and spelling (DfEE 1998). Group work and independent activities follow and at Key Stages 1 and 2 most children are differentiated into ability groups. Each group is working on activities that are set at their ability level but some children will require adult support from an assistant such as Stuart.

At secondary level there is no recommended lesson structure but there are clear recommendations for more interactive whole-class teaching with a clear focus on text-level, sentence-level and word-level work (DfES 2001). In addition, a range of intervention strategies provides support for the development of reading and writing, particularly in Year 7 (DfES 2003a) of which Stuart as a basic skills assistant should be familiar.

Shared Writing

Shared writing creates text in a communal process as the whole class contribute to the writing. Books written by the children together in groups are often well produced using word processing and stored in the library for all to read. Long after leaving a class, children will read a book they have made years before and reminisce with friends on the process of writing for the public. Indeed, once children have read texts together, they will return frequently to the same text, confident they have an understanding of the gist of the text. Confidence cannot be over-emphasised in any form of learning. A confident child who believes he or she can achieve will 'have a go' and not be afraid of making mistakes because with confidence he or she will take a few setbacks without giving up.

Shared writing with a more competent adult role model shows the messy process of writing and how a writer constructs a good piece of writing as an artist crafts a piece of sculpture. It explicitly demonstrates the process of composing and redrafting. It allows 'thinking out loud' to occur on the page. It demonstrates the activities that writers do while composing:

- deletion: the elimination of false starts and unnecessary or wrongly chosen words;
- rearrangement: changing the logic or word order and adding or expanding materials;
- consolidation: making the text more compact or streamlining while retaining the content.

Children understand the structure of the writing when they see it emerge on the page and in turn begin to comprehend how speaking and reading interrelate. Non-fiction writing across the curriculum introduces children to different vocabulary. Someone like Stuart is the ideal person to maintain a wall display of key vocabulary as a useful resource for writing.

Writing is a creative process and children have an innate ability to be creative in language. Pinkerton (1994) writes about the fascinating way children learn and use language creatively. The biggest drawback to using this creativity in shared writing is the size of the class. If children cannot see or do not feel involved with the creative process, they will lose motivation. No one wants to be a bystander in the game. Teaching assistants can help reduce the size of the class and thus give the child an interactive experience rather than that of an observer. Children learn through interaction, not through passive listening to another person. Active involvement of all pupils during shared writing should directly contribute to pupils' oral language development. However, it might be that the current focus in literacy lessons fails to allow pupils sufficient opportunity to develop their individual thinking through expression. Teachers and assistants like Stuart need to plan carefully to ensure a lesson structure that allows for extended speaking and listening opportunities.

Children with English as an additional language (EAL) particularly benefit from the opportunity to extend their speaking and listening skills within literacy lessons. These pupils will require provision for shared reading and writing to occur in small groups to allow quality interaction to take place. Some EAL pupils will take longer to acquire cognitive academic language processes (see Chapter 8). Consequently, to see and hear subject-specific vocabulary used only once by the teacher as a model is insufficient. These pupils will need the opportunity to see, hear and use language for a real purpose to internalise the language structures fully. For example, a bilingual support assistant might take a group of children and read the big book or develop writing in the home language before the whole-class literacy lesson, so that the children have a better understanding and knowledge of the content and process of the lesson. The assistant might also help the children identify commonalities and differences between the two languages at text, sentence and word level so that the child can use knowledge of the home language to support the development of knowledge in English.

Assessment

Assessment is a time for harsh realities. Have the children learned what you wanted them to? To become a professional in the world of teaching means that the children's learning is solely the responsibility of the adult, particularly in primary school. You can no longer blame the pupils for lack of understanding, intelligence or application to the task because the responsibility lies with the adult in the classroom. An analogy sometimes used is that when a firefighter reaches a fire in a house and the reason for the fire is that a person fell asleep smoking, firefighters do not leave and say 'Well, it's your own fault; you caused the fire'. In teaching, a child not learning or making progress is directly the responsibility of the adult. That is why assessment has to be brutal, honest and effective. To discover that the child has not learned despite your best efforts is frustrating and means that you have to find another, more effective method. It is daunting and assessment can be painful as it also measures the adults' competence. Small-group work is an opportunity for assessment when an adult can identify and record individual children's achievements. Stuart, as an assistant, is in a privileged position when working with a small group and can provide excellent feedback to the teacher about a child's performance of a task, thus enabling the teacher to make professional judgements. Look at the following extract and compare it with your own experiences at work:

T: How do you feel blue group are progressing in their guided reading?

TA: They love the new non-fiction materials and have been very keen to carry out wider research into 'sharks' this week. Adnan and Halima have really struggled to scan the text for key vocabulary prior to reading.

T: Well, I can emphasise scanning in the shared reading tomorrow. Why don't you join in and ask them questions in that part of the lesson? I'll watch to see how Adnan and Halima respond and whether they've remembered.

TA: Yes, I'll sit them at the front and prime them before the lesson starts and it should really give a boost to their self-esteem.

T: Yes, and on Friday, we'll spend some time together filling in our 'Reading Records'.

FIGURE 5.2 Sharing information and making judgements

From the extract, you will notice how the teaching assistant and teacher are working as a team, using the feedback to modify teaching approaches in the next lesson. This type of formative assessment is most important as it has a direct impact on the teaching and learning process. Assessment of individuals takes place when observing a small group closely. The reading conference motivates children as they have the undivided attention of an adult who is evaluating their reading progress. Keeping records is a task for the end of the week when the teacher writes an overview of the individual child's progress over that week.

The supporting adult questions the child's understanding of the text and encourages and gives positive feedback. It is essential to keep careful records of the child's errors and, when appropriate, use miscue analysis for a focused assessment of reading skills. Miscue analysis consists of recording the child's reading errors on a copy of the text, and allows the adult to analyse the patterns of mistakes the child is making. Many school schemes contain miscue analysis models to use. Diagnosis of mistakes leads to development of focused teaching strategies to rectify them.

Planning to Maintain Interest in Reading

To create a balance between each level, i.e. text, word and sentence, requires careful planning and depends very much on the individual children within the class. The professionalism and skill of teaching staff are required to assess the needs of each child and to provide the best method by which he or she will become a fluent reader. Thus, teachers approach reading in several ways because children are individuals and learn differently, and to use only one method can be demotivating. One method will suit some children better than others. When a variety of methods is used, eventually they all mesh and the result is a fluent reader.

Essentially, it is important to maintain interest in learning to read because if laboured teaching gets in the way of the motivation, then a child will reject reading for life. Teachers maintain children's interest through well-chosen books that are appropriate to the children's interest level. We have to remember that these children will grow into a future world which we cannot comprehend. Children are the next generation and they will be motivated by books that reflect the culture in which they live. Make reading appropriate to the modern world. In the following extract the teaching assistant is helping a child choose a book to read:

> TA: Can you find a book that you think will be interesting, Ehsan?
>
> E: No, there's nothing here I like. I want a book about wrestling, Miss.
>
> TA: You're interested in wrestling, are you? What about this book? It's not about wrestling but it is about martial arts and there are some lovely photographs with captions in it.
>
> E: Thanks, Miss, I'll read it tonight.
>
> TA: Tell me tomorrow what you think of it. If you like it, you can show it to the class. But remember, karate is for experts only and can be dangerous!
>
> E: Yes, miss.

The teaching assistant acts as an 'opportunist ally' in recommending the text for individuals to read in their own time. In this way, the child chooses a book with content similar to that he was looking for. Without an adult intervening here, he might well have chosen nothing. We can see that adult support is important in discussing the choice of books too. Relating learning to the children's experience and the modern world is important for motivation. To understand the purpose of reading and the benefits it brings are part of the reason why children continue to learn (Campbell 1998).

Are You Teaching a Future Doctor? Bilingual Children

A little boy from Bangladesh entered a Year 2 class some years ago without one word of English. After completing his education, he took a degree in medicine and he is currently practising as a doctor in the UK. Even now, his mother does not speak fluent English. So think that you might have a potential doctor in front of you when you teach bilingual children. Intelligence by-passes all language and intelligent children can learn an additional language in a very short time, especially if they have frequent interaction with adults or other children who speak English as a first language. To raise confidence and self-esteem in an English classroom, we must value the child's own culture as a positive reinforcement.

Cultural and linguistic diversity enriches society and to be bilingual is a great advantage. Monolingual speakers are in the minority in the world. In the UK, unfortunately, the term 'bilingual child' often describes a child from an ethnic group whom we consider to be at a disadvantage because his or her mother tongue is not English. We can overcome this by understanding the differences of culture and celebrating a child's bilingualism. Stuart clearly has an important role in supporting this in three different schools and could provide an example to others in recognising the benefits of cultural diversity.

Gender Issues

Research has shown that some boys are under-achieving in reading, causing them to be disadvantaged in all other subjects (Millard 1997). Motivating boys to read has the additional difficulty of overcoming the image reading has of being an 'uncool' activity and not sufficiently masculine to pursue. We can overcome this. Experienced teachers use non-fiction books, science fiction and other non-traditional reading material to encourage boys to read. They use magazines, football programmes, computer literature, any reading matter that has 'street credibility' and that boys do not consider feminine. Skelton (2001) suggests that we should look for different ways of being male, instead of trying to feminise their nature. Boys like to be best at what they do, and if they cannot be the best, they will drop out. In other words, we must appeal to their styles of learning and the need for a competitive challenge. The interim report from the Raising Boy's Achievement (RBA) Project appears to support the notion of working with the preferred learning styles of boys in literacy (DfES/RBA 2003). They found that boys from Key Stages 2 and 3 responded well to an integrated approach to literacy with less emphasis on the technical aspects of literacy learning and more on the processes. They found drama highly motivating in this respect.

Peer group pressure has considerable influence on Key Stage 2 children, many of whom are pre-pubescent at a much earlier age than even a decade ago, thus are motivated by a different range of reading matter. The *Harry Potter* books have encouraged all children to read and added cult status to the skill of reading. We can capitalise on this with other books of a similar nature. Many boys are particularly interested in the concept of the 'superhero'. They will read literature to which they can relate in this type of fantasy. Perhaps Stuart, our basic skills support assistant, can relate to this from when he was a child and bring that enthusiasm for adventure and heroism into his work with the children.

The Connection between Language and Thought

Vygotsky (1978) thought that children only begin to have a memory at the age of about 18 months when they have the words to enable thoughts and thus memories. He studied the relationship between language and thought in addition to the role of memory and thought in further developing language skills. Crystal (1987) agrees that language facilitates much of our thinking, in other words, language creates thought. There is clearly a complex interrelationship between the two and Vygotsky was also interested in the processes by which thoughts became language. To put this in the classroom context, there is no doubt that if children discuss a piece of writing together first before they commit to paper, they produce writing of a higher standard. The kind of thinking that involves language is the reasoned thinking that helps us to work out problems. Thought production and language are dependent on each other and one informs the other. In other subject areas such as science, children who are performing an experiment gain greater understanding if they discuss the concepts together and move towards their own understanding. Consider how these ideas might have an impact on planning for an activity in the classroom by reading the following extracts:

TA: What about developing a role-play for this work on pollination?

T: Yes, we could ask groups to present their work to the class to include a demonstration of the pollination process.

TA: That will give them the chance to collaborate and learn from each other.

T: Yes, you could observe their contributions and let me know who you think has a good understanding of the concept.

T: How could we create a speaking and listening opportunity with the letter writing?

TA: What about a debate where pupils are assigned roles so that we fully explore the issues relating to the change of use of the school playground for car parking?

T: Yes, but we might need to help some pupils develop their arguments in advance.

TA: I'll plan a guided group session with 'blue group' next week to develop their roles well in advance.

In the first extract the teaching assistant is making a useful suggestion to develop a role-play situation, possibly because it will be particularly useful for a specific group. The teacher agrees and suggests that the teaching assistant can have a role in determining children's understanding of the pollination process. They are capitalising on the relationships between thought and language to provide opportunity for secure development of conceptual ideas. In the second extract, they decide on a debate to explore an issue fully before the children write a letter (presumably a letter of complaint). Such an approach is much more interesting than simply planning a letter on paper with no real exploration of the issues. Thus, speaking and listening in all subject areas create a better understanding of concepts and create new knowledge in addition to helping children form important social relationships. The statutory speaking and listening curriculum is in the National Curriculum (DfEE/QCA 1999) but is not explicit in the National Literacy Strategy Frameworks.

Reading with ICT

A key Labour pledge at the 1997 election was to connect every classroom to the Internet. So far, 98 per cent of secondary schools and 80 per cent of primary schools have made the link. The level of popularity among teachers for computer-based instruction in reading may vary, but few will dispute the fact that computers have won a permanent place in most schools, if not in most classrooms. The attraction of reading and writing on a computer cannot be over-emphasised for all children. Research studies (Reinking 1988) indicate that computer instruction is effective for a wide variety of reading skills. The emphasis should not be on using computers to increase reading and writing achievement, but rather on using computers within the context of the curriculum for purposeful reading and writing activities. This is more motivating for pupils than computer-based drill and practice software. Pupils need opportunities to use the computer to apply reading strategies. Programs related to science, humanities and numeracy will all require the use of reading strategies.

Many pupils now have computers at home and parents and carers need to be aware that most games can be educational, developing skills and reading for meaning, but should be set up for two or more players, with the parents taking an active role to create important social and language interaction.

Developing the Role of Support Staff

Support staff will continue to have a crucial role to play in the development of young people's literacy skills. Now we have some Standards for Higher Level Teaching Assistants (Teacher Training Agency 2003), it is clear that there should be a professional partnership between teachers and assistants, based upon mutual respect and clearly defined responsibilities and expectations. This chapter creates a picture of how that relationship might look in the context of literacy teaching. Assistants such as Stuart have a very good insight into pupils' reading and writing development, and are involved directly in the evaluation of teaching and learning. They are an integral part of the literacy team, with a wide range of skills and the ability to take the initiative in response to issues as they arise. We think it is an exciting model that assumes on-going opportunity for career development for all parties who care about young people's literacy development. 'Over the coming years, we shall see new developments, enhancing opportunities for training and career progression in many different roles, and extending the range of what support staff can do in classrooms' (DfES 2003b).

Discussion Starters

1 What are the disadvantages of being unable to express one's thoughts effectively? Consider the main aspects of language speaking, listening, reading and writing. Consider personal as well as professional issues.

2 What motivation is there for a child to learn to read?

3 Some educators believe that teaching children to read by breaking words down into pieces and teaching strategies to sound out the letters can be tedious and turn children off reading. They claim that children learn to read more effectively without intervention if they are given motivational books, 'real' books and they frequently 'read' with an adult. What is your view on this?

4 Some children leave school at 16 less able to read than they could at age 11. Why might this happen? And what can we do about it?

Reflecting on Practice

1 Consider ways to value children's culture through their reading and writing experiences in school:
  (a) List all the approaches you can think of.
  (b) Discuss these with the class teacher or your line manager.
  (c) If possible, try some of your ideas and evaluate the impact on the quality of the children's work.

2 Explore the benefits of ICT in supporting your role:
  (a) Use ICT to create a sheet that can be used to record one group's attainments in a literacy activity.
  (b) Has each child attained the objectives?
  (c) What are the children's strengths and weaknesses?
  (d) Suggest activities to enable the children to make progress.
  (e) Have a discussion with a teacher about your task.

3 Choose a selection of books from the school library that you think will appeal to a specific group of children. Share your choice with the children and observe their responses:
  (a) Was your choice a good one, or were the children's preferences different from your expectations? Give reasons.
  (b) Consider the criteria you used to choose the books and compare these with the criteria the children would choose.
  (c) Reflect on the task and consider the impact on your future practice.

Websites

www.learn.co.uk – teaching resources and information.

www.standards.dfes.gov.uk/keystage3/ – for information on the National Literacy Strategy at secondary level, including EAL support.

www.standards.dfes.gov.uk/literacy/ – for information on the National Literacy Strategy at primary level, including EAL support.

References

Campbell, R. (1998) 'A literacy hour is only half the story', *Reading* 32 (2), 21–33.

Campbell, R. (2002) *Reading in the Early Years Handbook*, Buckingham: Open University Press.

Clarkson, G.J. (1996) 'Designer books for Reception children', *Language and Learning*, 12–18.

Clay, M.M. (1972) *Reading: The Patterning of Complex Behaviour*, Auckland: Heinemann Educational Books.

Crystal, D. (1987) *The Cambridge Encyclopaedia of Language*, Cambridge: Cambridge University Press.

DfEE (1998) *The National Literacy Strategy: Framework for Teaching English YR to Y6*, London: DfEE.

DfEE/QCA (1999) *The National Curriculum for England*, London: HMSO/QCA.

DfEE/QCA (2000) *Curriculum Guidance for the Foundation Stage*, London: HMSO.

DfES (2001) *Key Stage 3 National Strategy: The Framework for Teaching English: Years 7, 8 and 9*, London: DfES.

DfES (2003a) *Key Stage 3 National Strategy: Targeting Level 4 in Year 7: English*, London: DfES.

DfES (2003b) 'Developing the Role of School Support Staff: What the National Agreement Means for You', at www.teachernet.gov.uk/remodelling, accessed September 2003.

DfES/RBA (2003) 'Raising Boys' Achievement Project Interim Report/Key Findings', at www.standards.dfee.gov.uk/genderandachievement, accessed September 2003.

Goodman, K. (1967) *Reading: A Psycholinguistic Guessing Game*, London: Paul Chapman.

Goodwin, P. (1999) *The Literate Classroom*, London: David Fulton.

Graham, J. and Kelly, A. (2000) *Writing under Control*, London: David Fulton.

Haigh, G. (1996) 'This is the way they learn to read', *TES*, 6 September.

Hofkins, D. (2003) 'And then there was phonics', *TES*, 21 February.

Holdaway, D. (1979) *The Foundations of Literacy*, Sydney: Ashton Scholastic.

Millard, E. (1997) *Differently Literate: Boys and Girls and the Schooling of Literacy*, London: Falmer Press.

Pinkerton, S. (1994) *The Language Instinct*, St Ives: Penguin Books.

Reinking, D. (1988) 'Computer-mediated text and comprehension differences: the role of reading time, reader preference, and estimation of learning', *Reading Research Quarterly*, 23 (4), 484–98.

Skelton, C. (2001) *Schooling the Boys: Masculinities and Primary Education*, Buckingham: Open University Press.

Smith, F. (1973) *Children's Reading*, London: Holt, Rhinehart and Winston.

Southgate, V., Arnold, H. and Johnson, S. (1981) *Extending, Beginning, Reading*, London: Heinemann Educational Books.

Teacher Training Agency (2003) 'Standards for Higher Level Teaching Assistants', at www.tta.gov.uk/about/consultations/completed.htm, accessed September 2003.

Vygotsky, L.S. (1978) *Mind in Society, The Development of Higher Psychological Processes*, ed. Cole, M., Cambridge, MA: Harvard University Press.

Wertsch, J.V. (1991) *Voices of the Mind*, Cambridge, MA: Harvard University Press.

Wells, G. (1987) *The Meaning Makers*, London: Hodder and Stoughton.

Wray, D. and Lewis, M. (1997) *Extending Literacy*, London: Routledge.

6

Connections, Questions and Resources: A Recipe for Success

Sue Cronin

Meet Clare

I support a particular child with Down's Syndrome for all subjects in an inner-city secondary school. In addition to helping other children within the classroom. The child I support has difficulties with all aspects of mathematics and is unable to follow the same curriculum as the rest of the children in the bottom set. I assist the child through a separate mathematics scheme chosen for her by the school SENCO and Head of Mathematics. It involves the use of practical resources such as money. One of the main problems is that some of the worksheets used in the scheme are at the right level mathematically but are considered 'babyish' by my child and do not motivate her to engage with the tasks. I need help to create new resources which are at the same level of mathematics but engage the interest of a teenager.

I have attended the LEA training course but have not received any specific numeracy training. I am confident with my present child, as her mathematics attainment is very low. However, I would not be confident explaining higher-level mathematics to other children. I would like to understand more about how children learn mathematics.

Introduction

> The most valuable resource children have available other than their own intellect is the adults who work with them.
>
> (Brown 1998: 213)

The above is true of all subjects but particularly relevant for mathematics. For many children who have trouble with the subject, the presence of a supportive adult such as Clare to assist their mathematical development and understanding is crucial. Teaching assistants can make all the difference to the level of a child's outcomes and achievements in mathematics. This chapter will try to explore some of the issues involved in ensuring effective support in the mathematics classroom. It will consider the importance of the supporting adult's own perceptions and attitudes, and awareness of the issues and current thinking on effective teaching of mathematics. The chapter will also consider the importance of a resource-rich environment that will take account of children's learning styles to facilitate understanding and develop children's interest and capabilities in mathematics.

An Emotional Experience?

For many people the word 'mathematics' evokes an emotional response. Adults often have strong feelings about their school experiences that usually include many negative reactions to studying the subject. These include anxiety, panic and an inability to see any connection between the mathematics they learned in the classroom and the 'real world' they live in. Haylock (2001) notes that even among academically highly qualified individuals there is commonly a feeling of guilt that they are unable to do mathematics as well as they should.

It is interesting to reflect on some of the words that are associated with and describe mathematics. One group of teaching assistants who completed the task shown in Figure 6.1 produced a wide range of responses including subject-area-related words or phrases such as 'number', 'shape and space', 'algebra' along with skills-related words or phrases such as 'problem solving', 'mental calculations' but also, more revealingly, some very emotive words such as 'fear' and 'panic'.

Work with a colleague:

On a sheet of paper write down as many words as possible to describe mathematics. Compare and discuss with other groups any areas of commonality and differences in the words used. In particular, consider any emotive language used and reasons for its inclusion.

FIGURE 6.1 What do you think about mathematics?

It is important for all adults involved in teaching mathematics to reflect on these feelings as they may well reflect the attitudes and feelings of some of their own children. It is crucial for adults supporting children's learning to understand the children's own feelings towards mathematics. This understanding can provide a window into the necessary motivation needed and the best incentives required to ensure the child is stimulated and engaged. The supporting adults' role here is extremely valuable, as they will often form closer links with particular children who experience difficulties and will have a greater chance of finding the 'key' to unlocking the children's barriers to successful learning. The nature of the relationship of the supporting adult with these children is different to that of the classroom teacher and can complement the class teacher's knowledge of the children. Communication between both the supporting adults and children and the supporting adults and classroom teachers is vital. It ensures the maximum chance of a successful learning experience for the child. Some schools already use a link sheet such as the one provided in *Strengthening Mathematics Teaching in Year 7* (DfES 2002a) which is designed to promote a close dialogue between the class teacher and the teaching assistant.

Before supporting children's learning it is important to consider one's own attitudes to mathematics and its origins. This can help not only in terms of empathising with the children, understanding their fears and anxieties, but more importantly by reflecting on one's own experiences we can begin to rationalise why we feel the way we do. This process is a necessary start to feeling more positive and confident about one's own mathematical abilities. It is also a vital step in making sure that we do not necessarily teach and support the learning of mathematics in the same way that we were taught (Smith 1999). Through reflection, we can begin to evaluate the good and bad teaching and incorporate effective strategies into our own repertoire.

The supporting adult's feelings towards the subject will be transmitted to the child. If the adult admits to not enjoying mathematics or never having been any good at mathematics, this may contribute and reinforce negative attitudes in the child. That is not to say that we should pretend that the subject is easy and that it has always been our favourite at school! Children are very quick to recognise the truth and respond accordingly. Nevertheless, by analysing our own experiences and image of mathematics, we can begin to understand why we feel the way we do towards the subject and this can help to develop a more positive attitude. Ernest and Lim (1999) suggest that from their research adults did not differentiate between their image of mathematics and their image of learning mathematics. They found that learning mathematics related more often to a negative experience rather than a positive one. Thus, if our own learning experience of mathematics at school was poor, not only will we have a negative attitude to the subject but the prospect of being involved in a similar school process of mathematical learning may be uninspiring and itself generate negative expectations.

Carvel (1999) cites a primary school teacher recalling her public humiliation in front of the class by her 'sadistic' teacher for failing to understand a problem. This is often a common recollection and if not a reality, many adults recall an anticipated fear of failing in mathematics and then subsequently suffering such a public humiliation. Whether they experienced feelings of humiliation and failing or simply experienced the anticipated anxiety of such an event, the outcome is the same – a very negative attitude towards mathematics and poor self-esteem. Although it is easy to say that the cause is simply and largely the result of poor, uninspired mathematics teaching, the underlying reasons for this poor teaching are complex and varied. It is not simply a case of poor teachers. Fraser and Honeyford (2000) refer to 'sum stress' and give a list of typical reasons, which include past failures or a particularly bad experience in a lesson, parental attitudes, relationships with mathematics teachers and physical problems such as dyspraxia and dyslexia. They also cite Skemp (1986), who suggested that the underlying cause was rooted in the traditional methods used to teach with the emphasis on rote learning rather than on understanding. Smith (1999) refers to a 'virtual mathematics' experience for children whose teachers perpetuate an image of mathematics as a set of unrelated routines, which he calls 'mathematical rituals' based on their own learning experiences. They unintentionally pass on the concept of mathematics as an 'arbitrary collection of meaningless procedures' rather than a real understanding for the rich interconnections that form the subject.

In primary schools, this has partially been a result of the teachers' own lack of confidence of their subject knowledge. Bibby (2002) found that many primary teachers lacked confidence and were ashamed to admit any lack of proficiency. Thus, no improvement in their skills and confidence could result, since it is only by acknowledging that there is a problem in the first place can we begin to address it successfully and resolve the underlying the issues. Research carried out by Askew *et al.* (1997) found that even the most effective and enthusiastic teachers had in the past experienced 'arid' teaching and admitted to having had negative feelings towards the subject. Words describing their experiences included extremes such as 'traumatic' through to mundane feelings of boredom. However, what is encouraging is that, in spite of these earlier feelings and attitudes, they survived and moved on to enjoy the subject and to share their enthusiasm and knowledge of mathematics with their children. Perhaps a result of these experiences was that they understood what not to do and how not to do it! They recognised the need to make connections in mathematics, teaching strategies rather than sets of techniques and rituals, engaging children in thought and discussion about their mathematics. Haylock (2001) relates that by tackling these anxieties and confusions head on with trainee teachers, he has been successful in creating primary teachers who have a much more positive attitude to teaching mathematics and are able to employ more effective strategies than those they themselves experienced.

Teaching Trends

The various trends in teaching methodologies and content in the past decades have also played a significant part in the largely negative view of mathematics held by the adult population. From the late 1960s to the early 1990s the emphasis in primary mathematics moved away from whole-class teaching and, based on the theoretical ideas of the time, there was a strong emphasis on a 'child-centred' curriculum. The practical result of this approach in the classroom was the evolution of published individualised schemes. There were many advantages of such schemes. They included many well thought out, stimulating activities for children and covered a wide range of mathematics, lending themselves easily to a differentiated curriculum which could meet the needs of a wide range of abilities. However, the disadvantages included the fact that many children were often teaching themselves, and by choice of booklets dictating to some degree, the content of the work covered. The teacher's role was more of a facilitator and resource than classroom expositor. For many children this was not successful and they required greater direction and whole-class teaching to learn many of the concepts effectively. Adults who have not experienced this style of teaching and learning often reflect on feeling insecure in their knowledge and mathematical skills. As Haylock (1991), who is very critical of the primary teachers' reliance on commercial schemes, points out, the inherent feel-good factor of mathematics comes from learning with understanding and making connections reinforced by whole-class teaching.

In the past ten years, there has been a swing back towards an increased proportion of whole-class teaching. Cockcroft (1982) published a report, which indicated the beginning of a significant change in approach to teaching mathematics with a recommendation of a variety of teaching styles and integration of problem solving and investigation (Cockcroft: 71, para. 243). It acknowledged the need for exposition by the teacher but stressed the need for a dialogue between the teacher and child. It referred to the need for teachers to take account of and respond to children's answers. The introduction of the national strategies for primary and secondary schools between 1999 and 2001 reflected the changes in educational and more particularly political attitudes during the 1990s with a main emphasis on the importance of whole-class *interactive* teaching and a clearly prescribed curriculum. More recently, the numeracy strategies have increased their emphasis on the 'how' as well as the 'what' of mathematics teaching, with greater stress on developing problem-solving strategies and thinking skills. These are clearly important transferable skills which need to be developed in children and there is now a great deal of generic literature, which provides ideas and strategies to improve thinking skills.

A review of recent research by Mujis and Reynolds (1999) suggests that there is now a greater degree of agreement between the different research bodies as to the most effective ways of teaching and learning mathematics. The evidence is pointing towards a correlation between whole-class interactive teaching and mathematical achievement. However, this needs support through group work and individual related activities, as these play an important role in developing the child's higher order thinking skills. Mujis and Reynolds see a move by many countries towards a 'blend' of these approaches as reflected in the National Numeracy Strategy Frameworks for Teaching Mathematics (DfEE 1999a; DfES 2000). As supporting adults, there is an important role to play in assisting children to exploit this blend of methods. As we know, some children, e.g. those with Down's Syndrome, require additional guidance to participate in the main whole-class activities and need focused support in smaller group work or individual tasks. In both cases, the use of questions, discussion and selection of suitable resources by the adult are key to teasing out misunderstandings or misconceptions. Together we can help the child to start thinking about the best way to tackle a problem or approach a task. This principle holds true for children of all ages and abilities. All children require challenge at an appropriate level.

Learning Styles

When considering resources to stimulate learning and support discussion, it is important to take account of the learning styles of the children. Learning styles are simply the different approaches or ways of learning. They are the preferred sensory route to processing and making sense of the information. Some people have a visual preference, others auditory and others kinaesthetic or tactile (VAKs, as described by Pat Hughes in Chapter 3). Although most people have a preferred learning style, it does not mean that they are unable to access and process information via a different sensory style. There is no one style that is better, but for some children their preferred style will be their most effective method of learning. Obviously, within the classroom, the teacher needs to employ as many different stimuli and resources as possible to cater for all the different learning styles of the children. Good teachers have always used a variety of resources to stimulate their children, but with the present numeracy strategies, there is a greater expectation of all teachers to use a wealth of resources designed to stimulate learning. For example, opportunities for the visual learners arise through using the 100 squares, number fans, empty number lines, posters of mathematical ideas and vocabulary, seeing the objectives of the lesson written up on the board. For auditory learners emphasis on discussion and interactive questioning is important. Opportunities to repeat aloud, not just tables, can provide the right stimulus for their sensory needs. For kinaesthetic learners, the use of wipe-boards, the chance to come out and demonstrate, and apparatus such as multi-link cubes to investigate patterns are examples of how teachers can and do provide suitable learning experiences. As supporting adults, it is important to be aware of the learning styles of the children and to provide opportunities and resources which match their preferred style. However, it is important not to be exclusive, with resources designed only to support one learning style. In mathematics, visual connections are useful for all children as are the discussions linked to such visual images and there is a need to cover all learning styles to provide a variety of stimulus for all children.

Taking account of the preferred styles is important when supporting the children's learning and revision. They need help to think about effective revision techniques, which match their preferred learning style. It may be that for visual learners a mind map is a good way of learning about a topic, whereas for an auditory learner making up a rap and repeating notes aloud may be more effective. Within the lesson, it is important to provide the children with lots of stimulus but when helping children to revise and embed their learning it may be that a particular method is more successful and will play the major role in pupils' learning. As supporting adults, it is useful to discuss with the children their feelings about the best way of learning for a test or exam and encourage them to try some new techniques. For example, auditory revision techniques could include recording notes on tape, saying key ideas aloud, playing soothing background music as well as getting someone to test them. For a visual learner, revision styles may include making a poster, chart, diagram or cartoon as well as writing notes on key ideas and highlighting the main points/key words. Kinaesthetic learners may find Post-its useful or cutting up their notes and rearranging them. They may need to trace over key words and may have to stand up and stretch at regular intervals. Children need to be aware of the methods that they find most useful in helping them realise *how* to learn the mathematics as distinct from the content of *what* they have to learn. Using this knowledge of how they learn best can increase their success in mathematics.

Thinking Skills and Metacognition

Becoming aware of our own learning style is an important element of developing thinking skills. By becoming aware of the best ways in which we learn, we can capitalise on our knowledge and maximise our capacity to learn and retain information. It can also help to develop coping strategies to compensate for any weaknesses. Metacognition, thinking about your thinking, is recognised as an important element of the effective learning process. Tanner *et al.* (2002) cite research, which indicates that good problem solvers display high levels of metacognitive knowledge and skill. They are able to think about not only the problem but reflect on their approach and evaluate their own methods of tackling the problem. In mathematics, these are particularly important skills that children need to develop. For children to succeed, they need to reflect on their mathematical knowledge and be confident in their ability to tackle a new problem. They need to be able to plan and select the knowledge and skills required by the task and reflect and evaluate the process and outcomes. We can help children become aware of how they are thinking and learning through guidance and discussion. This is often a teaching strategy promoted in relation to gifted and talented children but it is not a strategy suitable only for the higher attaining children. There is a positive impact on the mathematical performances of low-attaining children who are explicitly taught these thinking skills. Some children may require more help to consider what they already know and what they need to know to solve a problem. They will need guidance to decide on the best strategies to tackle a problem and will need to talk through their planning, execution and evaluation of a task. Here a supporting adult can play an important role in developing these higher-order thinking skills by prompting children's efforts through careful questioning designed to engage the child in reflection. Questions, which can prompt the children into the metacognitive process, could include in the initial phase 'Do you understand what the teacher is asking you to do? What is the task/problem all about?' These are not as naïve a starting place as they might first sound, since many children in mathematics lessons have misconceptions as to the task or problem they think they are undertaking. If they are unclear and unsure at this point, they are unlikely to make much progress and be successful tackling the work. If the problem or task is clear in the child's head, the next step is to consider possible strategies for tackling it successfully. At this point, it is useful to ask if he or she has come across anything like it before. Making connections to other areas of mathematics and previous work is vital and needs constant reinforcement whenever possible. If working with a small group, the supporting adult needs to encourage children to share ideas and where possible consider the merits of different approaches. If they are clear on how to tackle the task, it is important to let them have a go. With lower-ability children, this will need scaffolding with suitable prompts to help them organise their thoughts and actions. Vygotsky (1978) saw a difference between children's capacity to solve problems on their own, and their capacity to solve them with assistance. He referred to this difference as the 'zone of proximal development' (ZPD). This area included all the activities that the learner could perform only with assistance. He saw the need for an active dialogue between the 'senior learner', the supporting adult, and the 'junior learner', the child, to bridge this gap in potential between what children already know and what they were capable of achieving with a suitable level of *non-intrusive* intervention. This is not an easy task for the supporting adults – finding a balance to ensure that the intervention is not so great that they give children directions rather than allowing them to think for themselves. In particular, Clare's role supporting a child with Down's Syndrome has the potential to become that of director rather than facilitator. With some children, progress in developing their thinking skills will be very slow. However, with practice and the use of appropriate prompts and questions, thinking skills can be developed and will have a considerable impact on the child's performance.

Questioning and Listening

As mentioned above, helping children to develop thinking skills, and particularly what Bloom (1956) refers to as the higher-order thinking skills (analysis, synthesis and evaluation) involves talk. The teacher and supporting adult need to be involved in a dialogue with the child, familiarising and modelling the language of the subject, encouraging the child to realise that talk is valuable and a tool for thinking. Cockcroft (1982: 72, para. 246) noted that one of the outcomes of good mathematics teaching was the ability of children to 'say what you mean and mean what you say'. Helping children to be able to talk mathematically about their ideas, with the teacher, supporting adult and other children, is essential. One of the dangers of working on individual programmes with children such as the one Clare works with is that they never have the opportunity to discuss their work with others in a group. The teacher and supporting adult must strive for a balance between whole-class, group and individual activities and discussions for all children. Such discussions will usually involve questioning both by the adult and hopefully by the child. It is possible to assess the child's grasp of the problem by the quality of the questions asked. Getting children to form their own questions can be enlightening, providing an insight into their understanding of the mathematics. For example, simply asking a child to supply a question/story for the division $12 \div 3$ can reveal if the child has a full understanding of the operation.

Research (Bauersfeld 1988; Wood 1994) cited by Tanner *et al.* (2002) sees two different forms of questioning: 'funnelling' and 'focusing'. Funnelling questions do not develop children's thinking. They are usually short closed questions requiring recall of facts such as 'if n is 2, what is n^2 (n squared)?' They may be appropriate in certain situations to ascertain children's existing knowledge but in terms of developing a child's problem-solving abilities and thinking skills, focused questions are required. These are usually more open-ended, requiring reflection and thought by the child, e.g. 'Is n^2 always greater than n?' Supplementary prompts to assist the children to think about the answer may be required. Suggesting the substitution of simple numbers to start with such as, 'If n is 3, what is 3 squared?' can ensure the child understands how to square a number and is not doubling to obtain 6 for the answer instead of 9. Follow-up questions may then include 'What happens when n is negative?', 'A decimal?', 'A fraction?' Choosing appropriate questions requires a great deal of skill and judgement, and relies on the adult's own good subject knowledge.

Many teachers find these focused questions more difficult. It is far easier to tell children how to do something than to extract from them how they have tackled something themselves. If the child is 'stuck', altering the question, so that it provides clues, can help the child find an answer. It is useful to build up a bank of such questions that can help children reach the learning objective. A good starting point is often 'How did you get that answer?', or 'Explain to me how you worked that out'. From their responses, the teacher or supporting adult can frame a supporting question, which will help to shed light on the task for the child. It may be a case of spotting where the child has made a mistake and saying 'Can you explain this bit again?' Explaining a second time may be sufficient to enable the child to spot the mistake or at least to realise the bit he or she does not understand. If not, it may be the child needs more guidance: 'Have you thought about trying this?' or, where possible, bringing in another child: 'Sarah, how have you done this? Can you explain it to us?' Questioning by the teacher and assistants needs to be sensitive and appropriate to ensure the self-esteem of the child is maintained and strengthened. An environment within the classroom of secure interaction needs to be established. Children need to know their responses are valued and that all the class will listen to them.

Connections

Research by Askew *et al.* (1997) found that the most effective primary teachers of numeracy were those who had a connectionist orientation of teaching. This was the most important factor, more so than their classroom organisation. They found that teachers across the range of effectiveness, from highly effective to moderately effective, were using whole-class teaching and group work. In other words, it was not the teaching organisational styles which made teachers highly effective, but their ability to share mathematical connections with their children.

The teachers in the research sample made these connections on many levels. They included the connections made between different topics such as decimals, fractions and percentages, stressing their equivalence. They also made connections between the different representations that were used, i.e. symbols and diagrams, words and objects. For example, in secondary school, connections to previous work in multiplication of two-digit numbers can be used when considering algebraic multiplication of two brackets $(x + 2)(x + 3)$, by considering a rectangle of sides $(x + 2)$ and $(x + 3)$ and finding the sum of the internal areas (see Figure 6.2). This connects to the child's previous experience building on an understanding of the grid method and providing a visual interpretation of multiplication in terms of area. This approach provides a way into multiplication of two brackets which gives a greater insight than simply teaching children a rule such as FOIL (first pair, outside pair, inside pair, last pair) which may become a useful routine later, but only when the children's underlying understanding of the operation is secure.

$$
\begin{array}{c}
\quad\quad\quad x \quad\quad +3 \\
\begin{array}{c|c|c|}
 & x^2 & 3x \\
\hline
+2 & 2x & 6 \\
\hline
\end{array}
\quad
\begin{aligned}
&(x+2)(x+3) \\
&= x^2 + 2x + 3x + 6 \\
&= x^2 + 5x + 6
\end{aligned}
\end{array}
$$

FIGURE 6.2   Making connections using the 'grid' method of multiplication

Connections with the children's own methods of thinking and working out were also important to effective teachers. The teachers discussed these methods with the children and linked them to their own. Askew *et al.* (1997) found that the connectionist teachers worked more actively with their children. Their primary belief was that the process of teaching mathematics depended on a two-way dialogue between the teacher and the child (this echoes the earlier views of the Cockcroft report). The child's work was valued and discussed. The class shared issues about methods and considered ways to improve.

Other connections are also important for effective learning. Making links to other curriculum areas is important, helping children to see the transferable nature of mathematical skills. Tanner *et al.* (2002) refer to children and adults holding two sets of parallel mathematical knowledge. One is for use in school, in the classroom, the other for the real world, and these sets do not overlap. For many children at secondary school, the situation is worse. They do not even see the mathematical overlap into other subjects and compartmentalise their knowledge, unable to recognise its applications in areas such as art, geography, science or technology. The supporting adult is in a position to remind children of these links as they arise in other subject areas by pointing out to children that this is a skill they have used before in their mathematics lesson. For example, children may have a quicker way of multiplying 460×5 than their geography teacher, who may suggest using a calculator when the child could use an appropriate mental strategy, find ten lots, and then halve it to obtain the answer. Constantly reminding children of the links and connections can help to embed the importance and relevance of the skills they are learning in the mathematics lesson and, for some children, this can be an important motivating factor. In a secondary school, the supporting adult has an important role, as specialists in other subjects do not necessarily put the same emphasis on numeracy skills and fail to make these connections explicit. This is less of a problem in the primary school where the generalist nature of the class teacher, who is largely covering all subjects, has a greater overview of the child's learning experience.

Resources

Connections and questions are essential for successful teaching and learning in mathematics, shored up by the use of appropriate practical resources. As mentioned already in this chapter, children have different learning styles and require different incentives to engage their enthusiasm and understanding. A resource-rich environment can meet the range of visual, auditory and kinaesthetic stimuli required to promote understanding and links to children's previous experiences. A good resource can spark a child's interest and generate questions and interactions between the children. Newspapers and comics are a rich resource. They can prompt many different jumping-off points. The television page in a magazine or newspaper can be a revelation to children looking at time. They can consider the number of hours they watch television on a typical day, which can develop into work on fractions, percentages, pie charts, bar charts, etc. Comparisons across the class to see if they watch more than an average child can produce more work on statistics and data handling. At a simple level, they may convert programme times to 24-hour time and calculate the length of time spent watching one or two television programmes. A more advanced piece of work may be to investigate statements such as, 'There are far too many soaps on TV and not enough news programmes'. This work can involve groups discussing the validity of the statement and deciding on what evidence they have to argue for or against, and on a suitable presentation of the facts to support their point of view. Children can develop mensuration skills by finding the dimensions of the pictures/images or columns of text and by comparing areas of text and images on a typical page. This can lead to work on ratio or comparisons of data to investigate what is a typical page, e.g. 'How much space is occupied by headlines, text, adverts, or pictures?' 'Magazines are bad value for money. They are just full of adverts' may be a statement that can provoke interest, argument and mathematics. House prices, car prices from a paper or a specialist magazine such as a motorbike magazine can provide opportunities to look at range and averages, not to mention scores such as football and cricket! Consideration of Annual Percentage Rates (APRs) on advertisements from loan companies can initiate essential discussion of money management and an increased awareness of the need for careful financial planning.

Books are also valuable for stimulating interest. Data can be collected from reference books that interest children such as the *Guinness Book of Records* or encyclopaedias of animals, birds, history or geography – whatever works for the particular child. Number work can come easily by comparison of facts. For example:

How much bigger is the world's biggest bird than the world's smallest bird?
What order would the animals be put in according to weight?
For how much of his life was Henry VIII married?

Children can answer these types of questions without realising they are working on mathematics if they enjoy the topic. With imagination, adults can use these topics to develop resources that engage the children, by being relevant to their experiences and interests.

Topical characters and popular media events can prove an ideal motivational medium, particularly with younger children. Events such as the Olympics or the football World Cup lend themselves easily to mathematics. Using a current hit film or cartoon character can make a less than exciting activity come to life. For example, the use of the characters from *The Simpsons* to illustrate a worksheet on basic number skills or problem solving can create some humour in a task – 'How many Duff beers can Homer buy for $10 if they cost 75 cents each?'

Harry Potter has provided a source for many great worksheets on 'Muggle Mathematics', covering topics such as ratio, exchange rates, number bases or directions. The correct recipe for a polyjuice potion which lasts one hour for one child over 3 years, 1½ hours for a child under 3 and so on, can lead on to a series of problems:

How much Boomslang required for 2 ten-year-olds for 3 hours?
If we only have 20 leeches, how much polyjuice can we make?

Foreign exchange based on 29 Knuts = 1 Sickle and 17 Sickles = 1 Galleon can be a more interesting alternative to the euro for some children. Working in the different bases of 17 and 29 when finding the cost of spell books and wands can stretch a child's numeracy skills and provide an unexpected appreciation and understanding of the advantages of the metric system and base 10! With squared paper and co-ordinates, a map of Diagon Alley can be used to discuss directions from one shop to another such as the 'Leaky Cauldron Pub'.

With older children, these stimuli can still play a part but the presentation needs to be more sophisticated and may need to look less contrived. This is where newspapers and magazines can come into their own. Playing cards can also work well with older children; simple games such as '21' and variations can be used to consolidate number bonds, as can a memory game based on selected cards that pair up to 10. Using a suit can make learning the eight times table more interesting – turn over the shuffled cards and complete the table. Cards are also useful to look at simple probabilities through the game of 'Higher and Lower'. For older children this could involve simple fractions – what is the probability of the next card being higher than the 7 of diamonds? If there are only 5 cards left to turn, and 3 are greater than the 7, then it must be 3/5.

Games are a rich resource in mathematics and Clare might find them particularly useful for the child she supports. They are motivational, often adaptable and thus are ideal for differentiated work. They can have a different focus according to the desired learning objectives. The focus could be on language and vocabulary of the mathematics. An example could be the use of target boards using questions based on *The National Numeracy Strategy*: *Mathematical Vocabulary* book (DfEE 1999b). This could be a starting game where children have to answer four in a straight line. By choosing open questions such as 'Give two factors of 24' or 'Find two fractions that add up to one', further discussion can be had by comparing different children's responses. Bingo is an example of another easily adaptable game to base on a current topic of work, such as area. The children may pick 4 areas, from 10 possible areas, e.g. 12cm^2, 15cm^2, etc. and then in turn a series of shapes given with dimensions, for the children to calculate the area, and check whether the units match the square filled in. First person to obtain four matching answers has a full house and wins.

Board games are also easy to adapt. If a game focuses on moving around according to number bonds up to 20, this can be changed and the cards be simplified to make moves with number bonds up to 10. Once the children's understanding is secure, the rules could be changed to involve multiplication. We can develop thinking skills through games by asking children to analyse and evaluate the rules, and to suggest their own changes to a game.

In fact, all of the existing numeracy resources in the classroom, such as the dry-wipe-boards, dice, cards or counting sticks are ideal for supporting children in smaller groups. The whole-class activities based on these numeracy resources may need adapting to suit the child's ability. Sometimes certain children simply require more thinking time than the majority of the class. They may need to repeat the whole-class activity, e.g. by physically moving their finger along the counting stick (a kinaesthetic approach) rather than just watching the class teacher do it. Someone in Clare's position can support her child in doing this during whole-class teaching, thus helping the child to benefit from it. Wipe-boards are extremely powerful resources with less able children who gain confidence in knowing that any mistakes may be wiped away and will not remain a permanent reminder, unlike work in ink in their class books. The key is to be flexible in the creation and use of resources, adapting them to meet the specific needs of the child and designing them to build on any existing knowledge or interest the children already have so that the resources stimulate and engage.

A Recipe for Success

This chapter set out to discuss some of the issues concerning effectively supporting mathematical learning. A resource-rich learning environment is the key. By providing children with appropriate stimuli, we can help them to break down the barriers and develop a greater understanding and appreciation of mathematics. However, it is important to remember that, as in the opening quote, the greatest resource existing to support the child is the classroom teacher and the supporting adult. It is the adult's presence, personality, knowledge and experience which will determine the conditions for successful learning. A classroom where there is a positive, enthusiastic atmosphere and an expectation for children to enter into a dialogue about their mathematics, not only to answer questions but also to pose their own, is essential. Children need to explore mathematics; they need support in making connections between different but related areas within mathematics itself, such as fractions and decimals, and between mathematics and their real world, such as the use of statistics in newspapers. Making these connections requires adult help through discussion and questioning but also the use of concrete, practical resources such as number lines and playing cards, wipe-boards and worksheets. The selection of the most appropriate resources and nature of support is crucial. We should take account of the children's learning styles as well as the subject content.

There is no single recipe for the correct amount of each of the above 'ingredients', for in every classroom and with each child the proportions required will vary according to attitudes and abilities. Figure 6.3 shows the range of ingredients that add up to effective mathematical learning – a recipe for success. Finding the best recipe for each group of children or individual is not an exact science and requires a mixture of careful planning, patience, persistence and professionalism, but the rewards are high. The value of seeing a child suddenly understanding a new mathematical idea is just as satisfying for the adult as it is for the child. For someone like Clare, dealing with children who find the whole idea of

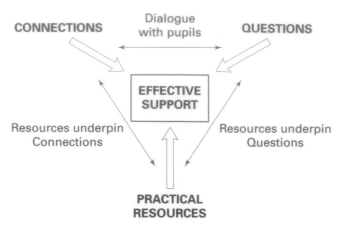

FIGURE 6.3   A recipe for success

mathematics challenging, making them feel negative and afraid to engage with it, the task can be very difficult but it is such a valuable one. We need reminding that the rewards of helping the child to unlock the door to a new and better understanding is the greatest job satisfaction and worth all the hours spent finding those right ingredients.

Discussion Starters

1   Reflect on your school experience of mathematics. What teaching and learning styles did you experience? Did they match your own preferred learning styles?
2   What would have been useful additions?
3   Should all children follow the same mathematics curriculum?
4   What are the potential difficulties faced by mathematics teachers when a child with special needs is in the class? How can the teacher overcome the difficulties?

Reflecting on Practice

1   Record examples of questions used by teachers in mathematics lessons (don't forget to ask the teachers' permission first). Sort the questions into 'open' and 'closed'. What was the purpose of each question?
2   Research cited by the Key Stage 3 strategy suggests that most questions asked by teachers are concerned with children's factual recall and comprehension. Few questions tackled the higher-order thinking skills such as analysis and evaluation. What is your experience? Identify opportunities to develop these higher-order questions when working with children.

Websites

www.ex.ac.uk/~PErnest/ – to access Philosophy of Mathematics Education journals on-line.

www.groups.dcs.st-and.ac.uk/history/ – useful information about the history of mathematics and mathematics in different cultures.

www.painsley.org.uk/mathsmirror/ – resources for secondary mathematics.

www.primaryresources.co.uk/maths/maths.htm – resources for primary mathematics.

www.standards.dfee.gov.uk/keystage3/ – information about Key Stage 3 mathematics.

www.standards.dfee.gov.uk/numeracy/ – to find information about Key Stages 1 and 2 mathematics.

References

Askew, M., Rhodes, V., Brown, M., William, D. and Johnson, D. (1997) *Effective Teachers of Numeracy: Final Report*, London: Kings College.

Bauersfeld, H. (1988) 'Interaction, construction and knowledge: alternative perspectives for mathematics education', in Grouws, D., Cooney, T. and Jones D. (eds), *Perspectives on Research on Effective Mathematics Teaching*, Reston, VA: National Council of Teachers of Mathematics, pp. 27–46.

Bibby, T. (2002) 'Shame an emotional response to doing mathematics as an adult and a teacher', *British Educational Research Journal*, 28 (5), 705–21.

Bloom, B.S. (1956) *Taxonomy of Educational Objectives: The Classification of Educational Goals: Handbook I, Cognitive Domain*, New York: Longmans.

Brown, T. (1998) *Coordinating Mathematics in the Primary School*, London: Falmer Press.

Carvel, J. (1999) 'Teachers "too ashamed" to admit inability in mathematics', *The Guardian*, 2 September.

Cockcroft, W.H. (1982) *Mathematics Counts*, London: HMSO.

DfEE (1999a) *The National Numeracy Strategy: Framework for Teaching Mathematics from Year R to Y6*, Cambridge: Cambridge University Press.

DfEE (1999b) *The National Numeracy Strategy: Mathematical Vocabulary*, London: DfEE.

DfES (2000) *The National Numeracy Strategy: Framework for Teaching Mathematics Years 7, 8 and 9*, Cambridge: Cambridge University Press.

DfES (2002a) *Strengthening Mathematics Teaching in Year 7*, Cambridge: Cambridge University Press.

DfES (2002b) *Mathematics Module: Induction Training for Teaching Assistants in Secondary Schools*, London: DfES.

Ernest, P. and Lim, C.S. (1999) 'Public images of mathematics', *Philosophy of Mathematics Education Journal*, 11, at www.ex.ac.uk/~PErnest/pome11/contents.htm, accessed September 2003.

Fraser, H. and Honeyford, G. (2000) *Children, Parents and Teachers Enjoying Numeracy*, London: David Fulton.

Haylock, D. (1991) *Teaching Mathematics to Low Attainers, 8–12*, London: Paul Chapman Publishing.

Haylock, D. (2001) *Mathematics Explained for Primary Teachers*, London: Paul Chapman Publishing.

Mujis, D. and Reynolds, D. (1999) 'Numeracy matters: contemporary policy issues in the teaching of mathematics', in Thompson, I. (ed.), *Issues in Teaching Numeracy in Primary Schools*, Buckingham: Open University Press, pp. 17–26.

Skemp, R.R. (1986) *The Psychology of Learning Mathematics*, Harmondsworth: Penguin.

Smith, J. (1999) 'Virtual mathematics', *Maths Teaching*, 166, March, 14–15.

Tanner, H., Jones, S. and Davies, A. (2002) *Developing Numeracy in the Secondary School*, London: David Fulton.

Vygotsky, L.S. (1978) *Mind in Society: The Development of Higher Psychological Processes*, ed. Cole, M., Cambridge, MA: Harvard University Press.

Wood, T. (1994) 'Patterns of interaction and the culture of mathematical classrooms', in Lerman, S. (ed.), *Cultural Perspectives on the Mathematics Classroom*, Dordrecht, Kluwer Academic, pp. 148–68.

7

Scientific Process Skills: Abbas' Journey

Roger Stevenson

Meet Fazia

Since my retirement from full-time work, I help voluntarily on a part-time basis supporting language development through science and art in Key Stage 2 classes. I support small groups of children, including children with EAL during practical activities in order to work on their communication skills and develop their subject vocabulary. The children I work with have difficulty in expressing themselves clearly in English speaking, listening, reading and writing and find subject vocabulary very difficult to learn. While I work with the children, I engage them in purposeful conversations about their work. I help them select appropriate resources and help them develop their research skills. I encourage children to use their home language to help them make sense of the activities.

I have no specific training for this work, only an interest in science and art as subjects. My previous employment was in a research laboratory, and painting is a hobby. I need help with creating ways to help the children associate the subject language with their understanding, especially in science lessons where some of the vocabulary seems to prevent the children succeeding in national tests yet they understand the processes.

The Nature of Science

What is science? The teacher can share this question with the children prior to the study of any new science topic and it will help to involve them directly in their own learning from the outset. Children's responses can be discussed, displayed and revisited after any activity. It is useful to look at definitions from a range of sources, shown in Figure 7.1.

Statements relating to each topic may also be classified by children as scientific/non-scientific, e.g. 'the candle glows and makes me feel happy' may relate to religious education (RE) or English while 'the candle gives light and heat' is a scientific statement. To have a philosophical discussion about the nature of science with children of any age is important as it sets the tone for further accommodative and divergent activities and builds

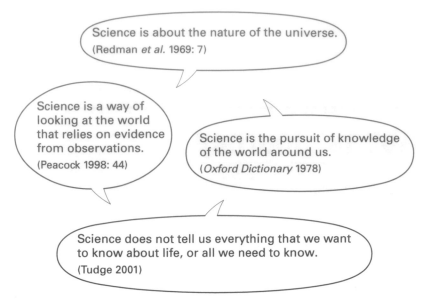

FIGURE 7.1   Displaying definitions of science

variety into lessons. Beresford's (2003) research into learning preferences shows that children value discussion of this kind and often do not get the chance to consider why we do what we do in school and to consider why the curriculum has taken shape in the way it has. To help Fazia understand some of the issues, I will present the story of one bilingual child and his scientific pursuits.

Scientific Inquiry

Abbas, a primary Year 6 child in my class, confided that he had a 'secret' contained within his school bag – a slice of stale pizza and that he would like me to look at it. Abbas, a child with an intra-personal learning style, was covertly investigating decay. Our subsequent conversation led to a consideration of several key scientific questions:

- How long had it been there?
- Was its condition changing?
- What would it be like by next week?
- What did this tell us about food in general?
- Why does food decay?
- What types of foods similarly rot away if left?
- Do some school bags work better than others do? If so why?
- Is this a hygienic line of inquiry?

Abbas was involved in an active, problem-solving process where learning is determined not by teaching but by the learner's knowledge, ability, attitude and context (Qualter *et al.* 1990). As an active learner, he was initiating his own activities and taking some responsibility for his own learning. He was probably unaware that he was developing Harlen's (2000) scientific skills:

- raising questions;
- developing hypotheses;
- making predictions;
- gathering evidence;
- interpreting evidence and drawing conclusions;
- communicating and reflecting.

He had not consciously formulated these questions. He was similarly unaware that he was using the 'processed-based' model where exploration, observation, asking questions and trying things out are central features. However, he was involved in genuine scientific inquiry and demonstrating a desire to carry out first-hand practical investigation to understand the world around him. The future study of microorganisms and the role they play in decomposition would develop his understanding and allow him to investigate more carefully, safely and with controlled variables.

Pupils will often construct their own meaning and have their own ideas for 'fair tests'. The real scientists in your class are probably similarly involved in investigations, which may or may not take them beyond the boundary of acceptable taste! Active learning is rooted in constructivist principles where children have ownership of the scientific problem and have been involved in identifying and defining it for themselves (Qualter *et al.* 1990). As such, this is a more powerful mode of learning than having the investigation chosen for you or having factual knowledge given to you directly by the teacher. Children are naturally inquisitive and they will try to make sense of new information in the context of their own understanding:

'The earth is flat.'
'Fluttering leaves make the wind.'
'The moon follows you as you walk.'
'Shadows follow you around.'
'Evaporation takes place at night.'
'Your eye sends out a beam of light.'

Concept construction involves careful mediation by teachers who will need to provide investigative frameworks that help children adapt their explanations along more orthodox lines. Consequently, teachers and assistants should be patient and deal sensitively with child misconceptions where science understanding is concerned. Worth (2001) argues that a teacher's role is that of a guide helping children learn through the experiences they have in the world. The teacher's role becomes that of a facilitator – a 'guide on the side' in preference to a 'sage on the stage'. The art to successful science teaching then is in providing the right opportunities for children to investigate at the right time, allowing for progression in skills knowledge and understanding. I would advise Fazia to take on this role of guide while supporting those children who need to develop their language skills.

The time spent finding out children's ideas is important and support for further development should ideally relate to children's ideas. The teaching assistant's involvement can then boost a child's understanding and self-esteem in the subject. In this case, the teaching assistant praised Abbas for his initiative and encouraged him to present his findings to the class. He is typical of the under-achieving band of children who require additional support in science. The quality of first-hand learning experiences proves highly motivating for him, as for most children.

An inquisitive disposition, however, does not automatically lead to good national test results. Later that year, Abbas struggled to read the language of the Key Stage 2 science paper. His low self-esteem was due partly to first and second language learning difficulties. He needed help to organise his findings and to record them so that the stress he felt about writing could be minimised. Abbas strongly felt the constraints of an assessment-led curriculum and this could have damaged the positive relationship he had with his teachers and his attitude towards learning in general. We can easily reduce scientific understanding to a set of 'facts' which ignore the whole child and measure mainly memory and linguistic/numerical ability. Teachers and teaching assistants will want to offset the potential damage caused to children through crude assessment tools and will want to carry out on-going formative assessments of children with regular feedback and shared goals. Learning partnerships with shared criteria for attainment are crucial for maintaining motivation of children such as Abbas. The following extract illustrates a typical piece of positive dialogue between the teaching assistant and Abbas:

> TA: You did very well with your own ideas for investigations this term, Abbas. Which parts of science have you enjoyed the most?
>
> A: I like the work on . . . on . . . mouldy things . . . organs . . .
>
> TA: Ah, yes, the investigation about microorganisms . . . what did you like about that?
>
> A: Seeing what happens to food, Miss, in different places . . . if it goes mouldy.
>
> TA: Have you placed any of that work in your record of achievement yet?
>
> A: Yes, here, look.
>
> TA: Good. Are you pleased with your progress in science?
>
> A: Sometimes if I can remember new vocabulary, I feel good about it.
>
> TA: Well, what about keeping a list of all new vocabulary each week? We could do it together on a Thursday morning. We could make it your target for science this term if you like.
>
> A: Yes, Miss, I'd like that.

Abbas' cultural background is that of a second-generation Asian Muslim whose family moved to the UK from Pakistan before he was born. The family spoke very little English language at home. This had created difficulties for him in absorbing new language and in particular subject-specific vocabulary. He did make progress and benefited from the shared goals and the chance to talk things through on a weekly basis with his teaching assistant.

Pupils can and should be involved in the decision-making and planning for future learning. Teachers and assistants such as Fazia should make sure children are aware of the skills, knowledge and understanding they need to improve on. Fazia is in a good position to support children in becoming actively involved in their learning process through building their self-esteem and developing their language skills within the subject.

Developing hypotheses

Formulating hypotheses takes practice and often requires additional support for some children who will need time to collaborate, organise their thoughts and put them into suitable forms of words. Pupils may need adult help to structure a hypothesis (there may be links with literacy 'sentence-level' activities). A hypothesis is a prediction based upon prior knowledge and experience and will be the idea that forms the basis of an investigation. A child *hypothesised* that all food will decay when the conditions are right, because some conditions allow microorganisms to grow:

> P: It could be that the warmer and damper the conditions, the more the microorganisms will multiply because I think that they will need the same conditions for growth as plants.
> TA: A good hypothesis. How could you prove that?
> P: Well, I could do a fair test, Miss. I could test some food in a dry place and the same food in damp conditions.
> TA: Yes, we could do that. What resources would you need?

Making predictions

A prediction exists within the framework of an investigation and the outcome of the investigation will determine whether it is correct:

> TA: You've decided what and how you will organise your investigation. Now can you make a prediction of the outcome?
> P: I think that the bread will decay if it is stored in a damp place.
> TA: OK, let's make a note of that.

At that time, the prediction was unproven. The hypothesis, on the other hand, is a more general statement than the prediction and can apply to all situations.

Gathering evidence: planning

How did Abbas gather evidence? His investigation was already a week old. He knew that the appropriate time scale for his inquiry was days and weeks not seconds, minutes or hours. He may not have been systematic in his planning and perhaps may not have thought through how often and when he would make his observations, but he knew intuitively that daily observations would be enough as change was very slow. Hourly observations would be tedious and unnecessary. He had limited his variables in order to keep his investigation manageable.

There are many different ways of reporting results and children have choices to allow them different ways of communicating results appropriate to their age and development. In

TABLE 7.1   Identifying two different investigations

	Same, i.e. controlled variable	Different, i.e. independent variable
Investigation 1	Food	Temperatures and conditions
Investigation 2	Temperature and conditions	Foods

the investigation that followed children had the choice of investigations, as shown in Table 7.1.

Did Abbas keep his test fair? To him his school bag represented the controlled variables of same temperature and conditions. He had realised that to make the test reliable he must make sure that the variables of temperature, light and moisture were controlled. The dependent variable was to be the slice of pizza changing subtly from day to day.

Gathering evidence: observing

Abbas had conveniently overlooked the need to record his results. As cited by Newton (1988), research in the 1980s by the 'Assessment of Performance Primary Science Unit' revealed that few children automatically record their data systematically in charts or tables, etc. It is important therefore to encourage children to ask questions about their own work and to evaluate what they are doing at all stages. With guidance and practice, children will begin to select an appropriate way of gathering and recording evidence appropriate to the nature of the inquiry. Abbas needed a 'scaffold' for the observations and guidance relating to vocabulary:

> TA: How are you going to record your observations, Abbas?
> A: Well, we could say what has happened every day or draw it.
> TA: Yes . . . what about recording our observations onto the computer each day and doing a drawing? We could set up a database.
> A: Can you show me how, Miss?
> TA: Of course . . . as long as you agree to show others how we did it so they can use it too.
> A: OK, Miss.

Later that day:

> TA: So how have we described the pizza today?
> A: Light grey mould. On 40 per cent of surface. Tiny hairs with white spheres on top. Green patches in parts. Cheese dry with white powder covering.
> TA: Well done!

Interpreting evidence and drawing conclusions

The groups went on to interpret their findings and draw conclusions based upon the work they had done together. Children need the opportunity to evaluate what they do and think in a kind of 'self-interrogation' (Qualter *et al.* 1990). The role of the teacher at this point in the proceedings is important and can help children further reflect and give them a clear idea of how they can move forward also in subsequent investigations:

> P: Our investigation shows that the cooler the conditions, the slower the microorganisms multiply, and we think this is because low temperatures make it difficult for them to move.

The class had answered their own questions asked originally in the form of hypotheses and some children were now able to ask further questions:

> TA: OK, so what else could we try to investigate?
>
> P: I need to investigate this further to find out more about microorganisms and would like to know if the microorganisms in the freezer start to reproduce again as the temperature increases.
>
> TA: Yes, that's a really good idea . . . anything else?
>
> P: I would like to know if restricting the supply of air will stop the microorganisms reproducing.
>
> TA: How could you test that, do you think?

Some could suggest applications in the wider world:

> TA: We've enjoyed the investigation and found out a lot but who needs to know this?
>
> P: It's really important for everyone at home and school canteen staff.
>
> TA: Yes, food technologists, cooks and anyone preparing and storing food need to know about microorganisms.

Bilingual learning issues

English as an additional language (EAL) pupils will often struggle to find an exact mother-tongue equivalent for technical and scientific vocabulary and may therefore benefit from specific bilingual support in science lessons. Consider the use of language involved in predicting: the use of conditionals and future tense necessary within the sentence. A focus on collaborative learning will give bilingual children the opportunity to develop language for a purpose and to talk in their mother tongue as they see fit. At all Key Stages, children may need to have the specialist vocabulary and forms of words modelled and displayed.

To extend opportunities for learning, the teacher could plan for each group to collaborate to simulate microorganisms in different conditions:

> TA: Group 1 . . . You are a microorganism living in a packet of Shreddies. Explain how you are feeling and what you need to do in order to survive.
>
> Group 2, you are a microorganism living beneath a boy's fingernail. Describe what happens to you and how your life changes when the boy bites his nails!
>
> You've got five minutes to work it out together and then we'd like to hear from you.

The simulations provided a different context for children to apply what they had discovered and served to develop scientific understanding and develop language skills in a social collaborative situation. Research by Cummins (1980) into bilingualism indicates that EAL children need opportunities to develop both basic interpersonal communicative skills (BICS) and cognitive academic language proficiency (CALP). Through simulation, both forms of language are developed as children interact to develop their role in the 'play' and find themselves using precise scientific vocabulary and hearing it used repeatedly by other children.

Communication and reflection

Each academic year feels like a form of journey for those involved (Finser 1994). Scientific inquiry requires planning, organisation, perseverance and teamwork. The relationships that have formed are crucial to the teaching and learning process. Both children and teachers alike will have developed and changed in some way during that time. Both should have taken time to reflect and evaluate progress made in teaching and learning. Just as teachers will reflect upon their own practice, we should also ask children if they enjoyed the work undertaken, and the way teaching activities were organised and what future work they would like to be involved in. Beresford (2003) argues that this enables children to have some control and responsibility for their own learning.

> TA: So what would you say about writing your own report for science this term, Abbas? What do you think are your strengths in science?
>
> A: Having my own ideas for investigations, Miss . . . and thinking for myself about my interest in science.
>
> TA: Yes, you really are good at that and have shown real understanding in most topics. What about the new vocabulary?
>
> A: Well, Miss, I can remember microorganisms, bacteria and microbes.
>
> TA: Abbas, that's fantastic. What do you need to work on then next term?
>
> A: Speeding up my work, Miss, and finishing things off properly.
>
> TA: I think you've just written your report, Abbas. Let's write it down together!

The Wider Picture

The media regularly makes us aware that the position of science and science teaching can be precarious. For example, some American states have outlawed the study of Darwin's theory of evolution because it contradicts a literal interpretation of the Bible. Public perception of the relevance of scientific technology can be manipulated. Weapons of mass destruction, for example, are discussed daily in the media and are an obvious product of humankind's new-age scientific capability. Genetically modified crops and the morality of human cloning continue to be debated in our times, as is the quest for the ultimate human DNA 'blueprint'. Cutting-edge science will continue to impact on our lives much as it did for the Victorians 150 years ago.

At primary and secondary levels, science teaching should include the achievement of wider aims. Jennings, as cited by Newton (1988), suggested that science education has neglected the creative aspects of our culture. The challenge then for science teachers and curriculum managers is to develop awareness of both the nature of science and the social and cultural implications of that science. We know that the majority of our children will not go on to be scientists. However, we also know that 'scientifically literate' people are more likely to have informed views in any ethical debate and will therefore be better placed to use their judgement well in the exercise of their democratic rights. The only constant thing in the development of science in society seems to be constant change. To reflect and research into its themes can be highly motivating for children of all ages.

Discussion Starters

1 Why is first-hand active learning necessary when we can deliver the curriculum content easily in the form of a set of facts?

2 How could the national tests demotivate a child like Abbas?

3 Why are records of achievement so motivational for Abbas?

4 Why is it important that children make their own decisions about recording results?

5 Why is it important to relate the work in class to the real world?

6 Do children with EAL benefit from the opportunity to use their home language in science lessons?

7 Why is collaborative learning particularly appropriate for bilingual children?

8 Why is it important that children are encouraged to reflect upon the impact of new scientific developments?

9 What constitutes a scientifically literate person?

Reflecting on Practice

1 Work with a group of children engaged in a practical science activity. Note the language they use and the type of questions they pose (if any). Consider your role in developing their language skills during a science lesson and identify any areas for development, e.g. do you have a scientific vocabulary and do you understand the meanings of specific words associated with the activity?

2 Create an interesting method of helping children describe their journey through a scientific investigation. The method must be appropriate to the age and aptitude of the children, e.g. oral reporting for younger children or those who have difficulty expressing themselves in writing.

Websites

www.aft.org/american_educator – on-line articles available in science and other subjects.

www.nsf.gov/pubs/ – the National Science Foundation publications page.

www.teachernet.gov.uk/remodelling – information about employment legislation, professional development and training for teachers and support staff.

References

Beresford, J. (2003) *Creating the Conditions to Involve Pupils in Their Learning*, London: David Fulton Publishers.

Cummins, J. (1980) *The Construct of Language Proficiency in Bi-lingual Education*, Georgetown, DC: Georgetown University Press.

Finser, M.T. (1994) *School as a Journey: The Eight-Year Odyssey of a Waldorf Teacher and His Class*, London: Steiner Press.

Harlen, M. (2000) *Teaching, Learning and Assessing Science 5–12*, 3rd edn, London: Paul Chapman Publishing.

Newton, P.D. (1988) *Making Science Education Relevant*, London: Kogan Page.

Peacock, G.A. (1998) *Science for Primary Teachers*, London: Letts Educational.

Qualter, A., Strang, J., Swatton, P. and Taylor, R. (1990) *A Way of Learning Science*, London: Blackwell.

Redman, S., Brereton, A. and Boyers, P. (1969) *An Approach to Primary Science*, London: Macmillan.

Tudge (2001) www.aft.org/american educator, accessed September 2003.

Worth, K. (2001) *The Power of Children's Thinking*, Arlington, VA: National Science Foundation USA.

Bilingual Learners: Inclusive Practice

Melanie Griffin

Meet Shadjeet

I am a bilingual support assistant working in primary and secondary schools and I provide bilingual support to specified groups of children in several schools. The children I work with have difficulty accessing the curriculum content in English and expressing ideas in coherent written English. I explain the teacher's instructions and explanations in simpler English and sometimes the children's home-language. I talk to the learners about their ideas before they start writing.

Although I am a qualified nursery nurse (NNEB), this qualification did not prepare me for my current role. Although I am bilingual, I still need more knowledge and understanding of how bilingual learners learn an additional language. I would like to understand the strategies for promoting language development and need ideas for the classroom. I would also like to involve the children's parents.

Introduction

This chapter invites the reader to explore the language and learning contexts of bilingual learners in a range of situations. It will discuss ways of gaining information on children's competence in their languages and will outline basic principles of first and second language acquisition, and the practical application of these explored. There will be an overview of ideas of language, culture and identity and an overview of research findings and practical suggestions for involving English as an additional language (EAL) parents in their children's learning. The chapter will introduce readers like Shadjeet, a bilingual support assistant, to key terms used in this field. The chapter will refer the reader to a range of further reading and to resource links including website information with the aim of giving Shadjeet a breadth of knowledge about language acquisition and supporting learning.

What Is Bilingualism?

What do we mean when we say someone is 'bilingual'? Within education, a generally accepted definition would be one such as that given by Hall (1995) who clearly identifies a bilingual pupil as one who has access to and uses two languages, at both home and school. Such a child will not necessarily be fluent, literate or competent in either language. Bilingual children need support in school for a variety of reasons, mostly related to comparisons in attainment. Attainment of minority ethnic pupils is below that of white UK pupils at all stages of education from pre-school to Higher Education (Gillborn and Gipps 1996). This is not the case for all minority ethnic groups, however; those particularly affected are Bangladeshi, Pakistani and African-Caribbean heritage pupils. Research has shown that pupils from these ethnic groups benefit from some strategies aimed particularly at their needs. Learners of EAL need support to ensure that their languages develop appropriately and these strategies will vary slightly according to the learners' first languages and educational backgrounds.

This variation in attainment of ethnic groups indicates that it is not the fact of being from a minority ethnic group that necessarily influences attainment, nor is it being a learner of English as an additional language. A range of factors is involved in under-attainment and it is the combination/juxtaposition of these which leads to a long-term under-attainment cycle for certain ethnic groups. As educators, we need to identify factors that adversely affect children's attainment and find ways to combat these. We need to find approaches that build on the learners' strengths and utilise the skills, knowledge and heritages they bring to the learning situation.

First and Additional Language Acquisition

First language acquisition

There are many theories of how language is learned: there are those who suggest that children learn by imitation alone, and others who propose the existence of in-built subconscious understanding that language has rules. Some suggest that role of 'baby talk' from parent or carer to child is essential to the language learning process. The ideas about language development generally accepted and used today come from the work of many psychologists and linguists over many years. Much of this thinking is based on ideas relating to children being born with the in-built understanding that language has patterns and a grammatical structure and that language learning follows a general pattern of development (Krashen 1981). The general model seems to be that language acquisition takes place through the learner hearing models of language, then uses that language to make generalisations about the grammatical structure of the language, experiments with these generalisations as rules, then further acquisition from exposure to the language, finally leading to fluency. Theorists and practitioners have examined the relationship between language and cognitive development and the role of the adult or fluent speaker in helping the learner develop the new language. The way that parents or carers speak to very young children seems to have a significant role in helping children develop the early stages of speech and understanding, although this is not universal, and teachers can have a significant impact on language development by following this approach.

Stephen Krashen's natural order hypothesis (1981) states that there is a predictable order in the acquisition of grammatical structures. For a given language, some grammatical structures tend to be acquired early, others late, regardless of the first language of a speaker. However, as will be discussed later on in the chapter, this does not mean that we should teach grammar in this natural order of acquisition. There are slight variations in the order of acquisition between first and additional language learners but it follows a general pattern. In both first and second language development, understanding precedes language production.

Additional language acquisition

We all learn language in slightly different ways, depending on our personalities, age and previous learning experience. However, there are patterns in language learning, significant factors which influence it and, as a result, ways in which we, as educators, can make language learning more successful for those we teach. Krashen's natural order hypothesis, mentioned above, shows that there is an order in which the grammatical structures of language are usually acquired. This means that children will learn them in that order if the conditions for successful language learning are present. Knowledge about this 'natural order' of language learning can also help us in assessing learners' progress in language acquisition and in focusing on relevant aspects of language in teaching as part of the whole curriculum. Children learn an additional language almost in the same way as a first language: by tuning in to the sound patterns, following models, using the language to communicate, making errors, which they correct over time by further following of models.

The age of the learner will play a part in decisions as to how much explicit attention we pay to grammatical morphemes. An adult or older child with fluency in a first language may want to discuss aspects of grammar. Although this will be meaningful to the older learner in a way it would not be with a child, it is still unlikely to promote fluency in the new language. Although study of language enables the adult learner to understand and discuss the structure of the language, it does not significantly improve the ability to converse in that language. We could debate endlessly on the relationship between accuracy and fluency or learning and acquisition. Accuracy and learning focus on the form of a language, the grammatical structures and on producing correct forms of the target language. Fluency and acquisition focus on communication and the practical application of language. 'Learning' a language, in this context, means studying it and learning about its structure and forms; it is a conscious process. 'Acquisition' is language learned subconsciously, when learners are not explicitly aware of the rules of grammar in the target language but are aware of what sounds right and what does not.

Research by Vygotsky (1978), Krashen (1981), Cummins (1996) and others shows that we learn language best through acquisition and this has clear implications for our work with bilingual learners. Krashen emphasises the need for accepting a slow pace with the learner only acquiring language when they are ready:

What theory implies, quite simply, is that language acquisition, first or second, occurs when comprehension of real messages occurs, and when the acquirer is not 'on the defensive' . . . Language acquisition does not require extensive use of conscious grammatical rules, and does not require tedious drill. It does not occur overnight, however. Real language acquisition develops slowly, and speaking skills emerge significantly later than listening skills, even when conditions are perfect. The best methods are therefore those that supply 'comprehensible input' in low anxiety situations, containing messages that students really want to hear. These methods do not force early production in the second language, but allow students to produce when they are 'ready', recognising that improvement comes from supplying communicative and comprehensible input, and not from forcing and correcting production.

(Krashen 1981: 6)

In his monitor hypothesis, Krashen describes how language learned through conscious focus on form acts as a 'monitor', checking the accuracy of what the learner is going to say or write, directing the language user towards correctness and thereby inhibiting fluency. Everyone has a monitor, Krashen believes, but it needs to be used selectively to develop language use. The monitor may be effective, for example, when composing a formal piece or writing or preparing a speech. However, when over-used and brought into the sphere of general communication, it prevents fluency and communication, which slows language progress.

As with first language learning, people learn an additional language most effectively in a natural immersion context, i.e. one where the learner has constant exposure to the natural use of the target language, where there is appropriate language input, scaffolding for language and concept learning and a supportive atmosphere for language output. It is important, therefore, to understand how to create a positive learning environment and to be aware of the factors that enhance or restrict the language acquisition process.

How long will it take bilingual learners to learn English?

Cummins (1984) shows that in an immersion-learning situation, most learners of EAL take around two years to acquire what he calls basic interpersonal communicative skills (BICS). This is when the learner can communicate and understand English for everyday purposes using a basic range of vocabulary and grammatical structures. Learners at this level may appear to speak English competently but that is because they only engage in language use at a basic and familiar level. They will have difficulty with subject-specific vocabulary, written styles of language, varying register to suit different situations, using English in decontextualised situations, and using and understanding more complex language structures, functions and vocabulary in English.

Cummins found that learners generally took between five and seven years to acquire cognitive academic language proficiency (CALP) when learning conditions were good. Learners at this level can use spoken and written English for a range of purposes and can participate fully in a range of classroom situations. Given this, children entering nursery or Reception class with little or no English are unlikely to have reached an age-appropriate level of English before they finish their primary education. In my experience, many children have not, and some are still at the BICS stage. There are many reasons why this may occur, and understanding of language acquisition may help us overcome some of them.

Transferable skills

When learners begin an additional language, they bring to that learning situation all their knowledge and experience of, and acquisition in, their first language. Teachers need to assess and utilise this source of knowledge in helping the learner in the acquisition of the additional language, otherwise language development will slow down and valuable support opportunities lost. Shadjeet, who works with small groups, is in a good position to discover children's first language knowledge and help other adults make use of it when working with the children. Depending on the age at which the learner begins learning the additional language, there will be a greater or lesser 'gap' to close. An older learner will bring to the situation more transferable skills.

Cummins' iceberg model (1996) shows how areas of understanding about language learned in a first language transfer to additional languages learned. He calls this shared area of understanding common underlying proficiency (CUP), which children do not need to relearn in the second language. CUP could be, for example, knowing that print carries meaning and has a direction; how to use a dictionary; associations between concepts; that there are different ways of addressing different people; the difference between fiction and non-fiction. Good development in the first language and in concept development based in the first language give a strong foundation for the additional language. Bilingualism in itself can have positive effects on cognitive development (Dulay *et al.* 1982; Cummins 1984). Given that bilingual learners have transferable skills that they can use to promote further concept learning and additional language acquisition, we need to know how to utilise and further develop these skills. Suggestions for supporting bilingual learners' first language development appear later in this chapter.

Factors Affecting Learning

Earlier in this chapter, we saw that some ethnic groups have patterns of significant under-achievement in our education system. There are many interrelated factors leading to under-achievement. Pupils from minority ethnic backgrounds achieve at different levels: Chinese and Indian heritage pupils generally achieve at higher than the national average, whereas Black, Pakistani and Bangladeshi children's results are usually at the lower end of the scale. Similarly, the Chinese and Indian pupils who achieve well are likely to be learning EAL as are the Pakistani and Bangladeshi heritage learners. The Black children are much less likely to be learning English but are still doing less well than most other ethnic groups. Despite these contradictions, there are influences upon learners' achievement which we can identify as being significant in terms of their impact. Some are applicable to all learners; others are relevant only to learners of EAL. It is important to be aware of these influences as some can be ameliorated by the classroom strategies and attitudes adopted.

Sociolinguistic situation

The learning situation for bilingual learners varies greatly from country to country. Where the children's first language is dominant or equal to another within their society, they are more likely to learn an additional language quickly and competently. In addition, where the children's first language is a minority language in their country but is equal within the educational setting, good progress in both languages is likely. However, within the education system in England, children are learning in an environment where English is the dominant language and the language of instruction. Some bilingual children receive some support in their first language but this is not a statutory part of their education and is likely to be inconsistent across the phases of schooling. This is not the ideal language-learning situation. Positive approaches to bilingualism, using first language for curriculum learning and strong links with families and communities, can go some way to alleviating this.

First language learning situation alongside second

Literature on the teaching and learning of EAL widely recognises two main stages of additional language acquisition on the road to fluency. The first stage, where pupils are often referred to as first stage and second stage learners in works such as Hester (1996), centres around the acquisition of everyday English to conversational level. The second stage includes pupils who have reasonably fluent conversational English but who are still acquiring more complex written and spoken English and subject-specific language. Cummins (1984) refers to these stages as BICS (basic interpersonal communicative skills) and CALP (cognitive academic language proficiency). Children at different stages of acquiring English will need differing support to access the curriculum and further develop their languages. The strategies employed will depend upon the learning needs of the children but will apply to most children learning EAL. As well as the factors relating to the status of the first language and the language-learning situation, there is a range of factors identified as having significant impact upon children's educational success. The US Department of Education's (2000) longitudinal study of children's education, ECLS-K, identifies these significant factors. Gillborn and Gipps (1996) outlined aspects influencing achievement in their research into the educational attainment of ethnic minorities in Britain. These indicators are:

- parents' (particularly mother's) education;
- socio-economic background;
- family situation;
- primary language of parents;
- gender;
- students' attitudes to learning;
- parental involvement in school;
- teacher–pupil interaction;

- prior attainment;
- fluency in English.

Other important factors affecting EAL learning are:

- language-learning situation;
- status of first language (L1);
- status of learners' culture;
- fluency in L1;
- teachers' expertise in teaching an additional language.

Understanding Children's Language and Learning Profiles

Assessment of learners' language levels and progress needs to be viewed in the context of their linguistic, socio-cultural and educational backgrounds. This background information will shed light on reasons for levels of development and progress, will help staff plan appropriate input and activities and will enable staff to include and value the learners' cultural, linguistic and ethnic backgrounds in the classroom. It will also facilitate appropriate communication with and involvement of parents.

When a child starts school, some basic information is required, in addition to that routinely collected by schools:

date of entry to UK if not born here;
asylum/refugee status;
previous schooling – where, how long, level, language of instruction?
how long been educated in UK?
if educated in UK, the EAL support received;
if educated in UK, any involvement of other agencies;
extended absences from school;
family background – ethnicity, languages used, religion, country of origin, residence in other countries, parents, siblings;
medical issues;
languages spoken at home/in community and to whom;
languages of literacy – in the home – being learned by the child;
family's opinion of child's language development in community languages and in English;
family's opinion of child's overall development since birth.

In addition, some assessments will be undertaken to determine competence, knowledge and understanding in:

first language;
English;
concept development;
curriculum knowledge.

Assessment Tools

There are a variety of scales used in English schools to assess the progress of EAL learners. This is largely because there is not, and never has been, a national scale for EAL assessment so each Local Education Authority (LEA) has devised its own or adopted an existing scale. Each scale has its advantages and disadvantages; some LEAs update or amend their scales, others do not. It is important to know which scale your LEA uses, particularly if the learners you work with receive support from Ethnic Minority Achievement Grant (EMAG) staff, as they will be using this scale to assess the learners.

I will give a brief outline of other scales that are available so that you are aware of their existence. Some LEAs have adopted more recently published assessments and in some situations you may need to try out a new assessment approach yourself or the teacher with whom you work. Shadjeet could well find herself in the position of working with different assessment scales in different schools unless her team have decided on a common approach across all the schools in which they work.

Hilary Hester scales

The Hilary Hester scales of EAL development have been used or adapted by many LEA EMAG services throughout the country. The scale has four stages: Stage 1 – new to English; Stage 2 – becoming familiar with English; Stage 3 – becoming confident as a user of English; Stage 4 – a very fluent user of English in most social and learning situations. The stages include speaking, listening, reading and writing all together within the stage descriptor and provide positive statements about what children can do.

Qualifications and Curriculum Authority (QCA) steps

The QCA has published pre-National Curriculum level 'steps' to enable schools to monitor the progress of early stage learners of English more accurately within the National Curriculum. Previously it was felt that some children remained at level W, even though they had made progress in English. These steps are not intended to assess children's language development in EAL, nor are they useful for this. They are a means of assessing EAL pupils' progress in English curriculum learning at and below Level 1. To accompany the steps, the QCA published a system of profiling which schools without EAL support staff may find useful.

The Northern Association for Support Services for Equality and Achievement (NASSEA)

NASSEA has produced an assessment package for EAL pupils, which links EAL progress to National Curriculum levels. These are broad links as we cannot use the National Curriculum descriptors to assess EAL pupils' progress. They are too broad and group a variety of conceptual elements in each descriptor.

First Steps

First Steps is an Australian approach now quite popular in Britain. It is not specifically for EAL learners but works on the basis that EAL learners will form part of the class. There are teacher books on oracy, reading, writing and spelling which include comprehensive checklists of language development as well as descriptors of progress for a range of genres in the book on writing. All of these may be usefully applied for assessment and planning the language development of EAL pupils.

Cummins' framework

Cummins' framework, detailed later in this chapter, is for formative assessment undertaken through classroom observation. The user needs knowledge of language functions, cognitive processes and contextualisation, but when used effectively, the framework gives a good indication of learners' language development in a range of practical situations, as well as enabling the assessor to determine the learner's zone of proximal development (ZPD) (as described later in the chapter). Several authors and researchers have tested and described the practical application of Cummins' framework. Two of the most useful sources are Hall (1995) and Frederickson and Cline (1990) who focus on assessment, but their work is equally useful for using the framework for planning activities.

The framework consists of two axes: one for cognitive demand, the other for context-embeddedness. These axes create four quadrants in which the assessor plots activities or levels of learner language development. The continuum for cognitive demand is self-explanatory in that it indicates difficulty of concepts involved in the activity. Context-embeddedness measures how far the task is placed in a context such as practical activity, prior learning, or familiar events or objects relating to the immediate and visible. Tasks that are context-reduced require the learner to go beyond the 'here and now', to work with unfamiliar situations and ideas or to apply previously learned but non-present concepts to different situations. The assessor can place language functions and concepts such as sequencing, describing, hypothesising and inferring in the various quadrants, showing the language demands of various classroom activities and curriculum learning.

The School and Classroom Environment

For an effective language learning situation to exist, learners need to feel valued, including their language, culture, religion and ethnicity. If a learner feels anxious or has low self-esteem, there will be a reduction in language acquisition. As Krashen explains, learners need a 'low or weak affective filter' to accept the input. His affective filter hypothesis states that the level of motivation and anxiety in a learner affects the ability to take on the comprehensible input. The higher the anxiety, the higher the filter level, allowing less language input to penetrate. EAL learners become more secure through the knowledge that their language, culture and identity are valued and that they have adequate space and time to develop responses. Possible ways of promoting this are as follows:

- Reflect community languages within school through signs, posters, displays and labels.
- Involve community members in school.
- Involve parents who speak other languages and ask them to speak these languages with the children.
- Provide information for parents in relevant languages.
- Provide opportunities for children to discuss curriculum learning in their first language sometimes.
- Allow EAL learners time to formulate answers, both written and spoken.
- Provide dual language books and other materials.
- Celebrate children's achievements in their first language and culture.
- Provide opportunities for children to study community languages in school – as extra-curricular session, within school time, as part of GCSE options.
- Explore a range of cultures, languages and viewpoints as part of the curriculum and everyday classroom practice.
- Encourage the continuing development of children's first language.
- Encourage parents to support the child in the language they use best.

Self-esteem and security can be raised through respect for all pupils' cultural backgrounds, and by having high expectations in the school and classroom. These high expectations should be of both teachers and pupils, so that each has a responsibility to the others within the class to provide the best learning situation he or she can. Blair *et al.* (1998: 8) found that in successful multi-ethnic schools, students of all ethnic backgrounds and with all kinds of learning needs were treated as potential high achievers. Similarly, the research of Lucas *et al.* (1990), cited in Cummins (1996: 146), stated: 'High academic expectations are communicated to bilingual students within its eight factors distinguishing successful high schools with significant numbers of Latino students.' This work strongly supports the assertion that a child who thinks he or she is a failure will not make progress, but a child who has failed yet believes he or she can learn will make significant progress.

Sources of Support for Planning

An understanding of learners' linguistic and cultural backgrounds, previous education and levels of fluency in first and additional languages is essential to planning and delivering effective teaching. Learners' needs will influence the amount of additional classroom support, resources, and types of activities, teaching input, expected output, timing and grouping.

Government publications are a ready source of information for teachers but influences on the practice of EAL teachers also come from research and practice in Britain and elsewhere in the world. This research by academics and teachers in the field of EAL often gives a wider perspective than the government-recommended strategies as it comes without political and economic constraints. Guidance on additional support, grouping and inclusion is found in the following:

- the National Curriculum Inclusion statement;
- the National Literacy Strategy guidance;
- the EAL training materials for classroom assistants;
- in publications such as those by Blair *et al.* (1998) and DfEE (2000).

More specific information on working with EAL learners in current influential theories on the teaching of EAL is given in Cummins (1996).

In classes where learners are organised in groups according to attainment, it is important to group EAL learners by cognitive level rather than by language level. Learners need to maintain an appropriate cognitive demand in their work and to work with others who are good models of language.

Supporting Bilingual Learners

Supporting the language acquisition process

Language acquisition is a long process which benefits from a cycle starting with comprehensible input and leading to confident production of the language. Effective language learning will take place only if the appropriate conditions are in place and this means clear planning, delivery and evaluation in the classroom, knowledge of learners' needs and strengths and an understanding of the language demands and opportunities of the curriculum.

Comprehensible input

'Input' means the language the learner is exposed to. 'Comprehensible input' (Krashen 1981) means language the learner is exposed to and can understand because it is within a range of comprehension, it is interesting or because it has been presented in a context which makes it comprehensible. For input to be comprehensible, it sometimes needs to be slower and clearer than normal speech. It may need to contain only standard, commonly used vocabulary and shorter, less complex phrases and sentences. Comprehensible input is appropriate and interesting to the learner so that the focus is on the meaning of the language rather than on the structure of it. A language-focused classroom with clear, consistent and comprehensible input is the best language-learning environment for the individual learners at their different levels and for the whole class. Teaching should ensure frequent exposure to natural language as this is essential to progress. If we follow Krashen's affective filter hypothesis, this natural input should lead to natural language output, without error correction. Language acquisition is most successful with comprehensible input and opportunities for rehearsal, practice and consolidation. Error correction heightens the affective filter, thus reducing the likelihood of effective learning, and can lead to over-monitoring and consequent lack of fluency for the learner.

Earlier in this chapter we looked at the natural order hypothesis and saw how this might be used for assessment and planning. Using language at an appropriate level for the learners is part of providing comprehensible input. Krashen's input theory (1981) and Vygotsky's (1978) theory of ZPD both require the teacher to be aware of the level of the learner's language development so that 'comprehensible input' can be provided. Krashen proposes that the learner who is at 'Level 1' needs comprehensible input at 'Level 1 + 1', i.e. one 'step ahead' of what the learner can currently produce and understand. This step ahead, needs to be received in a contextualised situation in order to be comprehensible.

Similarly, Vygotsky's ZPD describes the difference, or gap, between a learner's developmental level (things the learner can do alone) and what the learner can do with assistance. Activities, language and understanding which fall within a learner's ZPD are those that the learner is ready to acquire. The teacher and assistant need to provide language input at the appropriate level with non-intrusive support. The assistance the learner is given should not be too great, or too directive. Strategies such as modelling, scaffolding and co-operative activity are appropriate for this approach. In all such learning, there should be every opportunity for interaction. It can be difficult sometimes to focus on the learner's level of additional language development and then not plan to teach what seems to be the next step in the process in a grammar-focused way. As we have seen, research shows that decontextualised language teaching and a focus on grammatical structures do not aid fluency or language acquisition. The approaches proposed by researchers such as Krashen and Vygotsky follow the model used by many parents with their young children: comprehensible input at a level just above the child's developmental level, given in context. 'Caretaker speech', as it is now more commonly called, requires the adult to be aware of the child's level of understanding and language production and to provide talk at an appropriate level, with suitable repetition, about things of immediate relevance to the child (Ward 2000). Parents do not usually plan to teach their children a particular grammatical morpheme or structure because they know this should be next in the child's order of language learning. The classroom situation is, of course, somewhat different from the situation at home with one's own child. However, a focus on assessing children's language through everyday activity and an awareness of the language used when communicating with the learners will help to create an appropriate environment.

Rehearsal

Following comprehensible input, learners need time and space to rehearse new language. The learner needs to experience new language more frequently, so that it becomes familiar enough to become part of the language with which the learner is confident. Alternatively, the learner may actually 'rehearse' using the language by using it in play/informal situations, by talking to himself/herself or by beginning to use it in limited, secure situations. We often see this language rehearsal in young children, who chat, seemingly to themselves, or to toys, and will use language recently heard in conversation. We see it in young, first language speakers and in primary children learning EAL in the classroom. The use of explicit language rehearsal depends on the age and personality of the learner, but for those learners who do not actually verbalise their rehearsal, they are probably going through a similar, although silent, process in their minds. This highlights the need for EAL learners, in particular, to be given time to become comfortable with new language and to have time to formulate their language output when answering questions or engaging in discussion in the classroom. During this stage of learning, activities involving the new language, but not necessarily requiring the production of it, are beneficial.

Opportunity for practice

New language learning requires opportunities for learners to consolidate and practise their new skills. We can achieve this through the consistent use of vocabulary and phrases in the classroom. For example, teachers and assistants should highlight key vocabulary relating to a topic throughout the period of the topic; they can repeat phrases used to form questions about, make suggestions about and describe the findings of scientific investigations over the year's work. Learners will need opportunities to use the new language many times, probably starting with peer interaction in a one-to-one or small-group activity, leading up to situations that require the language to be produced in a range of whole-class situations.

Consolidation

As with the 'opportunity for practice' stage, consistent and repeated use of key language across a topic, subject of activity type, will help learners to consolidate their learning, to make the new language part of their everyday repertoire and extend their understanding of its application. The meanings and application of words and phrases can be specific and limited or multiple and varied. Learners of EAL will not be aware of these possibilities, restrictions or appropriateness unless they experience language used in a range of situations. Consider, for example, the wide-ranging meaning and use of 'get' and the very specific application of a phrase such as 'yours faithfully'.

The Teaching Cycle

Similarly, effective teaching follows a cycle of planning, delivering and evaluating, and where two or more staff are working in the classroom together, this should be done in partnership. Partnership working ensures that the expertise and time of each member of staff are valued and used to best effect.

Planning

Clear planning is essential to effective teaching and learning, particularly when there are two or more staff working together. The following are some of the elements of planning particularly relevant to EAL learners.

Cognitive/linguistic balance

This idea is encompassed in Cummins' (1984) framework, which provides a mechanism for planning activities for EAL learners while taking into account their cognitive and linguistic needs. It is based on the understanding that just because learners do not speak English (or any other specific language), it does not mean that their learning activities need to be pitched at a cognitive level lower than that of the majority of their peers. It also recognises the fact that EAL learners have more learning to do in school than their monolingual English-speaking peers and that too much new input at once will lead to confusion and is ineffective for learning. The framework also requires planning for contextual support for learning, which is outlined later.

Identifying key vocabulary and structures needed for curriculum learning

Vocabulary involved in many aspects of the curriculum is straightforward if using a scheme of work such as the QCA ones. This is useful for the main group of learners who are not early stage learners but who have not acquired CALP. Early stage learners will also need to learn everyday vocabulary used in the classroom. For them, curriculum-based vocabulary acquisition will depend on their previous education and level of common underlying proficiency.

Grammatical structures/phrases are more difficult to identify and the ones you focus on will depend on the age, previous experience and language levels of the learners. Schemes of work rarely indicate phrases and structures, other than in the National Literacy Strategy. These phrases should be part of the comprehensible input rather than specifically taught. Schemes of work are more likely to indicate language functions and the language structures can be selected using these. It is important to be aware of the language demands of the curriculum, of the language you are using to teach the curriculum, the language the learners need to access the curriculum and the language the learners need to express their understanding of the curriculum concepts.

Here is an example of language functions from a QCA scheme of work (www.standards.dfes.gov.uk/schemes3) from the Year 3 science topic 'Teeth and Eating'. The key vocabulary for the topic is given in the section labelled 'Vocabulary', and the language functions appear as part of the 'Expectations' and 'Outcomes', e.g.:

decide
describe
identify
explain how
recognise why
suggest questions
make relevant observations
present results
evaluate
say what they think they can conclude.

These words and phrases represent concepts that children need to understand. They are also language functions. Children need appropriate vocabulary and structures with which to express them. EAL learners need to learn the curriculum-related concepts at an appropriate cognitive level but need vocabulary and structures at their current language level in order to understand the concepts and to develop their language acquisition. An early stage learner of English may be able to name individual items, using structures such as 'It's a vegetable' and demonstrate understanding of their functions by non-verbal means such as grouping or matching to pictures. An EAL learner at the CALP learning stage may classify the items into relevant groups using language such as 'a tomato is a kind of fruit' and explain why with 'because it grows on a plant and has seeds inside it'. The first learner may be ready to progress to phrases such as 'carrots are a kind of vegetable' with appropriate input. The later stage learner may acquire structures and concepts for generalisation, such as 'fish gives us protein' or 'starchy food like rice gives us energy'. Before the EAL learner can progress to new language learning, supporting adults need to use the language in teaching and activities to provide a language model. In order for new language to be comprehensible, the teacher or assistant such as Shadjeet should present it in context.

Contextualisation

Contextualisation means putting new learning into a context, a familiar or comprehensible situation, so that the learner can understand it more easily. The level of context supplied will depend on the difficulty of the new learning for the individual learner. Context can take many forms within the learning situation. Some which may be used are:

- the learner's first language;
- the visual support;
- the practical activity;
- the activation of prior learning.

As the new concept or language item becomes more familiar to the learner (and the cognitive demand is therefore reduced), the context can be gradually reduced. Naturally, younger learners need more strongly context-embedded activities most of the time to enable them to learn the new concept or language and to maintain their interest and motivation.

Contextualisation is important for all learners, but particularly for those whose medium of instruction is not their first language. If there is a new concept to be learned, then we would aim to explain it using familiar language, using examples familiar to the learners and drawing on the learners' prior experience. However, for EAL learners, there is the additional barrier of the language of instruction. Where this contains linguistic features with which the learner is not secure, it does not provide a context but an additional item of learning not presented within a comprehensible context. Where the input is not comprehensible, learning will not occur; nor will it where there is more than one new item at a time. Focused contextualisation is essential for EAL learners, if they are to have any chance of learning either the new concept or the language items involved in the curriculum learning.

The need for contextual support on which to base new learning has been widely explored in EAL teaching and research. Cummins' (1984) framework facilitates planning for context-embedded activities, which are not at the expense of cognitive challenge. This is based upon examination of activities to analyse the new learning within each one. If there is a lack of context there will be either an overload of new learning, which will result in the learner not fully understanding most of the new concepts and language or there will be a lack of cognitive demand.

Cummins (1996: 58) explains: 'in context-embedded communication the participants can actively negotiate meaning . . . and the language is supported by a wide range of meaningful interpersonal and situational cues'. Such cues might be using prior knowledge, familiar language, visual support, familiar activities or resources but mainly having present and observable features to the learners, something on which to fix their new learning, either conceptual or linguistic.

Use of First Language for Curriculum Learning

Controversy still rages around the subject of bilingual and first language education, particularly in the USA, where a range of bilingual education programmes exist. The success of this approach partly depends on the type of bilingual programme involved, but those children who are taught bilingually generally succeed at higher levels in both languages than similar children taught through the medium of English alone, where English is not their first language. The most successful programmes are those in which the children's first language is valued in itself, not merely as a means to access the curriculum because of a lack of English and, more obviously, those programmes where the quality of instruction is high. The education system in Britain means that it is difficult to provide such an education for EAL learners here, although some research has been done into the effectiveness of such an approach and it has been found to be of benefit to pupils' learning (Fitzpatrick 1987). Similarly, Cummins' 'dual iceberg' (1996: 111) model demonstrates that there is a large area of knowledge about language that is common to all languages and therefore learning in one language can be transferred to another.

The use of first language materials can enhance not only pupils' access to the curriculum, its structures and support strategies through modelling writing structures in first language, but also the development of an equal status for the cultural and linguistic diversity in the classroom. Where schools and staff are not open to use of first language in the classroom, this is likely to have a detrimental effect upon the progress of the bilingual learners. Cummins and Swain (1986) support this assertion: 'To be told, whether directly or indirectly, explicitly or implicitly, that your language and the language of your parents, of your home and of your friends is non-functional in school is to negate your sense of self' (Cummins and Swain 1986: 101).

It is difficult for monolingual staff to support bilingual children in the children's first language, but with appropriate resources, careful planning and use of available school and community support, it is possible. It is possible to support learners through Level 1 without speaking their language if you are aware of the function and focus of the first language input, and staff, parents and learners are aware of the output needed. For monolingual staff working with bilingual learners, the focus of Level 1 work should be on developing transferable skills. This is because the teaching input can be in both Level 1 and English and the learners' output can be either Level 1 or English depending on the audience. This enables staff to support language and concept development through Level 1, while assessing understanding through English and non-language-based responses. To allow this to take place, staff need access to dual-language resources at appropriate levels; a tape-recorder and photocopying facilities will be useful and a translation service for small amounts of translation will be invaluable. This could be as basic as a phrase book or could be literate bilingual staff within the LEA. Many EMAG services provide this facility.

For example, Key Stage 2 children looking at themes in narratives could read or listen to folk tales and fairy tales in their first language and in English to gain a clear understanding of the plot, characters and style. Discussion and investigation of the texts could be through dual language homework materials, bilingual classroom support, peer discussion or shared reading/talk activity with older children fluent in the same first language. Written or spoken responses to the class or teacher could then be in English or shown through non-language-based responses such as matching, drawing, identifying and sequencing. Early stage learners will need modelling and rehearsal in order to formulate their responses in English and visual cues could support this. If bilingual staff such as Shadjeet work with the children, responses in the first language could be given to support this development and to assess concept understanding.

Visual support

Visual support for learning is beneficial for many EAL learners, as well as for many monolingual learners. Cooke (1997) develops ideas for using 'key visuals' to support learning, looking at key concepts, drawing on prior learning, key language and activities linking with the key visual. Similarly, writing frames of the type developed by Lewis and Wray (1997) and by the Education Department of Western Australia (1997) support writing development through contextualisation of the writing genre. Visual support may represent individual objects or actions; it may 'set the scene' for a topic or lesson, or it may go further than that and encapsulate the learning concept of the lesson (Cooke 1997). Key visuals are items that show the key focus of a lesson. A key visual may be a picture, diagram, flow-chart, key, table, etc. The teacher can refer to it at various points throughout the lesson or the topic and may provide a model to support the learners' output. Visual support used to demonstrate new language should ideally be available for learners to use for language rehearsal and as a support for formulating language production later.

Practical activity

Practical activity works as a context in a similar, although often more clear and direct, way to visual support. The learner has the opportunity to experience new language within a real (or simulated) situation. Similarly, the learner might rehearse new language while carrying out the related activities. This allows the learners and others involved in the activity to use and experience the language in a comprehensible and meaningful situation, as well as being able to use the activity, objects or resources used in it to support the learning and use of the language.

Parental involvement

A variety of research (Cummins 1996; Gillborn and Gipps 1996) demonstrates that parental involvement in schooling has a positive impact on children's learning. Gillborn and Gipps' research indicates that schools often perceive ethnic minority parents as not wishing to participate in their child's education, although the findings of research with parents in their study indicated otherwise. In my own work in schools, I have found that the school often perceives parents from ethnic minority communities to be uninterested in the school and their children's education. This contrasted with my own experiences with the parents, which led me to feel that they felt disenfranchised from the school and their children's educational experience. Many parents felt that they could not help their children with their schoolwork because they did not speak English or, more often, because they did not understand what work they were doing.

Similarly, research shows that pupils and parents from minority groups may feel alienated from the education process and parents may feel at a loss as to how to serve their children's needs. Blair *et al.* (1998) indicated dissatisfaction among various ethnic minority communities with the education provided for their children and the way schools reacted to their children's cultural and linguistic backgrounds. The views of these parents might have been surprising to the schools concerned. The parents were all very concerned about their children's education and keen to support it. This contrasts with the view that ethnic minority parents are not interested in their children's education because they do not join in school activities or attend parents' evenings. Schools with a multi-ethnic community need to be resourceful and innovative in their approaches to communicating with non-English-speaking parents who often feel intimidated by the alien culture of the school (DfEE 2000). There are many more barriers to parental involvement in school life for parents from ethnic minority communities than there are for White UK parents, particularly when these parents do not speak English as their first language. The involvement or otherwise of the parents is dependent on the school's effort and organisation in ensuring access for all.

Blair *et al.* (1998; 59) found that 'Making genuine links with local communities and involving parents can be exceptionally difficult, but appears to be a key factor in supporting and extending successful change.' Schools need to base their strategies to promote parental involvement on positive relationships and an understanding of the parents' ethnic, linguistic, cultural, religious and educational backgrounds. This kind of information is usually only gained after the establishment of positive relationships, but as a minimum expectation, schools should ask parents which language(s) they prefer for written communication and if they prefer a letter or a phone call or visit. This helps in planning for parental involvement in the children's learning. Many parents of EAL learners may have very different experiences of education to that of most teachers. Some may have been educated in Britain and will have a good understanding of the structure and methods of the system. Some may have been educated in another country and may not be aware of the assessment procedures and curriculum content and methods used here. An approach to learning which is often alien to parents educated abroad is that of learning through play in the early years. Some parents may have had limited education, education in more than one country or no education at all.

Gaining parents' trust, encouraging them to support their children's learning and giving them the confidence and information to do it are vital to the process, particularly for parents with limited education and those who are not literate. Videos and cassettes can provide input, which parent and child can watch or listen to together. Workshops for parents delivered in appropriate community languages can provide a safe environment where parents can find out how they can support their children's learning at home.

Of course, if you are in a school where bilingual staff have established positive links with families and the community, this is much simpler than if you are monolingual and have no support available to you in the language you need. Resources available on the Internet, published resources and LEA EMAG or translation services will help in creating useful links with non-English-speaking parents.

Language, Culture and Identity

The National Curriculum Inclusion Statement (DfEE 1999) suggests that teachers should have high expectations of all pupils and be aware of the different experiences and interests that children bring to the learning situation. They should plan for all children to have full involvement in lessons. All children have different experiences of language use, forming relationships, family life and learning, which form part of their individual identities and shape their view of the world. Socio-cultural development is a key part of the learning context and educators need to understand learners' cultural backgrounds and use this knowledge when working with the learners. Delivering the curriculum as if all the learners had the teacher's socio-cultural background is unlikely to be successful. We all modify our speech in terms of form and content according to the audience. Generally, this is done according to the age, familiarity, gender and apparent social, ethnic and religious group. More specifically, with people we know quite well, we are aware of their interests and experiences, opinions and prejudices – what is likely to gain a sympathetic response and what will cause antagonism. Similarly, when planning and delivering the curriculum, we must take into account the learners' backgrounds. Everyday situations depicted in texts and pictures such as mealtimes, clothes, holidays, sports activities, attitudes to animals and pets, for example, may seem 'normal' to one person but be unfamiliar, alien, to another. This can mean a departure from some of the resources, lessons and examples previously used. The culture of the school needs to change with the community.

On the one hand, schools reflect, promote and are shaped by the social values, goals and ideologies of the dominant cultural group in society. On the other hand, schools are currently facing an unprecedented and increasing number of children who grow up in linguistic cultures and communities that fall outside the dominant cultural group. Consequently, many of the assumptions, principles and practices on which schools have traditionally relied are no longer the most appropriate.

(Genesee 1994: 13)

Knowledge about learners' socio-cultural backgrounds and positive attitudes towards diversity is crucial to inclusion in the classroom. Learners can only feel included, and therefore secure, if they are part of the school and class and accepted fully, including ethnicity, language, culture, religion and family circumstances. If teachers ignore the learners' first language, view their appearance as 'different' or contradict their religious beliefs, the learners are unlikely to feel secure and included.

This approach must be an everyday, embedded one built into all aspects of the curriculum and school life. As Wrigley points out, cultural diversity does not mean merely 'a sprinkling of cultural icons from various traditions' (2000: 15). Celebrating festivals from other cultures and occasionally cooking 'Asian' food is not the way to inclusion. Accepting, discussing and expecting diversity in the way people look, talk, behave and think will promote inclusion. Using a variety of resources and examples in teaching will help to make the curriculum accessible to a wider range of learners and to broaden their outlook. Using languages other than English explicitly in the classroom will raise their status and promote the learning of bilingual learners.

Ultimately, promoting an inclusive approach is like teaching language – it requires clear and consistent modelling. To achieve this, the staff involved need to be confident and clear about the content and methods they are using to achieve their aims. Training, information and discussion for staff are essential to creating a school where everyone is able to implement the school's policies and ethos on inclusion.

Discussion Starter

Krashen proposes that language acquisition leads to communication and fluency, whereas language learning leads to over-monitoring and inhibits fluency. How does this idea compare with your own experience of language development?

Reflecting on Practice

Read your school's policies on EAL, equality of opportunity and anti-racism. How well are the policy statements reflected in the day-to-day life of the school?

Websites

www.edu.bham.ac.uk/bilingualism – University of Birmingham School of Education Bilingualism database.

www.emaonline.org.uk – Ethnic Minority Attainment website with resources for teachers.

www.irr.org.uk/education – Institute of Race Relations education page.

www.iteachilearn.com/cummins – Dr Cummins' ESL and Second Language Learning website with papers and other interesting information.

www.manchester.gov.uk/education/emas – Manchester City Council Ethnic Minority Achievement Service.

www.naldic.org.uk – National Association for Language Development in the Curriculum.

www.nassea.org.uk – the Northern Association for Support Services for Equality and Achievement, North of England contacts and working groups on various issues.

www.standards.dfes.gov.uk/ethnicminorities – various links to resources and publications on standards.

References

Blair, M., Bourne, J. and Coffin, C. (1998) *Making the Difference: Teaching and Learning Strategies in Successful Multi-Ethnic Schools*, London: DfEE/The Open University.

Cooke, S. (1997) *Collaborative Learning Activities in the Classroom: Designing Inclusive Materials for Learning and Language Development*, Leicester: Resource Centre for Multicultural Education.

Cummins, J. (1984) *Bilingualism and Special Education: Issues in Assessment and Pedagogy*, Clevedon: Multicultural Matters.

Cummins, J. (1996) *Negotiating Identities: Education for Empowerment in a Diverse Society*, Ontario, CA: California Association for Bilingual Education.

Cummins, J. (2000) *Language, Power and Pedagogy*, Clevedon: Multilingual Matters.

Cummins, J. and Swain, M. (1986) *Bilingualism in Education*, New York: Longman.

DfEE (1999) *The National Curriculum: Handbook for Primary Teachers in England*, London: DfEE/QCA.

DfEE (2000) *Removing the Barriers*, London: DfEE.

Dulay, H., Burt, M. and Krashen, S. (1982) *Language 2*, Oxford: Oxford University Press.

Education Department of Western Australia (1997) *First Steps Writing Resource Book*, Melbourne: Addison-Wesley Longman Australia.

Fitzpatrick, F. (1987) *The Open Door: The Bradford Bilingual Project*, Clevedon: Multilingual Matters.

Frederickson, N. and Cline, T. (eds) (1990) *Curriculum Related Assessment with Bilingual Children: A Set of Working Papers*, London: University College, London.

Genesee, F. (1994) *Educating Second Language Children: The Whole Child, the Whole Curriculum, the Whole Community*, Cambridge: Cambridge University Press.

Gillborn, D. and Gipps, C. (1996) *Recent Research on the Achievements of Ethnic Minority Pupils*, London: HMSO.

Hall, D. (1995) *Assessing the Needs of the Bilingual Learner*, London: David Fulton.

Hester, H. (1996) 'The stages of English learning: the context', presented at the School Curriculum and Assessment Authority (SCAA), *Invitational Conference on Teaching and Learning English as an Additional Language*, London.

Krashen, S. (1981) *Principles and Practice in Second Language Acquisition*, London: Prentice-Hall International (UK) Ltd.

Lewis, M. and Wray, D. (1997) *Writing Frames: Scaffolding Children's Writing in a Range of Genres*, Reading: Reading and Language Information Centre, University of Reading.

School Curriculum and Assessment Authority (1996) *Teaching English as an Additional Language: A Framework for Policy*, London: SCAA.

US Department of Education, National Center for Education Statistics (2000), *The Condition of Education 2000, NCES 2000–602*, Washington, DC: US Government Printing Office.

Vygotsky, L.S. (1978) *Mind in Society: The Development of Higher Psychological Processes*, ed. Cole, M., Cambridge, MA: Harvard University Press.

Ward, S. (2000) *Baby Talk*, London: Century.

Wrigley, T. (2000) *The Power to Learn: Stories of Success in the Education of Asian and Other Bilingual Pupils*, Stoke-on-Trent: Trentham Books.

Counselling and Guidance in Education

Shirley Potts

Meet Julia

Hello, I am a learning mentor in a secondary school and I work with children who are disaffected at school and often have health or social problems. Most of the work is with individual children across the school age range. Their main problem is low self-esteem, leading to poor attendance and engagement in the education process. I hold one-to-one guidance sessions with them where we review and set targets for future school progress. These are often targets about attendance, levels of engagement with lessons, and relationships with others.

I have attended all the learning mentor training provided by the Education Action Zone but I still would like to know more about the skills needed for counselling young people who arrive at the guidance sessions with many issues to discuss.

Introduction

Counselling, guidance, mentoring, behaviour management, coaching, advising, supporting . . . There are those who see very blurred lines between several of these functions, while other people might offer very clear delineation and differentiation between them. There is undoubtedly some overlap within the vocabulary of 'enabling' roles that are gaining increasing viability and credence in current educational environments. Nevertheless, there are also distinctions that need to be drawn – not only from the perspective of semantics, but also from ethical and professional angles.

The evolution of teaching from a didactic, instructive role into a holistic appreciation of the individual student has been a welcome and progressive development. Subjects such as Personal, Social and Health Education (PSHE) have entered the curriculum and the language of psychotherapy has merged into common parlance. Hence, we consider the 'baggage' students or staff may bring with them, we are aware of 'unfinished business', we listen to our 'inner child', we endeavour to 'empathise' and we nod sagely and 'hear' where someone is coming from. There is, however, a yawning chasm between talking the talk and walking the walk.

For the purpose of this chapter, it is necessary to clarify what will, and what will not, be addressed. I believe counselling, guidance and behaviour management are three distinct specialisms offering particular styles of support in specific situations.

- *Counselling* is, largely, a one-to-one, confidential, client-centred relationship whereby the counsellor encourages, enables and empowers the clients to find their own way to clarification or solution of a particular issue. There are various counselling approaches and theories but most will include the potency of a non-directive, sincere, listening relationship between counsellor and client. The professional, practising counsellor must be trained and qualified and in receipt of regular supervision. Additionally, a period of personal therapy is recommended by most training courses and is compulsory for membership of the major professional bodies.

- *Guidance* is more directive than counselling and – in an educational setting – bears more relevance to career or subject choices, academic development, decision-making and wider personal issues such as safe sex or financial independence. The guidance professional, then, is likely to be trained in a particular category of supportive intervention and might be a careers adviser or health professional.

- *Behaviour management* relates most frequently to behaviour 'problems' that are difficult to tolerate or accommodate in an educational setting. Perhaps the disenfranchised adolescent with poor attendance or the withdrawn eight-year-old victim of bullying? Behaviour management might then become the domain of other professionals through referrals to educational psychologists, social workers or family therapists.

Therefore, to clarify, this chapter will not be addressing the essential training requirements of the above professions. However, we will examine some of the core skills common to various helping professions that educationalists may incorporate – from teaching assistant to head teacher, from university professor to nursery nurse – in their interactions with children and young people. In this way, the chapter addresses the needs of the learning mentor, Julia.

Relationship and Rapport

Carl Rogers (1978) who initiated the person-centred counselling approach spoke of a 'way of being' not only in the counselling relationship but also as a person of integrity beyond the counselling room. He suggested the core conditions of a counselling relationship are empathy, unconditional positive regard and congruence – sometimes interpreted as non-possessive warmth, non-judgemental acceptance and honesty. Without over-simplifying the issue, are these not three basic characteristics that will inform, enrich and enhance relationships between educationalists and students? What better foundation to the classroom rapport than to display warmth, acceptance and honesty to those in our care? Of course, this may sound too naïve and idealistic for the unruly urban classroom or the nursery full of noisy, egocentric three-year-olds, but it is the quality of the practitioner, more than the variables of the situation, that is being addressed here.

In recent years, the concept of emotional literacy has rapidly gained ground and infiltrated the educational establishment through the works of authors such as Gardner (1983), Goleman (1996), Orbach (2001) and Mortiboys (2002). Holistic approaches to student care have heralded approaches such as accelerated learning, educational kinesiology, neuro-linguistic programming and the learning revolution. Smith (2003) suggests a continuum of facilitative input from presenting, through authenticating, directing, leading, training, facilitating, developing and mentoring, to coaching – the first being a large-group activity and the last being a one-to-one process. Practitioners may feel more comfortable with a specific style of interaction and it is relevant to remember that individual educationalists have differing skills and need not all practise in the same way. However, much of the current movement resonates with Rogers' earlier words:

> We know that the initiation of such learning rests not upon the teaching skills of the leader, not upon scholarly knowledge of the field, not upon curricular planning, not upon use of audiovisual aids, not upon the programmed learning used, not upon lectures and presentations, not upon an abundance of books, though each of these might at one time or another be utilized as an important resource. No, the facilitation of significant learning rests upon certain attitudinal qualities that exist in the personal *relationship* between the facilitator and the learner.

(Rogers 1969: 197)

Relationship is the potent tool that each practitioner brings to his or her interactions with young learners. With or without intention, practitioners communicate a 'way of being' in such a way that the young learner will have formed an opinion of the practitioner that will colour all future interactions. For this reason, some basic communication and counselling skills are the surest foundation for practitioners who will inevitably be drawn into counselling or guidance situations in the course of their career. The formal acquisition and application of skills are insufficient to guarantee a therapeutic encounter, but more on the personal qualities of the helper later.

Skills

Three principal counselling theories are: psychodynamic, cognitive-behavioural and person-centred, with many other approaches emerging over the past half-century, e.g., transactional analysis, gestalt, existential, transpersonal, psychosynthesis and psychodrama. Some counselling practitioners would now favour an integrative approach where they would not exclusively follow one theory, but appropriately integrate elements of several theories. The micro-skills highlighted below are common to most counselling approaches but are also, significantly, applicable to the educationalist's repertoire of interpersonal skills.

Empathy

Colloquially described as walking a mile in the other one's moccasins. Essentially, empathy is the ability to see from the client's frame of reference. It is not to be confused with sympathy, or having experienced a similar situation – 'I know how you feel' is not an appropriate counselling response. Nobody knows precisely how another person feels. The skill of empathy actually requires concentration, perseverance and honest self-reflection. We may support a young person with a problem that would appear trivial in our own life, we might have chosen strategies very different to those adopted by the client, we may be shocked or disgusted by what we hear – but the cornerstone of empathy is to remain fixed upon the client's viewpoint and circumstances. A deeper level of empathy can only operate subsequent to the formation of a trusting relationship. This may precipitate opportunities to identify hidden agendas where there is perhaps a discrepancy between a client's talk and body language or manner. In these circumstances, a counsellor/helper may be able to illuminate these discrepancies gently and sensitively and suggest the unacknowledged feelings implied by them.

Congruence

Colloquially described as being the same on the outside as the inside. Congruence has variously been translated as honesty, sincerity, being real and transparency. 'The counsellor should be herself in the relationship, putting up no professional front or personal façade' (Rogers 1978: 9). All of these skills are interwoven and congruence can offer a profound link to empathy. Wosket (1999) describes how empathic responses have their limitations where the experience a client describes is far beyond the imagination capabilities of the counsellor striving for empathy. In such a situation, the congruent response from the counsellor – 'I cannot imagine what you feel' may prove effective in deepening trust and acceptance. Congruence must always be balanced with a compassion and understanding for the client. It is never the intention to brutalise with honesty or penetrate someone's self-constructed protective mechanisms with excruciatingly painful haste.

Positive regard/non-judgementalism

This skill entails valuing the other person, regardless of differences of moral stance, belief or opinion you may have. There is a power in prizing unconditionally another person's right to exist. Clearly, in educational settings there are limitations to 'unconditional positive regard' where certain conditions exist regarding behaviour and actions in order for the structure of the establishment or session to remain intact. This is where, again, honest self-reflection is required on the part of the adult to ensure decisions are made and conveyed in a non-judgemental way. It is possible to value a child or young person but dislike his or her actions. This may carry echoes for parents who have appreciated how it is possible to love their child while occasionally disliking the child's actions.

Active listening/attending

This is a deceptively complex skill. Many people pride themselves on being a 'good listener' without ever having truly evaluated their skill. Helpful listening requires focus and concentration as well as an appropriate environment. There are various physical factors to consider such as the seating arrangements, being at the same level, physically – particularly if you are an adult addressing a child, privacy without intimidation, body language, time available. If a client is to be aware that someone is listening to him or her sincerely, the helper's body language should be open and relaxed without appearing too unperturbed. Maintain adequate eye contact without staring intently. Try not to fiddle with pens or keys, or glance at your watch. These may seem obvious trivia but until we have had the opportunity to observe ourselves, perhaps in a role-play situation, it is remarkable how many of our personal idiosyncrasies go unchecked. Most importantly, active listening requires a counsellor to become comfortable with silence. In everyday conversation there are few silences – there is a natural tendency to complete a sentence, fill a gap, prepare a response . . . but in a helpful, counselling exchange, there must be a readiness to allow space for thought. Sitting in silence for just 30 seconds is difficult and can be a source of much discomfort to the novice counsellor. However, the developing ability to sit with someone and be supportive while they pursue an uninterrupted train of thought is a skill well worth acquiring.

Paraphrasing and summarising

These skills link very closely with active listening as they offer the client a positive demonstration of your attendance. Paraphrasing involves reiterating what the client has said, but in the counsellor's own words – it is a tool to ensure the client is aware of your level of understanding of the situation. Summarising is very similar but involves a précis of the client's story by the counsellor, with repetition of the client's own words. This can feel quite artificial during initial usage, yet can be a remarkably helpful tool when the clients hear their own words from another perspective.

Prompts, clarification and open-ended questions

These are also evidence of active listening. Prompts may simply be nods of the head or brief interjections (the 'mm-hmms' of the much maligned archetypal counsellor!). The congruent listener may seek clarification and admit to confusion or uncertainty over what he or she is hearing. Thus, it would be quite acceptable for the counsellor to say, 'I'm not sure I got that bit – can you explain again to me?' Far better to let a client know that you are listening intently than to allow them to meander on when you lost the thread some time ago. Within the same context, any questions posed by the counsellor should be open-ended, i.e. not able to be answered with a simple 'yes' or 'no'. For example, 'How do you feel at playtime?' invites a more full response than 'Do you get lonely?' It is essential to avoid asking questions simply to satiate the curiosity of the counsellor. Also worth a mention here is the danger of collusion. It is possible to collude with a client unwittingly in our endeavour to sound empathic and supportive. For example, it is not unknown for a client (especially a child) to laugh inappropriately while recounting a serious issue but it would not be fitting for a counsellor to share the laughter. Similarly, when a client recounts a liturgy of discontent it could be dangerously collusive for the counsellor to join in the 'ain't it awful' script.

Immediacy

This refers to the ability to stay with a client emotionally and intellectually. A common distraction is to be planning one's response while the other person is still speaking. This, again, is the popular format of everyday conversations but the tempo must be slower in a counselling exchange. Immediacy is another skill that will only evolve through practice and experience as it is inevitable that trainee counsellors will be ransacking their mind for the appropriate response, the correct body language, the wise word – while failing to give full attention to what clients are saying.

Challenging

This combines with the deeper level of empathy mentioned earlier and is not a tool that one can use flippantly in an encounter. As its name suggests, challenging entails pointing out discrepancies in a client's language or actions. For example, a counsellor might say, 'You're telling me you weren't bothered by what they said, but it seems to me you're close to tears.' Clearly, this can be a demanding exchange for a client and one must introduce it with sensitivity and caution. The technical vocabulary of much counselling theory holds little relevance to the uninitiated and it is important that counsellors/helpers/listeners are able to communicate with their clients through a mutually relevant 'feelings language' (Hobson 1985). Counselling or communication skills should not be applied mechanically or superficially but with humanity and integrity. These are skills that should become integral to a helper's way of being.

Example Situations

Within an educational setting, it is likely that staff, including Julia the learning mentor described earlier, will regularly encounter certain dilemmas among children and young people. Friendship difficulties will frequently arise, as will anxieties or pressures related to learning, personal embarrassments such as blushing or shyness, isolation through cultural differences or through bullying. The reasoned support of a caring and skilful listener can allay many of these anxieties. A teacher or teaching assistant may usefully address some issues, maybe in a classroom situation. Generalised discussions on bullying, self-esteem and loss or friendship are standard ingredients of the PSHE curriculum and, from circle time with primary children to the heated debates of undergraduates, it is possible to confront some contentious or painful problems within the relative safety of a group encounter.

Situations that are more complex occasionally arise and it is the responsibility of learning mentors and others to be aware of the need to refer on to other professionals. Some situations will be beyond the remit of the school situation and require wider discussion or involvement. Examples of more complex situations might include bereavement, abuse concerns, special needs, health issues such as anorexia, drug abuse or sexual matters, bullying and the risk of suicide. While any of these areas might become a class discussion topic, individual circumstances may also dictate the involvement of other agencies or professionals. This necessarily impinges upon issues of confidentiality, which always present a dilemma to the adult supporting a child or young person. As far as possible, a child or young person is afforded the privacy of a confidential exchange with the person who is helping them. However, McLaughlin *et al.* (1996: 70) remind us that:

Legally teachers do not have to maintain or breach confidentiality. They must comply with school policy and the head teacher's instructions on this matter and use their professional judgement.

It is desirable professional practice to maintain students' confidences and it is desirable always to tell the student first if confidentiality is to be broken. It is also important, especially in child protection matters, to reduce the number of times a student has to repeat a distressing disclosure.

It is important that staff should understand the boundaries of their role and this is explicit in school policy documentation and practice. Schools may offer an integrated or differentiated model of counselling support or guidance. Within an integrated model personal, emotional and social support is a shared responsibility through a staff team and an inherent part of each staff member's role. On the other hand, a differentiated model would see specific professionals identified for a particular supporting role with staff obliged to encourage appropriate referrals. The learning mentor in the pen portrait is working in a differentiated model where the pastoral system in the school refers children to the learning mentor.

On a practical note, it is wise to remain as transparent as possible in your actions. In this age of accountability, it is feasible to inform other staff of your supportive role without necessarily breaching a student's confidentiality. Similarly, it is sensible to avoid situations where extreme privacy leaves you open to allegation or accusation. Children are quite likely to ask if you can keep a secret. It is an ethical requirement for the counsellor to explain that should any topic raise concerns that he or she has to share with others, the counsellor will always inform and involve the child first. Confidentiality is important, but equally, there are ethical responsibilities where children are involved:

> If the educational establishment has responsibilities similar to those of parents, due to the age of the pupil, or granted to them by a court because the young person's family has broken down or the young person is considered 'at risk' for any reason, it is understandable that the management of the organization is reluctant to have significant information withheld from them. Indeed, numerous enquiries following the deaths of young people subjected to physical or sexual abuse have emphasised the importance of professionals liaising with each other to ensure that they are not each individually aware of different aspects of a situation which, had these been communicated, could have been joined together like pieces in a jig-saw to provide a more complete picture of the young person's circumstances.

(Bond 1998: 13)

The school environment is likely to dictate the level of counselling support offered by staff. Some establishments adhere to a mission statement and policy that encourage the holistic support of students and an attendant interest in their social and emotional development. Other establishments have a more academic focus with a belief that emotional or social support is an extra-curricular activity beyond the remit of educationalists. The prevailing mood, however, is to regard students holistically in the understanding that it is virtually impossible to separate emotional or social contentment from academic progression. Links between home and school have been increasingly emphasised and encouraged in recent years with, particularly for younger children, strategies such as home/school diaries giving a clear message to children of co-operation and mutual care and concern.

The Power Imbalance

Geldard and Geldard (2002: 18) suggest the desired attributes of a child-counsellor are that the counsellor must be the following:

1 congruent;

2 in touch with his or her own inner child;

3 accepting;

4 emotionally detached.

We must not confuse emotional detachment with a distant or aloof manner. It only implies that a child can perceive the supporter to be sufficiently detached from a situation to receive the child's words without incurring personal distress. It is impossible to avoid a power imbalance within counselling support and guidance in education. There is the clear contention between adult and young person, as well as the hierarchical roles intrinsic within the education system. Additionally, there is a language of deficit implicit in the teaching role. Patently, children arrive at school assured of the limitations of their knowledge, which they must enhance and enlarge through the assistance of those who are older and wiser. Children have a need – and the educational establishment can supply the solution.

This may be an over-simplification, but is a foundation that supporters must be aware of in their role. It is particularly difficult for young people to share intimate concerns or awkward fears with someone who holds a powerful role in the child's life. Conversely, the paradox of supporting is that *too* much support can be equally debilitating. One of the primary outcomes of a holistic education is to enable young people towards independence and self-regulation. Rather like the withered muscles within a long-term plaster cast, excessive support can undermine the natural maturation processes of life. Obviously, the maintenance of balance requires insight and consideration on the part of the counsellor/helper, which brings us, finally, to the personal qualities of those who would counsel and support young people within educational settings.

Personal Qualities

As mentioned earlier, clinical knowledge alone will not produce the required environment for a supportive encounter. Counselling, guidance, helping, emotional support – whatever term we use – requires a warmth and compassion that must be sincere. The word *sincere* takes its root from *sans cerre,* meaning 'without wax'. The linguistics evolved from the ancient Greek practice of pouring wax over marble statues or busts to conceal any cracks or flaws in the marble – thus enabling them to deceive prospective purchasers. A *sans cerre* piece of work then, without wax, was much to be prized, as, indeed, is the quality the word has come to represent. A helper must be genuine – caring without smothering, encouraging without patronising, friendly but professional, making reasoned assessment of a situation without judgementalism. One of the most desired attributes within counselling training is self-awareness. It is crucial to become aware of one's own flaws and weaknesses:

- the tendency to rescue someone who is struggling to find words;
- the inclination to breach boundaries in offering too much support;
- the gender preconceptions that we are barely aware we hold;
- the racism or disablism that we do not even address, so convinced are we that we have no discriminations.

This is the penetratingly honest self-awareness that the prospective counsellor or helper must tackle if he or she is to evolve into a fully functioning practitioner. McLeod (1993: 77) reminds us that 'brief skills training and self-help programmes can do little to address relationship and attitude issues in any serious or systematic manner'. We can only attend to these issues within a candid and supportive environment. Some elements are for addressing privately and individually but others we must rehearse and hone within a tolerant group of colleagues. All the discomfort and awkwardness of highlighting our inadequacies or deficiencies within the exercise of our evolving counselling skills we should appreciate as an opportunity to experience the hurdles a young person may encounter in revealing problems to a listener.

In conclusion, there is a wealth of additional literature and training courses accessible via the websites or references below, but there are also personal qualities that can be refined through independent self-analysis and self-awareness in the discerning practitioner. The learning mentor, Julia, clearly recognises the need to develop and refine the necessary skills. Emotional support and behaviour management in schools must commence with the appropriate attitudinal stance of the practitioner, reflecting interpersonal skills and wider understanding of supportive interventions. One would hope that learning mentors such as Julia already have or will quickly develop the most appropriate attributes for their situation.

Discussion Starters

1 Based on your own experiences in classrooms, what do you feel are the most common emotional or social difficulties experienced by children and young people?
2 A student is undergoing personality changes and expressing anti-social behaviour beyond the usual expectations of adolescence. How do you respond?

Reflecting on Practice

Find references in school documentation that provide guidance for teachers on counselling, guidance and managing pupils' behaviour. Discuss the effectiveness of this guidance in relation to your observations of school practice and discussions with colleagues. If considered necessary, collaborate with colleagues to make recommendations for change and justify your suggestions.

Websites

www.alite.co.uk – accelerated learning website.

www.angermanage.co.uk – link to the British Association of Anger Management.

www.antidote.org.uk – emotional literacy website.

www.bacp.co.uk – British Association for Counselling and Psychotherapy.

www.educationalists.co.uk – resources and support for education specialists.

www.playtherapy.org.uk – PTUK, the Society for Play and Creative Arts Therapies website.

References

Bond, T, (1998) 'Ethical issues in counselling and education', in Crawford, M., Edwards, R. and Kydd, L. (eds), *Taking Issue*, London: Routledge, p. 13.

Gardner, H. (1983) *Frames of Mind*, New York: Basic Books.

Geldard, K. and Geldard, D. (2002) *Counselling Children*, London: Sage.

Goleman, D. (1996) *Emotional Intelligence*, London: Bloomsbury.

Hobson, R. (1985) *Forms of Feeling*, London: Tavistock/Routledge.

McLaughlin, C., Clark, P. and Chisholm, M. (1996) *Counselling and Guidance in Schools*, London: David Fulton.

McLeod, J. (1993) *An Introduction to Counselling*, Buckingham: Open University Press.

Mortiboys, A. (2002) *The Emotionally Intelligent Lecturer*, Birmingham: SEDA.

Orbach, S. (2001) *Towards Emotional Literacy*, London: Virago Press.

Rogers, C. (1969) *Freedom to Learn*, Columbus, OH: Charles E. Merrill Publishing Co.

Rogers, C. (1978) *On Personal Power*, London: Constable.

Smith, A, (2003) *Alite: Train the Trainer Resource Pack*, Beaconsfield: Alite Ltd.

Wosket, V. (1999) *The Therapeutic Use of Self*, London: Routledge.

10

Inclusion: Special Needs

Wendy Hall

Meet Pam

For the past 12 years, I have worked with a range of different children with special needs from Reception to Year 6 in a primary school. I work throughout the school depending on the nature of support required. Many of the children have difficulty interpreting and completing tasks, accessing and recording information. Some have dyslexia, dyspraxia or Down's Syndrome. Some children seem frustrated – they appear to be intelligent but are always on the slow learners' table with children who are less astute than they are. During literacy and mathematics lessons, I mostly work with small groups, interpret worksheets for the children, and help them record their work. I also support in other lessons.

I have attended in-service training provided by the SENCO. The focus was general issues of Individual Education Plans and tracking children rather than details about conditions and how to support particular children. I really need advice about the real difficulties of their conditions. If I knew more about how some of these children learned, I could focus my energy instead of trying everything I know in the hope that something will work.

Introduction

The word 'inclusion' covers sexual orientation, race, ethnicity, gender, as well as the issue of special needs. The focus of this chapter is special needs and the aim of this chapter is to provide the reader with a taste of each specific condition and to provide some practical suggestions to help make provision for these children more relevant and meaningful. This chapter cannot replace in-depth study of any of the conditions but I hope to bring Pam, the learning support assistant, and others like her closer to understanding that using appropriate teaching methods and materials helps children with each of these conditions. Most of the suggestions are quite easily achievable in any classroom. This chapter reviews the most commonly met needs but does not represent the full range of needs which may be found in schools today.

The terminology of this chapter refers to 'special needs'. Current terminology varies from special needs through additional educational needs to learning difficulties and disabilities.

Inclusion refers to provision for all children, regardless of their ability or needs within the mainstream school. This differs from integration that places the responsibility for acceptance on the child, requiring the child to conform to the norms and procedures of the school. Inclusion should address access to information, curriculum and buildings. Here I address the issue of access to the curriculum. We can enhance access to the curriculum through a greater knowledge of special needs, learning styles and appropriate adaptations. The responsibility for identifying and addressing the needs of children rests with the classroom teacher; however, very often the teacher will delegate work with special needs children to the learning support assistant. It is essential, therefore, that the assistant is familiar with the varying special needs. In addition, like Pam, any supporting adult needs to know how to adapt learning situations to make them accessible to different children. Some knowledge of the child's condition is also very important in addressing the individual needs. Easier worksheets are no longer a viable alternative to the main work of the class. Sometimes gifted and talented children will also have special needs and may in fact need challenging activities presented in a different format. Let us not assume that all children with special needs work at the lower end of the ability scale; many will work at a similar level to their peers but will be underperforming against their potential ability. Some children will also require specialist teaching in addition to adaptations in the class. Again, the suggestions here do not replace good specialist teaching.

The following discussion will address several aspects of each condition. The discussion of conditions will examine educational needs for each special need, behavioural needs either as a direct consequence of the special need such in Attention Deficit/Hyperactivity Disorder (AD/HD) or secondary as a result of a condition (e.g. behaviour problems arising with boys who are dyslexic) and socialisation needs.

Special Needs: Symptoms and Strategies

Dyslexia and Irlen syndrome, the most common special needs, are similar but different conditions. There is some disagreement about the incidence of dyslexia mainly due to disagreement about how to define dyslexia (Hornsby 1997). Suffice to say, there will be at least one child in every class with dyslexia and the figures for Irlen syndrome are similar. For this reason, this chapter will outline the symptoms and strategies available to any classroom teacher or assistant.

Dyslexia

The stereotypical concept of a dyslexic person is someone who has difficulty with reading and spelling. However, there are different types of dyslexia even within these areas of difficulty and some dyslexic people have little difficulty in reading or spelling but have other difficulties common to most dyslexic people such as memory and organization problems. Hyperlexia is a subgroup with a strange presentation of symptoms. Hyperlexic children will often appear to be good readers and competent at spelling; however, they have difficulty with processing language. They will often have great difficulty in constructing language in written tasks, they may remember or understand little of what they have read and often seem to be unco-operative or deliberately obtuse in carrying out instructions because they have not correctly processed them. They may not understand idioms or figures of speech and may take language very literally. There is of course also the subgroup of dyscalculia, which affects mathematical attainment, but not all children with dyscalculia are dyslexic.

When helping dyslexic children it is essential to know to which subgroup the child belongs. These subgroups are:

- difficulty with phonic strategies relying mostly on visual processing;
- difficulty with visual processing relying on phonic strategies;
- a mixture of each category with strengths in one area and difficulties in the other.

In reality, most children fall within the third group. Hyperlexic children need help with thinking logically, with interpreting instructions and 'reading situations'; they also need to learn ways of constructing and recording their thoughts.

The main characteristics of dyslexia for all groups are:

- In early childhood, there is a difficulty with manipulation skills, and differences in development of walking, talking and sleep.
- During the school years, the following indicators suggest the possibility of dyslexia when the previous early symptoms have also been present: reading, writing and spelling problems, poor handwriting, confusion with left and right, difficulty with remembering tables, telling the time and other sequence-based activities, along with poor memory, poor personal organisation and low self-esteem.

The clustering of signs indicates dyslexia rather than a singular difficulty, particularly when this is not consistent with the age and educational experience of the child. A teacher suspecting a child may be dyslexic should refer the parents to a specialist assessment teacher who can undertake a full assessment profile or to an educational psychologist who will undertake similar screening.

Strategies

Depending on the subgroup, different strategies for attacking unknown words will be required. A difficulty with phonics would preclude 'sounding out' as a strategy to decode text. A child with difficulties in visual processing will not recognise a word even when met on several occasions on the same page. He or she may make silly errors when spelling, e.g. using the correct letters but in the wrong order or reversed in orientation, using b for d and vice versa. Multi-sensory teaching uses the area of strength and supports the area of weakness, bringing all senses to bear on the process. The child is required to see, hear, feel and do. Almost all dyslexic children will have problems with processing information and in organisation; they have difficulty remembering what to do and may keep asking for instructions. Even with written instructions, they may have difficulty in interpreting them into action. It is more useful to present material in diagrammatic or pictorial form as this is already concept-based not word-based. The time taken to access and process incoming and outgoing ideas is far greater in dyslexic children and it is unrealistic to expect a dyslexic child to complete identical work as other children in the same time. The challenge is to provide a stimulating task to complete in a different format. Notes, bullet points and tables in addition to extra time are especially useful with dyslexic children, as is Information and Communication Technology (ICT) where a child may be able to word process more quickly once they have learned keyboard skills or they could use a voice-activated tape-recorder to record information.

Irlen syndrome

Irlen syndrome, also known as Scotopic Sensitivity Syndrome, is similar to dyslexia and often misdiagnosed as dyslexia (Irlen 1991). A child with Irlen syndrome will manifest the same errors as a dyslexic child but will also complain about print moving, distracting rivers of white, colours or the dazzle of a white page. He or she may often exhibit discomfort with red itchy or sore eyes, and may feel dizzy or sick. There are several areas of difficulty for the Irlen syndrome child; these include print resolution, span of recognition, area of focus, light accommodation. Children with Irlen syndrome expend more energy in processing information and they will usually only attend to one input. It is virtually impossible for this child to write and listen to instructions simultaneously. This has implications for classroom management when giving out directions and instructions while children are still copying from the board or finishing work. They also have difficulty seeing certain colours; therefore writing on the board in different colours is unhelpful for these children. They suffer from glare from blackboards more than other children do. Many children with Irlen syndrome will wear tinted non-prescription lenses or use coloured overlays for reading. Tinted lenses virtually eradicate all symptoms of movement of print.

Strategies

The Irlen syndrome children gain most comfort working under natural light near a window using enlarged text (font size 14 points minimum) on non-white paper – usually yellow or pink. They may tire quickly and will need work chunked with regular rest breaks or a change of activity to rest the eyes. If they are not already using coloured overlays, you may find that reading through tinted acetate will improve accuracy, comprehension and speed. Eye exercises such as those taught through Brain Gym® classes also help to alleviate the symptoms of eye-strain. These children have difficulty seeing the board, especially in bright conditions. It is helpful to use symbols such as triangles, squares and stars rather than colours to denote areas of text. This helps children to find their place again when they have looked away to write something down.

Children with Irlen syndrome very often have very stilted reading. This is because of their reduced span of recognition, preventing them from scanning text and reading smoothly. They are reading each individual word separate from others and trying to string the words together to make some complete whole. These children need to practise their reading privately several times, maybe onto a tape-recorder so that they can replay and listen for the sound and meaning, before asking them to read aloud. This aids not only their reading performance but their self-respect too. Because children with Irlen syndrome will have difficulty accessing information through the written word and will physically tire more quickly, they require short pieces of work and to be given extra time to complete this work. Different ways of presenting information and recording information will help maximise the potential of these children.

Incomplete concept formation due to reduced focus and span of recognition is another difficulty for Irlen syndrome children. If they have been given diagrams, they may not have viewed the compete picture, focusing on part of the diagram at any one particular time. It is necessary to check concept formation through discussion before proceeding. This may apply to science, geography and time lines in history.

Dyspraxia

Dyspraxia is another common condition often coexistent with dyslexia, particularly in boys. Up to 10 per cent of the population is most likely affected, with 2 per cent being affected severely. It is associated with problems of perception, language and thought. Another name for dyspraxia is Developmental Co-ordination Disorder (DCD), Perceptuo-Motor Dysfunction and Motor Learning Difficulties. The Dyspraxia Foundation website (www.dyspraxiafoundation.org.uk/dyspraxia-information/whatis.html) offers practical support and advice to teachers, parents and pupils. Dyspraxia is an impairment of co-ordination that affects gross motor activity, fine motor activity and/or oral performance. It is possible for a child to have only one variety but often a child is affected in two or all three areas. Portwood (1999) provides a comprehensive list of behaviours and symptoms. Fine motor dyspraxia affects handwriting and manipulation. Gross motor dyspraxia affects larger movements such as control of limbs and often leads to a clumsy child who cannot run, skip, bat or walk without accident. Oral dyspraxia affects the production of language, particularly speech. Dyspraxia needs early identification and a programme of occupational therapy is the most common remediation. School staff might help with daily exercises and should know of any activity that would cause undue problems and take appropriate action to teach co-ordination. Dyspraxic children often do not learn cause and effect and require teaching to think like other children. They do not automatically make the learning connections that other children will make so the adult has to present these connections very explicitly.

Strategies

It may be that discovery techniques are inappropriate without close supervision. Science experiments will need to be progressive and linkages made clear for the child to experience investigation and formulate rules. The learning of spellings will need to be by analogy and the application of explicit rules. When dyspraxia is coupled with other special needs such as AD/HD or dyslexia, particular attention must be given to the various difficulties and specific tuition to remediate each different aspect. Specific exercises and tuition to improve handwriting, progressive and cumulative spelling instruction, assistance with processing skills and memory to assist in creativity of language and help with accessing information to improve reading are all necessary to move the dyspraxic child forward.

Practical strategies can be found in Boon (2001) and include advice such as a sloping surface to write on and appropriate pencil/pen grip, paper that is temporarily stuck to the surface and a good seating position with feet placed firmly on the floor. These produce huge improvements in the appearance of writing. The use of ICT also helps to hide the effects of dyspraxia. Schools can purchase specialist equipment such as rulers with handles to assist or simply winding a rubber band round a pencil can help improve grip. Dyspraxic children need extra time or adapted activities as well as physical therapy to improve their co-ordination. As with all children, the teacher and assistant need to be aware when to intervene and when to stand back and watch the child making his or her own learning connections.

Attention Deficit/Hyperactivity Disorder (AD/HD)

The diagnosis of AD/HD is a medical one made by a doctor. Most use the criteria in the *Diagnostic and Statistical Manual of Mental Disorders*, fourth edition (American Psychiatric Association 1994, cited at www.adhd.org.nz/dsm1.html). Such children are typically highly distractible, with features included in the 'Inattention' category of criteria, and fidgety, finding it difficult to concentrate or complete a task; however, they do not usually need to dash out of their seats and run around the room. AD/HD children have aspects of hyperactivity and/or impulsivity added to the signs of Attention Deficit Disorder (ADD). The diagnosis of AD/HD or ADD depends on at least six of a variety of signs being present for at least six months before the age of 7 years in two or more situations. AD/HD children can fall within three categories: hyperactivity, impulsivity and a combination of the two. The combination is the most common. Hyperactivity and impulsivity are most challenging for the teacher and involve calling out, interrupting, not waiting for their turn and being domineering in group activities. In practical situations impulsivity can also be a safety issue as children may dash out in front of traffic when out, or they are likely to pick up hot glue guns without a thought to their own safety or others'. These children are not intentionally naughty but seem to be unable to help themselves or their own impulses. Hyperactivity is exasperating to the teacher but not as challenging as impulsivity. Hyperactive children will need to be constantly on the move, interfering in other people's business even when they know they should sit and quietly complete their work.

Strategies

Staff need to be aware that often the behaviour of this child is not deliberately disobedient or wilful. The task and expectations will affect whether or not the child stays on task and whether he or she completes the task or leaves the task unfinished or gives up on it. Short focused tasks are best for this child. There should be regular change of activity to take account of the natural behaviour pattern of the child. Often seating the AD/HD child away from other children to work with a support assistant is best for both the child and the other members of a group. AD/HD children often prefer to sit alone to complete work without fear of getting into trouble. They also need regular recognition of their achievements and reward systems may work well; rewards given for easily achieved tasks to start with, increasing to greater and greater achievements as the term or year progresses. Practical tasks such as science experiments or maths activities need structuring sequentially and logically. AD/HD children are very curious and natural experimenters; however, this needs channelling into useful investigation to avoid them taking computers apart to see how they work and not being able to reassemble them! These children will make the connections dyspraxic children will not make; the supervision and structuring of the task for these children are solely for focus and safety purposes. It may be useful to partner AD/HD and dyspraxic children under the supervision of an assistant. The AD/HD child is likely to be dexterous where the fine motor dyspraxic child will not. The one would complement the other.

Down's Syndrome

Down's Syndrome children are often included in mainstream classrooms. Very often Down's Syndrome children have an assistant like Pam assigned to them for all or part of the school day. Down's Syndrome children do not usually present a challenge in terms of their behaviour. Usually there is a very specific Individual Education Plan (IEP) and schools often seek advice from nearby specialist schools and Local Education Authority (LEA) advisers. The advice given here is therefore limited.

All children with Down's Syndrome have learning difficulties; however, this may range from difficulty with number work as detailed by Nye *et al.* (2001, at http://www.down-syndrome.info/library/periodicals/dsrp/07/2/068/). In addition, it may affect the ability to learn the skills of reading as described by Laws *et al.* (1995). All Down's Syndrome children will show delayed development but the extent of delay often depends on the expectations of their carers. Barker (1999, at www.down-syndrome.info/library/periodicals/dsnu/01/3/133/) outlines how music and singing can assist in the language development of children with Down's Syndrome. The Down Syndrome Trust website is a valuable source of information.

The social development of Down's Syndrome children, particularly as they get older towards the top of Key Stage 2, needs careful monitoring. The physical development they go through at this age does not correspond to their conceptual development or their understanding of bodily change. They may be encouraged into activities that they would not normally engage in of their own volition. In their eagerness to be part of a group they may be led astray and find themselves unwittingly getting into trouble, having copied bad behaviour or cheekiness.

Strategies

Specific advice relating to suitable learning strategies should be sought from specialist teachers. Work for Down's Syndrome children will not only need to be presented in a simpler form but will need to address the same concepts but at an easier level. Down's Syndrome children are unlikely to grasp the intricacies of electrical circuits along with their peers but they can grasp how different products are powered by either gas or electricity and whether this electricity is through mains supply or battery. They will need work presented in simple forms, possibly pictorially in the same way as dyspraxic children. They will be able to follow directions and diagrams when they would not cope with a large amount of text. If text is necessary, then it should be enlarged and presented in smaller chunks so that the child can assimilate one piece of information or instruction before moving on to the next.

One of the main difficulties with teaching Down's Syndrome children in mainstream schools relates more to their socialisation than to educational attainment. Down's Syndrome children very frequently suffer from nasal congestion which leads to a runny nose and breathing with the mouth open. The enlarged tongue flops out and they need continually reminding to wipe their nose and to put the tongue away and shut the mouth. They very often eat with the mouth open and again need reminding to eat with the mouth closed. The assistant will need to be sensitive to these aspects and needs to judge when to be beside the child to offer support and when to stand back and allow independence.

Sensory Impairments

Visual impairment

Visual impairment is relatively common but covers too large a variety of conditions to be included in this chapter. These impairments may vary from slight reduced vision, monocular vision to juvenile cataracts or macular dystrophy (an inherited condition) (Liverpool Voluntary Society for the Blind [LVSB] undated). Children who have grown up with reduced vision will have adapted to the condition but with delayed development. Typically, young children will be up to two years behind their peers. Blind babies do not develop at the same rate when they cannot see a stimulus to talk to, to look at, to walk towards, etc. Some children with visual disability will have learned to adapt to their condition and may hold their head at what appears to be a peculiar angle; this may be so that they hold the object to be viewed in their line of vision, which may be peripheral. They may walk with their feet turned out, as this prevents you from stubbing your toes. It is much less painful to stub the inside of the foot than to crash toes into an obstruction, so some children with reduced vision may walk in this peculiar fashion.

Strategies

Children with severely reduced vision might have disrupted concept formation. Blind children may think a squirrel is a bird as they have heard that they live in trees and hop from branch to branch; knowing that birds do this, they infer that squirrels are a variety of bird. Similarly, they often have no concept of some of our common expressions. When a sighted person exclaims 'the bulb has just gone', the blind child may take this literally. We must explain many concepts explicitly to children with reduced vision:

> How can a child who cannot see appreciate the concept of solubility? . . . or appreciate how light is made from the combination of many separate colours?
>
> They are likely to need individual apparatus and activities that require enlarging for them to see with any reasonable clarity. Yellow paper helps children who are suffering from loss of vision.

Yellow is the last colour to stop functioning when vision is lost. The font should be 16 point or above.

(LVSB undated)

One of the issues with visually impaired children is that of safety and access. Monocular children need careful positioning and the teacher needs to be alert to possible dangers that the child may not appreciate if used to disability. A child with sight in only one eye needs a position in which the good eye has maximum view of the classroom.

Children on the blind side may be at risk when using hot glue guns or scissors. Children with more substantial loss of sight will benefit from bright yellow tape at the edges of surfaces including steps to help them locate edges. Contrasting colours also help children denote areas whereas colour co-ordinated furniture and displays are not helpful as everything looks the same and there is little to denote one area from another. Tape-recordings are essential for children with reduced vision especially if they are not Braille users. While closed circuit television (CCTV) can be helpful for some children, it can also be unhelpful for children with reduced focus as enlarging text on a screen only serves to reduce the amount the child can see at any one time but in an enlarged font. Young children with visual impairment often learn touch typing and the glut of voice recognition software has made life a lot easier for those people who wish to word process but have not learned touch typing.

Everyone should be aware of the posture of the visually impaired child. A child stooping over a desk to scrutinise a text is likely to suffer from stiff shoulders and neck. He or she needs regular rest breaks to sit up and release the tension in the upper back. Social education is an important aspect of the education of children with substantial sight loss. Whereas most children take their cues of appropriate behaviour from what they see around them, blind children will not. The normal touching and cuddling of a young child will not be appropriate with older children but they will not learn this automatically; they will need telling what is appropriate and what is not.

Hearing impairment

The range of hearing impairment is too vast to discuss in detail here. Some children will be accompanied by a signer but a national shortage of signers affects school provision. An important aspect to note is that British sign language (BSL) is a concept-based language rather than a word-based language. Reading and writing can be delayed and disrupted for children using BSL as their first language. They will need to learn a new language and grammar of standard spoken and written English. Most children who were born with a hearing loss have learned quite naturally to lip-read. Most children with hearing impairment will use a combination of strategies and aids; they may lip-read and use an amplification aid, or lip-read and sign. Cochlear implants are still relatively rare in this country. Teachers and assistants should pay particular attention to the child who has lost hearing through illness or accident after acquiring language. These children are not obvious as their spoken language has generally developed and they use normal intonation and stress patterns. They may have learned to read and write before losing their hearing. Teachers and other adults in school might easily overlook the psychological consequences to a child of suddenly losing hearing. Such children might miss essential information or appear rude when they do not respond to requests or instructions. Children who have been born with a hearing loss very often have at least one parent who is also deaf and may belong to the deaf community whereas the person who has lost his or her hearing will not share this identity.

Strategies

Many children will be quite independent, given the correct consideration by the staff and children of the school. Awareness of developing skills of independence is crucial to inclusion. If a child lip-reads, the management of talk in class needs to be a focus of attention. If not handled well, the child can miss the majority of the lesson material. Teachers and assistants such as Pam should organise groups in such a way that the hearing-impaired child can see each speaker's face. People should not cover their face with hands or chew while talking. Lighting should be on the speaker's face so that the lip-reader has a good view of the mouth. The common use of radio aids is riddled with problems such as low battery power, whistle interference and 'clutter noise'. The most commonly used aid is the amplification box worn by the teacher connected to hearing aids worn by the child. This can work well if the teacher and assistant remember to switch off the box and are sensitive to the general level of noise in the classroom, which is generally higher than the teacher's voice. The child needs to be able to concentrate without interference for some of the time during lessons. Other children have the luxury of ignoring background noise but a hearing-impaired child, with the box permanently switched on, will hear everything the teacher says at full volume. Staff must be conscientious about switching the amplification on and off as needed. Once teachers and assistants such as Pam have addressed the practical issues of communication, there is no reason why a hearing-impaired child should not share the work with the rest of the class at an appropriate level. The social skills of deaf children need monitoring as other children can easily ignore them and leave them out of the social groups.

Strategies for All

From the above it is clear that it is not necessary to make individual provision for each child who has special needs in your class. Often you can use the same strategy to address the needs of several children and modify a single activity in a variety of ways to suit several different children. Activities are adaptable and used in a variety of ways, such as picture cards, grapheme cards and word cards, all on individual tiles. Children can use these materials to:

- listen to initial phonemes of words which label pictures;
- match these to grapheme cards;
- listen to medial vowels in words which label picture cards;
- play rhyming word snap;
- play letter snap – a visual matching game;

TABLE 10.1 A summary of support strategies

Strategies	Will help with
Task-boards – detailing sequence of activities, groups – helps to keep track of what the child or group has to do	All conditions
Personal written instructions – enlarged text – font size 14 on non-white paper – good spacing and chunking of information	Dyslexia Irlen syndrome Dyspraxia Hearing impairment
Coloured markers/symbols against text – particularly on the board when viewed from a distance but also useful on individual texts so that children can locate their place again	Irlen syndrome Dyslexia ADD/HD Visual impairment
Lighting – natural light or ordinary tungsten lighting/lamps rather than fluorescent strip lighting. Personal lamps in study coves are ideal	Hearing impairment Visual impairment Irlen syndrome
Sloping surfaces for writing	AD/HD Dyspraxia Dyslexia
Sticking paper to the surface at the correct angle	AD/HD Dyspraxia Dyslexia
Seating – children with particular difficulties may need to sit near the front but not necessarily at a low-attainers table	Hearing impairment Visual impairment AD/HD
Tape presentations giving content and instructions – no adult needed	Hearing impairment Visual Impairment Dyslexia Irlen syndrome Dyspraxia
Small group/one-to-one – some children need the adult to moderate their behaviour and help them with work	Down's Syndrome Various conduct disorders
Use of computers – Many activities can be adapted for use on personal computers (PCs) – This could include cloze procedure activities, matching activities as well as specifically designed programmes such as 'Wordshark'	Will help most children but need to change background, font type and size, resolution and colour for dyslexia, Irlen and visual impairment Use of speaking programmes good for hearing-impaired (with headphones), visual impairment, dyslexic/Irlen and dyspraxia

TABLE 10.1 continued

Strategies	Will help with
Use of tape-recorders to record activities	Good for all children who have difficulty with writing, composing and recording
	Need to be vigilant of AD/HD children with other children – they will be impulsive and not want to wait turn
Large egg timers – a visual time scale	Helps time organisation for dyslexic, AD/HD
Use of special rulers with handles – and other modified equipment	Dyspraxic children, children with grip problems
Personally addressing children – signals your attention to them – be explicit about actions/directions	Visual impairment that is quite severe – will miss visual cues
– ahead of asking a question – gives time to mentally prepare an answer	ADD/HD, dyslexic and children with Irlen syndrome

- play word snap – a visual strategy;
- play find the pairs of initial letter and word or picture cards – a memory activity.

A variation on this could be that a child picks a picture card and then changes one sound in it to create a new word. Thus, three sets of carefully selected materials can be used together to create at least seven different games. Similarly, different groupings and careful use of resources can considerably assist many children. The strategies in Table 10.1 will help you identify different techniques useful with groups of children.

Apart from making the learning task easier by adopting some of the suggestions here, you will also have made the life of special needs children happier because they know that their needs are being considered and not just brushed aside. They will no longer be 'invisible' but will be aware that they matter. Some children will for the first time recognise that they are different but not necessarily 'stupid' because they cannot keep up with their peers. When they realise this, they are likely to be confident of their place in society and better able to be an advocate for themselves.

Discussion Starters

1 Imagine you are the learning support assistant Pam. What have you learned from this chapter and what other information will you need to discover?
2 How would you ensure full integration of a child with special educational needs into the classroom community?
3 What are your views on inclusive schooling? List the potential advantages and disadvantages of children with Down's Syndrome attending mainstream schools.

Reflecting on Practice

1 Examine the Special Needs Policy in your school. Is there guidance about specific conditions?

2 Identify the range of different conditions present in your school. What teaching methods do people use for children with different conditions? Evaluate the effectiveness of these methods and if appropriate suggest some new strategies.

3 How would a new member of staff know how to teach/manage children with these disabilities?

Websites

www.bda-dyslexia.org.uk – the British Dyslexia Association – information and research articles about dyslexia.

www.down-syndrome.info – on-line resources, ideas and on-line books.

www.dyscalculia.org.uk/index.html – the dyscalculia site – information and articles.

www.dyslexia-inst.org.uk – the Dyslexia Institute – information on dyslexia.

www.dyspraxiafoundation.org.uk – information and research articles about dyspraxia.

www.irlen.org.uk/Researchlist.htm – Irlen Centre North West – research papers relating to Irlen syndrome.

www.irlenuk.com/ – clear information about Irlen syndrome.

www.mk-adhd.org.uk/home.htm – information and research articles about AD/HD.

References

American Psychiatric Association (1994) *Diagnostic and Statistical Manual of Mental Disorders* (*DSM*) 4th edn, Washington, DC: American Psychiatric Association, at www.adhd.org.nz/dsm1.html, accessed September 2003.

Barker, J. (1999) 'Singing and music as aids to language development and its relevance for children with Down syndrome', *Down Syndrome News and Update*, 1 (3), 133–5, at www.down-syndrome.info/library/periodicals/dsnu/01/3/133/, accessed September 2003.

Boon, M. (2001) *Helping Children with Dyspraxia*, London: Jessica Kingsley Publishers.

Dyspraxia Foundation (undated) 'What is dyspraxia?', at www.dyspraxiafoundation.org.uk/dyspraxia-information/whatis.html, accessed August 2003.

Hornsby, B. (1997) *Overcoming Dyslexia*, London: Ebury Press.

Irlen, H. (1991) *Scotopic Sensitivity Syndrome Screening Manual*, Long Beach, CA: Perceptual Development Corporation.

Laws, G., Buckley, S., MacDonald, J., Broadley, I. and Bird, G. (1995) 'The influence of reading instruction on language and memory in children with Down's syndrome', *Down Syndrome Research and Practice*, 3 (2), 59–64.

Liverpool Voluntary Society for the Blind (LVSB) (undated) *Visual Equality Training Manual*, Liverpool: LVSB.

Nye, J., Fluck, M. and Buckley, S. (2001) 'Counting and cardinal understanding in children with Down's syndrome and typically developing children', *Down's Syndrome Research and Practice*, 7 (2), 68–78, at http://www.down-syndrome.info/library/periodicals/dsrp/07/2/068/, accessed September 2003.

Portwood, M. (1999) *Developmental Dyspraxia Identification and Intervention: A Manual for Parents and Professionals*, London: David Fulton.

Informing Practice: Assessing Learning

Christine Bold

Meet Margaret

I am a part-time primary school teaching assistant providing Additional Literacy Support (ALS) and Further Literacy Support (FLS). I use the training materials and have total responsibility for the small ALS and FLS groups I support. I follow the guidance in the support pack and make notes about the children's progress each week. The children struggle to write with confidence, planning a story, having believable characters, using dialogue and producing well-constructed sentences.

I have completed the National Literacy Strategy training for ALS and FLS. But I still need help with knowing who has achieved the objective and who has not. These decisions are difficult because the only time I see the children is during their session with me.

Introduction: The Nature of Educational Assessment

Educational assessment is about using evidence to make judgements against a set of criteria about whether children have achieved a learning objective. It relies on the ability to make professional judgements using pedagogical and subject knowledge. The values and beliefs underpinning the philosophical stance of the assessor in relation to the assessed inform the process. Let us examine two possible approaches to assessing a child's performance in relation to a key objective for Year 5 from the National Numeracy Strategy (NNS) Framework for teaching mathematics: 'Carry out long multiplication of a two-digit by two-digit integer' (DfEE 1999 Section 2: 4). A teacher who believes that performance of the calculation in a particular way to achieve a correct answer every time is an indication of achievement might have the expectation that the children use the most compact method as shown:

74×36

$$
\begin{array}{r}
74 \\
\times\ 36 \\
\hline
2220 \\
444 \\
\hline
2664 \\
\end{array}
$$

In such a situation, the teacher might assess children producing alternative methods as not having achieved the objective, even when the answer is correct. Such a teacher might also have focused on teaching the method by 'rote' rather than through understanding. Teaching by 'rote' means teaching children how to perform calculations without understanding why the methods work. Such a teacher might value mathematical teaching and learning processes that might appear to produce quick and effective improvements in test results for many children in the class.

In comparison, a teacher who believes that understanding the processes of long multiplication is more important than the product may assess the child differently through questioning and discussion about different methods and connections with other aspects of mathematics. Such a teacher might accept a range of informal methods of calculation, e.g. the 'grid' method in Figure 11.1 and might even accept the occasional incorrect answer when a child has applied the correct processes and can identify and correct errors with understanding.

74×36

An approximate answer $70 \times 40 = 2800$

×	70	4
30	2100	120
6	420	24

(child calculates the answer mentally)

e.g. $2100 + 400 + 100 + 40 + 24 = 2664$

$74 \times 36 = 2664$

FIGURE 11.1   The grid method for long multiplication

In using the above method, the child has shown the ability to approximate the answer and to use knowledge of number structure in order to calculate effectively. A teacher valuing the teaching of such methods might argue that understanding how to do this method demonstrates ability with two-digit numbers beyond that of a child who can learn the compact method by rote. These two cases illustrate two extremes of thought. Most teachers' values and beliefs lie somewhere along a continuum between the two, and are quite naturally affected by parental, school and government pressures to ensure that children succeed in national assessment tests. The two cases also highlight the close connection between the assessment process and teaching.

This chapter will focus on issues surrounding the assessment processes occurring daily in all classrooms with a range of participants. The processes involved in making judgements of capability are a necessary part of the process of teaching. Assessment is not something we always undertake as a separate activity, but is part of teaching and learning events in which children achieve clear objectives or targets and new targets are set. This chapter does not provide a comprehensive guide to the full range of classroom assessment methods and opportunities, but instead provides an overview and discussion of the principles guiding the assessment practices occurring in many British schools.

Margaret is typical of many teaching assistants who were employed specifically for certain government initiatives and found themselves with the responsibility of using prepared teaching materials to provide extra support for identified groups of children who were deemed to be under-achieving. When paid to undertake such an activity with no other contact with the identified children, the processes by which the teaching assistant makes judgements might be different from those used by the classroom teacher who will know more about the whole child and who will have undertaken the initial screening and identification of children before implementing the programme. More about such screening materials will be included in the paragraphs on diagnostic assessment. The teaching assistant must focus on the objectives for the lesson and use evidence from various sources to determine success. The Further Literacy Support (FLS) Module 4 week 14 materials provide a useful example to illustrate some issues. In the Guided Writing session notes for the teacher to use, and for the teaching assistant's reference, are the following aims and objectives:

Aim: To write dialogue to take the story forward
Objectives: Y5 T3 Text 9 To write in the style of an author
Y5 T2 Sentence 6 To be aware of the difference between spoken and written language, including conventions to guide the reader.

(DfES 2003: 12)

The Supported Session notes for the teaching assistant express the children's targets differently: 'their targets this week are to write dialogue and to use smart word choices and well-constructed sentences' (DfES 2003: 13).

There are potential problems with the use of different language to describe aims, objectives and targets in relation to the assessment of learning within a lesson or unit of work. The aim of this particular lesson is the practical outcome, a piece of writing with dialogue that takes the story forward. If a child completes this piece of work, there is the potential to achieve the stated Literacy Strategy objectives, which may or may not translate well into the targets of using smart word choices and well-constructed sentences. Achieving the aim of completing the piece of writing does not necessarily indicate achievement of the specified objectives. The teacher and teaching assistant must be clear about their joint understanding of the relationship between these different ways of expressing lesson outcomes and potential achievements for a meaningful assessment to occur. This will only happen when they have time for discussion and the teaching assistant supports the original guided writing lesson. It is interesting to note that the relationship between some of these elements is clear on the associated support sheet in 'The Story Jigsaw' (DfES 2003). This supports the child's involvement in setting and achieving targets, but again the relationship with the stated Year 5 objectives is not explicitly clear. It is not surprising, therefore, that the teaching assistant Margaret has some difficulty in determining whether the children have achieved their objectives.

The FLS teaching materials break down the learning steps and provide activities that are interesting and manageable. Many teaching assistants have told me success stories of the children who take part in these programmes, and of their own enthusiasm for these materials. In using the FLS material as an example, I am highlighting potential issues related to assessment processes in the classroom. The FLS guidance materials (DfES 2002a) stress the importance of assessment and monitoring, but give no practical advice on how to set up the processes and systems needed. The assessment evidence base for ALS or FLS programmes will vary according to the activity but generally, it will include observation, noting responses to questions, contributions to discussions, practical activities and *children's products*. In the example provided there seems to be little guidance on exactly what evidence base to develop, although both teacher and teaching assistant produce weekly reviews. The aim is to ensure that children are working at age-related expectations according to the identified Year 5 objectives.

The role of the teacher is to respond to assessment outcomes and provide an appropriate curriculum. To expect the teaching assistant to concentrate on delivering a 'package' without any guidance on formative assessment and subsequent activity modification is asking him or her to fulfil only part of the cycle of planning, assessment and evaluation. In order to explore further the various issues raised for Margaret, the chapter first presents an overview of the different formative assessment processes in schools in Table 11.1.

The order in Table 11.1 reflects the level of importance in relation to the teacher and teaching assistant in the classroom who are both mainly concerned with individual children's learning needs. They need to develop formative assessment skills to inform their planning and diagnostic skills and to help individual children overcome specific barriers to their learning. This chapter will therefore focus on the issues surrounding these two aspects of assessment. In addition, there is some discussion of the varying terminology used in schools to label learners based on their assessed capabilities and consider the implications for learning.

The Nature of the Formative Process

Formative assessment is the process by which teachers and teaching assistants use their knowledge of the children and their responses to classroom activities to inform their future planning. It is essential to the daily and weekly cycle of planning for learning as described by Mitchell and Koshy (1993). They emphasise the dynamic nature of the formative assessment process and warn people not to confuse this with the formal recording and assessment processes required by central government agencies. Formative assessments are often informal in the sense that they might occur at any point in the day when working with children and they rely on knowledge of the objectives that the children are aiming to attain. This is why both children and adults in the classroom need to have knowledge of the objectives. Children cannot attain if they do not know the nature of the objectives in language that is accessible to them. Formative assessment occurs when the teacher or teaching assistant identifies a mismatch between the expectations of the activity and the child's level of attainment and intervenes during the learning process (Brooks 2002). The supporting adult modifies the activity to suit the child's current level of attainment and move skills, knowledge and understanding forward from this point. Good formative assessment processes are at the heart of inclusive practice, providing 'feedback' and 'feeding forwards' to ensure progress. Theoretically, through formative assessment and effective planning processes we should be

TABLE 11.1 A brief overview of the assessment processes

Type	Purpose	When	How	Records
Formative a judgement about a child's performance against a specific objective based on evidence gathered	To inform future planning	All year round	Observation, questioning and discussion, children's responses to classroom activities Children's self-assessment	Planning sheets Class teacher assessment sheets Teaching assistant feedback forms Comments on children's products
Diagnostic identification of the specific aspect of understanding of a concept that is causing a child difficulty	To identify the reason for a particular child's difficulty	At any appropriate point in the child's learning	Individual activity and discussions with the child	Teacher notes Child's responses to learning activities or assessment tasks Annotated work – recording discussions with children Individual test error-analysis sheets
Summative a summary judgement or end result of the child's attainments over a period	To identify a level of attainment at a specific moment in time	End of term End of year	Assessment tasks and tests Aggregation of teacher assessment records	Class yearly objective record sheets Class test results sheets
Evaluative an objective judgement of the effectiveness of teaching based on evidence of attainment in identified aspects of the curriculum	To identify whether the curriculum is being taught effectively	All year round (internal) End of year (internal and external evaluation of performance)	Observation Children's books Analysis of test results	Teacher notes; teaching assistant records School self-evaluation report Ofsted report Class error-analysis sheets

able to ensure that all children reach their full learning potential. Brooks (2002) cites a survey of research on formative assessment that identifies clear learning gains in schools where formative assessment practices were improved. The challenge for adults supporting learning is to discover children's capabilities and to move their learning forward in a way that suits their particular learning styles.

Mitchell and Koshy (1993) describe in detail the processes that support effective assessment for effective learning. They emphasise the need for assessment activities to be contextually relevant to the children and not separate from the curriculum. However, they do acknowledge that a teacher might assess either through their everyday activities with the children, or through activities designed to determine attainment of a specific objective. The NNS materials designed to support end-of-term assessments (DfES 2001a) seem to follow this philosophy by encouraging teachers to use classroom activities in order to determine the specific achievements of a specific group of children. The emphasis in the materials is on the use of dialogue and probing questions to determine children's levels of understanding. The aim is that these special assessment lessons provide an opportunity for teachers to fine-tune their formative assessments that should be happening every day. Unfortunately, a number of teachers still lack confidence and skill in daily formative assessment through working with the children. Instead, they rely heavily on children's products that do not necessarily provide a realistic view of a child's attainments. Products are summative in nature. They tell us that a child 'can do' in a supportive situation, but do not often inform us of the understandings a child has, or whether they can apply their knowledge and understanding to another contextual situation. Assessing learning in a formative way, that identifies 'next steps', requires detailed understanding of progressive steps through the curriculum, and the interrelationship between different aspects of the curriculum. It requires knowledge of children and their learning styles, and above all, it requires a certain level of confidence in one's ability to make judgements and take action on them.

Issues for Schools

The introduction of several national initiatives to improve the quality of teacher assessment in schools since the publication of the Task Group on Assessment and Testing (TGAT) report in 1987 has had little impact on practice. In many classrooms, primary and secondary, teacher assessment still consists of a series of tests and homework, from which teachers collate results and report a summative judgement to parents at the end of the year. Schools will justify their approach by stating that the children all have to learn how to cope with tests and claim that this is the only way to judge a child's attainment without support. Another issue for schools is that they are so overwhelmed with external demands on their time, that they cannot implement the more useful and focused assessment practices promoted over the last 15 years. For example, the main problem with the approach to recording and making judgements on assessments suggested by Mitchell and Koshy (1993) is the volume of writing. Their recording sheets are more detailed than most teachers at any phase can possibly maintain as a formative assessment system, but they do provide a valuable diagnostic approach that one might use with some specific children. The system of recording assessments promoted by the NNS (DfEE 1999) is very efficient and effective, but unfortunately, before 1999, many schools had set up much more detailed systems for recording that they are reluctant to change. A detailed record does not necessarily reflect a better assessment process. My preference is to follow the process promoted by the NNS – that of high-quality assessment through classroom-based activity with minimal but effective records of achievement. In my experience, this approach has always produced an effective learning situation for the child. However, I acknowledge that educational establishments often trap themselves in situations by their own success. A school praised by the Office for Standards in Education (Ofsted) for its detailed record keeping system in 1998 is not going to change it just because the NNS suggests it in 1999. The importance of summative reports outweighs the importance of formative processes in such a situation. The challenge for all schools is to develop a system of formative assessment processes that lead to efficient and effective recording systems, and still gain praise and support for their approaches from external agencies.

Involving Children

When considering the formative assessment of design and technology in primary schools I put forward the idea that children should be fully involved in the whole process (Bold 1999: 83, Fig. 4.4). Through identifying and setting appropriate targets for children to achieve, the teacher can enter into a cyclical dialogue with the child, resulting in the child identifying the next steps for making progress alongside the teacher. This approach works particularly well in practical subjects when discussion about the development of a product inevitably results in consideration of how to improve both the process and the outcome. It also works at General Certificate of Secondary Education (GCSE) level when children are encouraged to review their progress through a practical assessment through discussion with their teachers. Such an approach has been in place for years in early years settings where young children play and adults intervene with questions to develop the children's thinking. Formative assessment and encouraging children to consider their own development begin as soon as children enter a learning situation with a more capable person promoting development. The processes are sometimes evident when children play alone. The following event illustrates my point:

> My two-year-old daughter was walking downstairs with a teapot full of water when it began to spill. She said, 'Oh, it's coming out' and promptly went back upstairs. I thought she had gone to fill the teapot again, but instead she emptied some out. She walked down the stairs and said, 'That's better.'

My daughter's self-directed 'target' was to walk downstairs without spilling water. She recognised she was not attaining her target and so she adjusted the level of water to ensure that she did attain it. This shows that young children have insights into their own capabilities and the attainment of relevant goals. Of even more significance is the fact that my daughter seemed to lose the ability to make judgements about her own learning once she began school. At school, she waited for others to tell her of her capabilities, or, more often than not, her failings. School reporting processes seemed to encourage her to focus on the negative aspects of her learning rather than her positive achievements. From my observations of children progressing through the education system over a number of years, it seems that identifying levels of attainment through tests and reporting serves to widen the gap between those who are deemed successful in their education (e.g. those who pass more than five A–C GCSEs) and those who are not. Including children in identifying their own strengths and weaknesses, setting realistic and attainable targets and concentrating on self-improvement appear to have a more positive impact in encouraging all children to succeed.

The Importance of Marking and Feedback

The National Strategies at both primary and secondary levels emphasise whole-class discussion about alternative approaches to mathematical calculations, or interpreting and writing texts, for example. The interactive teaching approaches currently promoted are ideal opportunities for formative assessment to occur. As the teacher is working with the class, weaker children are easily identifiable as are those who require an extra challenge. Teachers are encouraged to modify and adapt materials to different levels of challenge and to address misconceptions as they arise. Marking guidelines supporting the development of children's writing at primary level (DfEE/QCA 2001) and materials supporting the assessment processes involved in improving attainment (QCA 2001) emphasise the importance of good quality marking and feedback. Quite clearly, the National Strategies are promoting formative assessment as the tool to aid progression and improve standards. The Qualifications and Curriculum Authority (QCA) make a distinction between assessment *of* learning, i.e. summative judgements, and assessment *for* learning, i.e. formative processes. They cite research in Israeli schools from 1988 where children given grades or praise only did not show as much improvement as those given comments and action points for improvement. Despite this type of research, grades and marks are still prevalent in some schools and in particular subjects such as mathematics. When teachers do make comments, children might not always have clear opportunity to act upon them and make improvements. This often seems to be the case when teachers present homework as an 'add on' to the lesson rather than an integral part of a unit of work. When the children receive their marked homework, their topic will have moved on so comments on such work will have little impact. It is far better to use the homework within the next lesson and build upon the experience positively.

Clearly, the QCA and the DfES regard formative assessment processes as the key to effective learning. Weeden *et al.* support this view and provide some useful principles for marking and feedback:

- Marking should be linked to clear learning objectives.
- Assessments should be 'fit for purpose' and have appropriate mark schemes.

- Marking should help identify pupil misconceptions.

- Marking should be focused and prioritised.

- Marking needs to be planned for and should be integral to teaching and learning.

- Marking and feedback should take place quickly so that pupils remember the context.

- Recording may need to take a variety of forms that are manageable but informative.

(Weedon *et al.* 2002: 101)

With younger children in the Foundation Stage and early Key Stage 1 where less paper and pencil recording might occur, children can have opportunities to share making a short record of a practical activity with an adult as means of recording significant achievements, as suggested by Clarke (1998). In this way, children can become involved in a dialogue with the supporting adult in order to improve their learning while at the same time providing a record of their formative development.

Intervention and Differentiation

Set against the advice to use formative assessment to improve learning are the national testing arrangements requiring the teaching of a specific curriculum and 'intervention' strategies for children who are 'falling behind'. There are certainly conflicting philosophies at work within the different government agencies that impose curriculum change on schools. When the TGAT (1988) proposed the system of ten attainment levels, they expected 80 per cent of children aged 7 to be assessed at Level 2 , but now there is growing pressure from the government to interpret the Level 2 at age 7 and Level 4 at age 11 as entitlements rather than averages. Schools are under pressure to increase the numbers of pupils exceeding these 'averages'. In such a climate, teachers have difficulty justifying their own judgements about success, and the nature of attainments for children. There is pressure to teach a curriculum that is inappropriate for some pupils because the national tests will have some content at a higher level. For example, Key Stage 1 teachers feel obliged to teach the content of English and mathematics to Level 3, although the majority of children will attain Level 2 and some might attain Level 1. The same happens at other Key Stages, but during Key Stages 3 and 4, some differentiation occurs to allow children access to a differentiated curriculum designated at the level of projected attainment. Differentiating the curriculum because of assessments raises another issue, the 'self-fulfilling prophecy' (Wragg 2001), with regard to assessment and targeting for future performance. If we tell children they are identified as being capable of a 'D' or a 'C' in their GCSE examinations, then they might not achieve as well as they could because they reinterpret the 'label' negatively as 'being unable to gain an A or B'. As soon as we attach levels or grades to an assessment result, the interpretation often rests on the lack of achievement rather than the positive achievements.

Teachers and teaching assistants must identify the place of formative assessment within the system. My own view, based on my classroom and advisory experience, is that formative assessment should inform the taught curriculum and aid differentiation, but at the same time, teachers and teaching assistants should not limit children's opportunities to learn by providing a curriculum that does not enable them to move forward in their learning. Unfortunately, this is what often happened in the past. Those identified and labelled as needing a differentiated curriculum often did not receive a rich range of experiences. All children should have realistic and achievable targets to aim for across the curriculum. There is therefore logic in the argument for the inclusion of all children in some whole-class teaching as part of the National Strategies. Children learn from each other. If we separate some children and give them a very different curriculum, they are missing a learning opportunity.

The Impact of Summative Assessments

National tests as a summative assessment of children's attainment have a negative impact on the quality and value of formative assessment. A summative assessment is one that summarises the achievements over a period, and this might be by teacher assessment over the year including half-term assessment activities against key objectives or by an annual test across several levels and objectives. A test provides a snapshot of how a child performed on a particular day. By contrast, formative assessment is a qualitative, objective judgement over a period. It culminates annually in a summative 'best-fit' assessment against a set of criteria. In England, we use the National Curriculum Attainment Targets (DfEE/QCA 1999) to help us identify the level of performance in each subject. The majority of people tend to judge children's yearly achievements by the reported levels of attainment based on national test results. These summative results should have equal weighting with the teacher's reported assessment levels for the same subjects, but the reality is that the test results take precedence. Assessing children to allocate a level is a summative judgement that often labels children very early in their school career as being 'high ability' or 'low ability'. These labels seem to be prevalent in many schools despite the fact that Ofsted use the terms 'higher attainers' and 'lower attainers'. You may question the difference between them. They do mean something very different. In fact, the labelling begins on entry to school with baseline assessment designed to provide a means of measuring 'value-added' in relation to evaluating school performance. In order to measure value-added, Lindsay and Deforges (1998) suggest the baseline assessment needs to be a valid and reliable assessment so that schools can determine the impact on a child's original capabilities over a period. They also discuss a range of issues in relation to this measure as part of determining school effectiveness, and in using the measures to determine children's educational difficulties. It is useful to identify children having difficulties early in their education, but unfortunately, it can lead to labelling and self-fulfilling prophecies where children only perform to the level expected of them throughout their school career. We must also remember that the criteria we use in our summative judgements of children's attainments are age-related, not child-related. They do not take into account that different people learn at different rates and in different ways.

Do the labels matter?

My own belief is that the labels we use to identify different groups of children based on our assessment processes matter because they hold different meanings. Let us consider 'ability'. Everyone is born with the ability to learn. We might be able to determine that innate ability by an intelligence test, but growing emphasis on multiple intelligence theories, outlined by Pat Hughes in Chapter 3, and knowledge that we can alter our intelligence test scores with practice make this approach to determining 'ability' very unreliable. Tests and examinations in school do not assess our ability. They determine our level of attainment at a specific point in time. The label 'low ability' or 'high ability' implies that the child cannot alter that position. The reality is that many adults previously labelled as incapable of academic success are now gaining Higher Education degrees, thus dispelling the myth that 'ability' is the main factor in determining success. Attainment is a much more tangible concept in assessment. We can measure attainment against a set of clear objectives. We can identify a child as having attained a set of criteria, or not. The TGAT (1988) recommended the use of the term attainment before the introduction of the National Curriculum in 1989, and Ofsted favours 'attainment' as a measurable item. The TGAT supplementary report identifies the difficulty of defining ability although the group admitted to inadvertently using the word ability in some sections of their original recommendations.

Sometimes people talk about 'under-achievers' in relation to children whom they perceive as not reaching their full potential. The main dispute with labelling children in this way is that none of us knows the exact potential that a particular child has. The nature of a person's achievement depends on a variety of characteristics as identified by Gagné (1994, in Eyre 1997) who provided a complex model of the interrelationships between personal traits, the environment and developmental processes. Eyre (1997: 7) presents a simplified model and suggests that there are three interrelated factors influencing success: (1) innate ability; (2) opportunity and support; and (3) motivation and hard work. She also indicates that the balance between these is different for different children and so there is no clear recipe for success. Many high achievers in life did not show outstanding talent in their early schooling so labelling children as 'high achievers', 'low achievers' or 'under-achievers' really does not mean very much. Attainment is clearly about the assessment process of making judgements or testing according to a set of clear criteria. If labels are necessary, then it is better to use 'higher attainers' and 'lower attainers' as this reflects the level of attainment and does not make judgements about innate ability or predict potential success in later life with regard to achievement.

Diagnosing Strengths and Weaknesses

The DfES and QCA have continued the trend of the past 20 years in producing materials to support teachers in their formative and diagnostic assessment of pupils. Unfortunately, many of these materials sit on shelves unused by schools. Teachers are overloaded with paperwork and suffering from the continual stress of constant change, and unless a school has a high commitment to fine-tuning the teachers' formative and diagnostic assessment skills, the materials produced lie untouched and gather dust. Some of these materials are excellent. For example, the materials produced to help teachers learn from children's mistakes, misunderstandings and misconceptions in mathematics clearly identify some core aspects requiring attention and exemplify these with video examples (DfES 2002b). In particular, these materials focus on the common mistakes that children make in tests, the difficulties children have with the language of mathematics and the diagnosis of errors to identify what the child does not understand. Similar NNS materials support the assessment of children with English as an additional language (EAL) (DfES 2002c). These materials aim to determine whether the child can access the mathematics in the planned teaching programme for the class. The potentially contentious point is that they include learning English mathematical language as an important element. The support assistant using the materials may use the child's home language to identify that the child's mathematical understanding is at the required level, but within English spoken whole-class teaching the child might not demonstrate the same level of understanding. Previous assessment guidelines analysed by Gravelle and Sturman (1994) gave some sound advice on assessing bilingual pupils but more often than not 'fluency' referred to fluency in English. The English assessment system clearly disadvantages many bilingual pupils, especially those who begin school with little or no spoken English, and has done so for some time.

Teachers might feel they have little time to develop or fine-tune their diagnostic skills, but the production of the learning objectives in the strategy documents, together with exemplary materials, aids the diagnosis of specific difficulties and the small steps of learning that children need to take in order to overcome them. Many of the recent guidance materials focus on diagnosing errors in tests, rather than the individual diagnosis through close work or interviews with a child. Diagnosis through test responses can be a useful starting point, but the real diagnostic situation occurs when the supporting adult is able to delve into the child's thinking to discover the misunderstandings and consider how to support learning. Although many teachers will consider they cannot fit diagnostic procedures into their working pattern, having another adult in the classroom provides an ideal situation to include such practice. Because of the increase in the numbers of teaching assistants and the growth in specific intervention programmes, the opportunity to look closely at individual children's learning has improved greatly in the past five years.

For example, the Early Literacy Support (ELS) programme provides a Screening Pack (DfES 2001b) to confirm the teacher's on-going assessments for children who are not attaining the expected levels at the end of Year 1 term 1. Although the pack clearly provides an opportunity to look more closely at a child's attainments, it relies on the assumption that the child should be at a particular age-related level of learning. Many teaching assistants have described the ELS programme's success in improving levels of attainment, but most often, they suggest that this is due to the child having their confidence built through one-to-one support, rather than any clear strategies to use the diagnosis from the screening. The sessions are pre-planned and therefore do not take into account the individual differences in the children. The supporting adult has to develop the skill to adapt and modify if necessary, if the diagnostic element of the assessment is to be useful. Other materials not associated with the National Strategies include the Mathematics Recovery Programme, which takes a focused diagnostic approach, looking at young children's mathematical strategies in depth (Wright *et al.* 2000). It focuses on small steps of understanding that a child needs in order to make further progress in learning about calculating with numbers in mathematics. The initial assessment is lengthy and detailed, requiring the adult to take the child through several activities, with a video recording taken so that the child's response is available for review. Once the teacher identifies the stage of learning, the child then undertakes a teaching programme designed to help the child progress from that stage to the next. The difference between this approach and the DfES intervention strategies is that it recognises the small steps of learning between the objectives as child-related, instead of focusing purely on the curriculum objectives provided for a particular age group. The Mathematics Recovery Programme is also successful with older children who exhibit the same weaknesses in understanding as much younger children that prevent them from making progress. Diagnosis is therefore a very powerful assessment tool and can improve a child's learning potential if used well as part of a focused and structured programme. Although programmes of intervention in learning can improve a child's rate of progress over a short period, there are indications that the rate of progress falls once support stops. For example, many children who followed the ALS programme in Year 3 or 4 have also been chosen to follow the FLS programme in Year 5. It might be that individual intervention strategies used by the teacher during formative assessment in daily classroom practice will prove more effective for long-term gains in attainment.

A Summative Statement

The focus of adults working with children in the teaching and learning situation on a day-to-day basis is that of making formative judgements in order to help a child make progress. However, we must also acknowledge that the summative results from national tests can also be informative. For example, if many children in a class or a whole school perform badly on the same or similar questions, then the teacher must consider the effectiveness of his or her teaching. The mistakes children make on national tests are analysed by the QCA who produce annual reports on the type of questions causing children difficulty. Although these reports are informative and teachers might act on them, there is a sense of them having little real impact on learning because in the next test a 'new' type of question tests something a little different that most children have difficulty with and the whole cycle repeats itself. Thus, the value of the national diagnosis is limited. Formative assessments by the teacher and the teaching assistant are therefore the most likely way to have a quality impact on learning. Linked with in-depth diagnosis of problem areas, such formative assessments have the potential to raise achievement, thus fulfilling the government's agenda more effectively than the 'cramming' that occurs before national tests. More importantly, helping children raise their level of achievement and along with that their self-esteem can only improve society in general as these children become adults who value positive achievements in preference to negative levelling and labels.

Discussion Starters

1 How do formative assessment processes fit into your working day?

2 What are your views on the reporting of national test and examination results in relation to their value as summative judgements of children's attainment levels?

3 What are your observations of the impact of national tests and examinations on the formative assessment processes in school?

Reflecting on Practice

1 While working with a group of children, make observations of their responses to the activity. How do these observations help you determine their level of understanding in relation to the lesson objective? Is there any other information you need and how might you acquire it?

2 When you look at the school assessment data, is there any noticeable gender difference in attainment levels in your institution? If so, what do you think might cause this and what might be done to alter the situation?

Websites

www.nfer.ac.uk – access to on-line research reports and publications about assessment-related issues including issues such as the implementation of the Foundation Stage Profile.

www.ofsted.gov.uk/ – for reports, publications and data on school performance.

www.standards.dfes.gov.uk/ – search for assessment-related pages, find information on whole-school target setting.

www.standards.dfes.gov.uk/research/ – log in to access research digests on a variety of topics including formative assessment.

References

Bold, C. (1999) *Progression in Primary Design and Technology*, London: David Fulton.

Brooks, V. (2002) *Assessment in Secondary Schools: The New Teacher's Guide to Monitoring, Assessment, Recording, Reporting and Accountability*, Buckingham: Open University Press.

Clarke, S. (1998) *Targeting Assessment in the Primary Classroom: Strategies for Planning, Assessment, Pupil Feedback and Target Setting*, London: Hodder and Stoughton.

DfEE (1999) *The National Numeracy Strategy: Framework for Teaching Mathematics Years R to 6*, Cambridge: Cambridge University Press.

DfEE/QCA (1999) *The National Curriculum for England*, London: HMSO.

DfEE/QCA (2001) *The National Literacy Strategy: Marking Guidelines for Writing*, London: DfEE.

DfES (2001a) *The National Numeracy Strategy: Using Assess and Review Lessons*, London: DfES.

DfES (2001b) *The National Numeracy Strategy: Early Years Support Programme: Materials for Teachers Working in Partnership with Teaching Assistants*, London: DfES.

DfES (2002a) *The National Literacy Strategy: Further Literacy Support: Teacher's Book*, London: DfES.

DfES (2002b) *The National Numeracy and Key Stage 3 Strategies: Learning from Mistakes, Misunderstandings and Misconceptions in Mathematics*, London: DfES.

DfES (2002c) *The National Numeracy Strategy: Assessment Toolkit to Support Pupils with English as an Additional Language*, London: DfES.

DfES (2003) *The National Literacy Strategy: Introduction to the Further Literacy Support Programme: Module 4 Top-up Sessions*, London: DfES.

Eyre, D. (1997) *Able Children in Ordinary Schools*, London: David Fulton/The National Association for Able Children in Education.

Gravelle, M. and Sturman, E. (1994) 'Assessment of bilingual pupils: issues of fluency', in Keel, P. (ed.), *Assessment in the Multi-Ethnic Primary Classroom*, London: Trentham Books Limited, pp. 61–7.

Lindsay, G. and Deforges, M. (1998) *Baseline Assessment: Practice, Problems and Possibilities*, London: David Fulton.

Mitchell, C. and Koshy, V. (1993) *Effective Teacher Assessment: Looking at Children's Learning in the Primary Classroom*, London: Hodder & Stoughton.

QCA (2001) *Using Assessment to Raise Achievement in Mathematics: Key Stages 1, 2 and 3*, London: QCA.

Task Group on Assessment and Testing (1988) *National Curriculum: Task Group on Assessment and Testing: Three Supplementary Reports*, London: DES and Welsh Office.

Weeden, P., Winter, J. and Broadfoot, P. (2002) *Assessment: What's in It for Schools?*, London: Routledge/Falmer.

Wragg, E.C. (2001) *Assessment and Learning in the Secondary School*, London: Routledge Falmer.

Wright, R., Martland, J. and Stafford, A. (2000) *Early Numeracy: Assessment for Teaching and Intervention*, London: Paul Chapman Publishing Ltd.

12

Study Support: Opening Minds with Out-of-Hours Learning

Mari Cunliffe

Meet June

I work full-time with disaffected children in one secondary school and two feeder primary schools. My role is to encourage individual children to remain in school and engage positively with the learning experiences on offer. The children's difficulties are many – disengaged from the learning process, poor attendance, under-achieving, lacking in confidence and low self-esteem. I build positive relationships with the children based on trust. I find out their interests and try to engage them in out-of-school activities, run by the teachers, through which they build their self-esteem and gain a sense of ownership.

I recently attended the LEA three days' training on 'Tackling disaffection and truancy' and one LEA Study Support twilight session. These training sessions have encouraged me to think about setting up my own Out-of-School Club to cater for the needs of Year 6 and Year 7 children. I need to find out what will interest a particular group of children, seek funding and set the club up with the full involvement of the children. I also need a means of monitoring the impact of club involvement in relation to the child's response to other activities in school.

Defining Study Support

The terms 'Study Support' and 'Out-of-School Hours Learning' are synonymous and will be used interchangeably throughout this chapter. My own preferred term is the latter as it includes that key word 'learning' but Study Support is shorter and snappier. In addition, there are those who still think the term 'Study Support' relates only to academically based activities such as Homework Clubs, Study Clubs and revision sessions and this is not the case. In 1998 the Department for Education and Employment (DfEE) published *Extending Opportunity: A National Framework for Study Support* which opens with the following definition:

Study support is learning activity outside normal lessons which young people take part in voluntarily. Study support is, accordingly, an inclusive term, embracing many activities – with many names and many guises. Its purpose is to improve young people's motivation, build their self-esteem and help them to become learners that are more effective. Above all it aims to raise achievement.

(DfEE 1998: 1)

This definition accepts and supports the width of activities and clearly expects schools to look beyond the 'Homework Club'. This breadth and range are made explicit by Education Extra:

Study Support or Out of School Hours Learning (OSHL) are those activities which take place outside of compulsory school hours and which children attend voluntarily. Activities range from homework assistance and exam preparation to sports activities, arts and drama, reading clubs and breakfast clubs, environmental and community work – in short, any school linked activity that takes place outside of school hours. Study support activities can take place before and after school, lunchtimes, weekends and holidays.

(Education Extra 2003: 3)

This definition is particularly useful in that it specifies the times at which such activities may take place, thus encouraging schools to be flexible in their approach to meet the needs of the children.

Study Support can include activities that support key skills or core curriculum subjects:

■ Study Clubs – providing space and support to complete homework tasks or coursework;

■ help with key skills such as numeracy, literacy and Information and Communication Technology (ICT);

■ revision sessions including Easter Schools and 'Catch-Up' Clubs;

■ residential visits, study weeks or weekends.

Or include activities that encourage participation in creative, sporting and leisure activities:

■ the Creative and Performing Arts – music, dance, drama, art;

■ sports, games, outdoor pursuits;

■ special interests, e.g. science, robot wars, fishing, astronomy.

Or activities that are developmental and encourage the pupil to take an active role in his or her own learning and decision-making. These may include:

■ learning about learning, developing thinking and study skill, emotional literacy, revision techniques, circus skills;

■ mentoring, by adults or other children;

■ volunteering activities, environmental projects, community art, crime prevention;

■ lifestyle choices, healthy schools initiatives, life/school balance, motivational projects.

A school aiming for a well-balanced out-of-hours programme should be offering children a range of activities from across these three areas. This list is not exclusive and certain key questions need to be applied to any activity to know whether it qualifies as Out-of-Hours Learning. The school should ask these questions:

- Is the activity voluntary on the part of the children?
- Does it take place outside compulsory school hours?
- Will the activity have an impact on attendance, attitude, achievement or aspirations?

Thus, a Breakfast Club would qualify as it is purely voluntary for the pupil, it takes place before compulsory school hours and it has a measurable impact on school attendance. The teaching assistant June appears to have identified a need for a specific group of children. This chapter aims to support this development by providing information and advice that take her through the process of setting up a Study Support initiative.

Who Benefits?

Children and their schools benefit not only from increased academic performance, but also from the tangible improvement in student motivation and their positive attitude to learning. In particular, most schools report an improvement in pupil–teacher relationships. The Prince's Trust (with the DFEE 1999) set the scene for national developments by providing clear and succinct guidance about the nature and benefits of voluntary participation in developing young people's ability to achieve. They had set up 'xl clubs' in schools across the UK (www.princes-trust.org.uk/) and suggested that the benefits are not only to the children but such activities have an impact on parents and other carers, in addition to the wider community. A number of recent government reports and initiatives have also highlighted the place of Study Support in 'building learning communities'. These include the report of the Schools Plus Policy Action Team 11 (DfEE/Schools Plus 2000) which paved the way for the Extended Schools report (DfES 2002a).

Due to the wide variety of activities that can be included under the title Study Support and its overarching nature, I would contend that Study Support is neither a subject, nor simply an approach to subjects but an approach to learning. This means that Out-of-Hours Learning is not 'more of the same' but when embedded in the learning culture of a school it can have a direct and measurable impact.

The impact of Study Support

The most rigorous evidence into the impact of Study Support is a longitudinal study undertaken by the Quality in Education Centre, University of Strathclyde, between 1997 and 2000. They tracked two cohorts of over 8,000 children from 52 schools for three years. The larger cohort was tracked from Year 9 through to GCSE level and the smaller cohort from Year 7 through to their Key Stage 3 national tests (McBeath *et al.* 2001).

The study had two aims:

■ To measure the impact of participation on the attainment, attitudes and attendance of a large sample of secondary pupils in schools serving disadvantaged areas.

■ To develop and disseminate models of good practice through the support to schools of critical friends, training events and publications.

(DfES 2002b: 4)

From the research emerged clear evidence that children who attend voluntary learning opportunities outside of school hours do perform significantly better in national tests and GCSE than students who do not participate. Further, there is a positive impact on school attendance and the children's attitude to school and learning. Interestingly the report also found that 'Study support related to curriculum subjects shows strong effects on attainment but so also do sport, aesthetic activities and drop in sessions as well as other activities' (McBeath *et al.* 2001: 7). This supports the results of previous and subsequent qualitative studies, which consider that the voluntary participation of children is the key factor. There is a clear message here for June who will have to ensure that the children will want to attend voluntarily for the greatest impact in school subject learning.

Setting up an Out-of-Hours Club

This section of the chapter offers practical advice to anyone wishing to set up an Out-of-Hours Club, and should be particularly useful to June.

Having a purpose

Study Support exists for a purpose. Its purpose is to enhance children's abilities as learners and it will take shape and change over a period of time as Study Support grows, matures and extends its boundaries. Growth will depend in some measure on whether the goals are explicit rather than implicit and public rather than private.

(McBeath *et al.* 2001: 10)

Too often, schools and other providers identify a club they wish to run and proceed from there. This can be a mistake. Evaluative research studies indicate that a club or activity should arise from an identifiable need. Study Support is not a 'bolt-on' activity; it exists for a purpose – to enhance children's abilities as learners and this philosophy is fundamental to setting up a balanced programme of Out-of-Hours Learning opportunities. As an experienced LEA Study Support Manager, if I am approached by a school for funding to set up a new Out-of-Hours Club, my first question is 'What need does it fulfil?'

The recent study by Education Extra (2003) on behalf of the DfES reported that in some schools only 25 per cent of children attended voluntary Out-of-Hours activities. The reasons included:

■ A negative attitude to school in general and any additional activities in particular. This group appeared not to know what was on offer in their school or to consider the choices 'boring'.

- Many children expressed an interest in or had attended a club, but had dropped out.

- Children complained that the quality and range of provision were poor.

The quality of the activity was the key factor in retaining pupil interest.

It is clear that there is a significant proportion of the school population whose needs schools are not addressing. Where the school has first identified a need, activities can directly address that need. Case study 12.1 is a successful example of this process.

Case Study 12.1: The importance of identifying and meeting needs

A primary school in an area of social deprivation identified a group of Year 6 boys who had low self-esteem, were unmotivated, under-achieving in school work, and had low standing with their peer group, as they did not excel at traditional sports such as football. The head teacher and Study Support Co-ordinator sought to address this problem. Their purpose was to help raise self-esteem and build confidence and, in their own words, give these pupils 'some street cred!'

After wide discussion with teachers, students, parents and other stakeholders a decision was made to start a street hockey team, targeting these pupils. In partnership with a local initiative, the local police supplied funding for vital equipment and coaching.

The team looked splendid in their colourful outfits and fearsome helmets and with first-rate coaches soon mastered the fundamentals of the sport. Not only did the target group show greatly increased confidence and self-esteem, not only were they looked-up-to and envied by their peers, but their school work improved to such an extent that they achieved beyond expectation in Key Stage 2 national tests.

Thus, having a clear purpose should be the starting point. Before making progress, know what you want to achieve. Once you identify the goals, write them down, discuss them with others and refine them. June needs to consult with others before moving forward with her project.

DO

- Have a clear purpose.

- Let other people know your purpose.

- Involve senior management.

- Involve other staff.

- Start small.

Finding out what is needed

Nearly all schools have existing clubs and activities already running. Very often, these have stood the test of time and are well attended by certain groups of children. Any school considering expanding their provision should conduct a careful analysis of what already exists and what young people want. Questions that could be asked include:

- What activities already take place in school and in the local community?

- How well do these meet the needs of young people in the school or community?

- What is the best way to consult with the young people about their needs, interests and expectations?

- Who are the individuals and groups most in need? And who would benefit most?

- Who can help develop our programme in school, the LEA or the local community, in terms of resources and expertise?

Someone might have already done some of this work, especially if there are existing clubs in the school. Seek out any person who might have the role of 'out-of-hours' co-ordinator. Make your interest known and enlist his or her help and support. If no one exists with the remit for developing learning beyond the classroom, then it is likely that existing clubs have developed on an *ad hoc* basis and there is no co-ordination of Study Support within the school. This should not be the case as the government has made available substantial funding for schools to develop out-of-hours activities through the New Opportunities Fund, Standards Fund and Awards for All – to name but three funding streams. This could also bring into question the school's Health and Safety Policy regarding extra-curricular activities. If there is indeed no central co-ordination within school, then there is great scope for a new person to develop auditing skills, and the ability to analyse the results. However, this is not a task for one single person and it is better to work as part of a whole-school team, seeking help and advice from colleagues.

In their Study Support Toolkit, the DfEE (2000a) suggests that a range of different people become involved in a particular project. Evidence from the research programme makes it quite clear that the impact is greatest when there is a whole-school approach, and a commitment from the whole-school community and beyond. Sefton LEA Out-of-Hours team have a checklist (see Figure 12.1). It has proved a useful tool in identifying key personnel and possible resources.

Practical issues

By now a plethora of ideas and suggestions will have emerged as part of the consultation process and you will have the support of the school Leadership Team and have formed partnerships with colleagues within the school community and possibly within the wider community. You may even have secured funding to 'pump prime' your project, enabling you to buy resources or outside expertise. Now is the time to consider purely practical issues.

Funding

When you seek the support of the school Leadership Team, you must also address the issue of funding. Unless the activity is to be run in a classroom, by a volunteer, using resources which already exist in the school, then it is likely that you will need money to resource your activity. Some good clubs run on a shoestring using the goodwill of staff, but even better clubs operate where there is access to additional funding for additional resources, both material and human.

1. Are the following fully aware of the school Study Support Programme?

Head teacher ☐	Governing Body ☐	LEA Co-ordinator ☐
Senior Managers ☐	Chair of PTA ☐	G&T Co-ordinator ☐
Leadership Team ☐	Parents ☐	Learning Mentors ☐
Teachers ☐	Pupils ☐	Bursar ☐
LSAs ☐	Link Adviser ☐	School Secretary ☐
☐	☐	☐

Which of the above need to be brought on board?
(Use the blanks to insert others relevant to your school, e.g. EBP, Special Needs Co-ordinator.)

2. How can others best be made aware and brought on board?
   - Staff/departmental meetings
   - PTA/Governors meetings
   - INSET
   - Staff training/development
   - Invitation to events, etc.
   - Open evenings
   - Fliers, leaflets, newsletters
   - Letters
   - One-to-one discussion
   - Staffroom discussion
   - Awareness-raising sessions
   - Building a team

3. What sources of funding for out-of-hours Learning are already in school and what is in the pipeline?
   - Excellence in Cities
   - NOF Study Support
   - Summer School funding
   - Awards for All
   - Standards Fund
   - Gifted and Talented money
   - ESF/SRB

4. What resources are available in school that could be used?

5. What resources are available in the local community?

6. Who can help you find out? You may find the list at the top a useful starting point.

FIGURE 12.1   Sefton LEA Out-of-Hours Learning Team checklist

Most schools have access to funding specifically targeted at out-of-hours learning from a range of national or local initiatives. The Local Education Authority (LEA) may have funds available to support certain activities and the National Lottery has a variety of ever-changing funding streams, which you could access. Do not be put off initially by the paperwork. There should be someone in school or the LEA who can help you to 'write a bid' and it is a most satisfying experience when you receive your first grant.

The most likely use you will have for additional funding is to buy materials and equipment for your club, to pay for staff – especially outside providers – and to take children outside the school environment to extend their learning. All this will bring an added dimension to your activity, which will play a major part in the recruitment and retention of your children. This is especially important if your target group of children are those who do not normally participate in out-of-hours learning.

Target group

It is likely that your initial perception of a need or 'gap in provision' grew out of the recognition that the school was not meeting the needs of certain children. You may therefore already have a target group of children in mind, as does June. Identify the group in writing because it will form part of the monitoring process later on. This group might include, depending on your original purpose, one or more of the following:

- children in danger of being socially excluded;
- children exhibiting challenging behaviour;
- children in danger of under-achieving;
- children on free school meals;
- children with records of poor punctuality and/or attendance;
- the gifted and talented;
- children in the special educational needs (SEN) register;
- children for whom English is not their first language;
- children 'at risk';
- young carers;
- children in public care;
- young people from minority ethnic groups;
- children with low self-esteem and lacking in confidence.

Leaders must take care with the ratio of targeted children to non-targeted within the club. If the activity were to cater for, as an example, 100 per cent of children exhibiting challenging behaviour, one might question whether the leader had thought carefully. Experience has shown that a well-thought-out mix of targeted children with non-targeted children (good role models) can be most beneficial to both sets of children and to the staff running the activity. Case study 12.2 shows that success can follow from having the right mix.

Case Study 12.2: Getting the right mix

A large comprehensive school in a socially mixed area had perceived a need to 'develop responsibility for their own behaviour and learning' in a group of Year 10 boys who were in danger of being excluded from school. The boys had one common interest – sport in general and football in particular. They could relate especially well to a male learning mentor who was willing to work, after hours, with this small but challenging group. After discussion with senior staff, form tutors, children and parents, the learning mentor decided to train a group of children for the Junior Sports Leader Award. This award demands commitment on the part of the children and leads to an accredited qualification. It was decided the group would consist of the eight boys in danger of exclusion and an equal number of girls who were considered good 'all-rounders' and gifted and talented in sport. The project obtained funding from the New Opportunities Fund. It was such a success that it has become an established out-of-hours activity with that school and is now in its third year. There is both hard statistical and anecdotal evidence that this activity achieved its prime purpose with this group of boys.

This ratio of 50:50 worked well in this particular situation. In general, experience shows that 25–30 per cent is the optimum percentage of targeted children within a group, or the group can come to take on the 'flavour' of the target group. The purpose of targeting is normally to aid inclusion, not to have a club labelled by other children. There are of course exceptions. If the free school meal rate is 65 per cent and the club aims to target children who suffer social and economic deprivation, then limiting the number of children on free school meals to 25 per cent would amount to exclusion. We can also argue that gifted and talented children might benefit from a club where all children are very able students. Whatever the mix, keep numbers of children manageable in the first instance. If the activity proves to be worthwhile, numbers can always increase at a later date. Other resources, equipment and human, will be required at that point.

Where, when and for how long will your club run?

One of the issues to address is where to base your club. This depends on several factors:

- the nature of the activity;
- the number of children;
- options available to you;
- obstacles you are likely to have to overcome.

Case study 12.3 illustrates the practical problems facing one school.

Case Study 12.3: A simple solution

A school for children with moderate learning difficulties had decided to run a Reading Club for Year 7 children, the aim being to continue to foster the 'reading for enjoyment' the children brought with them from the primary phase. Although it was very much an 'all comers' club, staff had especially encouraged the attendance of children who appeared to have few friends. The problems encountered were that most children came to school by hired mini-bus and could not stay after school and if the club was at lunchtime, there was very little space available, especially during rainy spells. The library was the obvious place, being small but well equipped with bean-bags and comfortable chairs, but that was open to students during the lunch hour, and the constant coming and going of others would, it was felt, destroy the ambiance of the club.

They reached a simple solution. The library, it was decided, would be for the exclusive use of the 'Bookworms' on Wednesday lunchtime and other students would have to work around that. This had two benefits. First, the Bookworms felt very special and bonded as a group, and second, it provided a real-life learning experience for children with moderate learning difficulties who had to take into consideration the fact of opening and closing hours.

If your club is likely to be using large and bulky equipment, the storage may be an issue:

- How long will it take to get out and put away?
- What are the health and safety implications?

- Can someone else put out the equipment?
- Can you enlist an army of helpers?

Do not be put off by these obstacles. Some of the most exciting and productive clubs are those which offer 'hands on' experience to children and the task of dealing with large or bulky equipment is more than compensated for by the quality of the learning experience and often the behaviour of the children.

The activity may not necessarily take place on school property. It might be easier for children to go off-site. Your initial consultation may have unearthed facilities which exist within the community. An example of this might be Youth Group facilities such as table tennis, which are not in use until later in the evening. Perhaps a local library can offer space and support for students to complete homework, coursework or research. It is always desirable in any case to look at extended learning opportunities afforded to children by bringing an added dimension to the activity. This might mean taking the children into the community or inviting a specialist into the club. For instance, a Drama Club might experience a live performance at a local theatre, work with a group of Performing Arts students or attend a course on stage make-up.

When your club will run is dependent on your target group. The majority of activities do run after school hours, but there are exceptions. Younger primary age children may have difficulties getting home after school, particularly in winter. Children in special schools are often reliant on hired transport and some secondary children may have the responsibility for siblings after school. It might be worthwhile considering lunchtime or breakfast sessions if these prove more accessible, although each brings with it its own set of problems. More schools are organising Study Support activities at weekends and during holidays. There is a growing tradition of Easter Revision Sessions, Weekend 'Catch up on Course Work' events and Summer Schools. While your target group may not be enthused by any of these opportunities, you may be able to take advantage of the school being open, facilities available and staff on the premises to run a special event of your own alongside other out-of-hours activities.

Finally, consider how many sessions your club can offer. Aim for quality provision. Better to run ten well-thought-out and well-resourced sessions leaving the children wanting more than having children leave from lack of interest. Study Support is not 'more of the same' and poor quality provision is one of the most common reasons for pupil drop-out. Good attendance numbers are often indicative of a well-run activity.

Staffing your club

Study Support puts the emphasis on learning rather than teaching. Young learners need people who can support them in a variety of ways and the selection of the right tutor is crucial. Tutors do need a range of skills and knowledge, but equally important are their attitudes and beliefs. A major reason for children's non-participation in out-of-hours learning is 'dislike of the teacher'. Not all good teachers translate well into good Study Support tutors and for certain activities it is worth exploring the options of adults other than teachers. These can include teaching assistants, learning mentors, sports and drama coaches, parents, older children, students, and so on. At least one primary school to my knowledge runs a well-attended lunchtime club manned by the school caretaker and targeted at disaffected boys.

Potential tutors should have a genuine liking for children, be open and approachable, and have a belief in the ability of learners and a willingness to learn themselves, from colleagues and children. In some instances, they may simply be a facilitator. Case study 12.4 is a good example of the children being proactive and encouraging the teacher.

Case Study 12.4: Where there's a will . . .

A Year 11 pupil approached a young English teacher at a rural secondary school asking if she would supervise an after-school 'knock about' at hockey. A former PE teacher had run training sessions but had left the previous year and the students wished to resurrect the club. They had been told that they needed a teacher to supervise it. The teacher explained that she had not played hockey herself since high school, could only do a Friday night owing to commitments to Drama Club and the School Council and they (the students) would have to take responsibility for the organisation and training of other children. The Year 11 boy assured her he would 'sort everything out' and true to his word, he did.

Every Friday an average of 14 students from Year 7 to Year 11 (12 boys and 2 girls) attended. The older children organised the warm-up and taught specific skills. Carried along by their enthusiasm, the teacher contacted the area hockey co-ordinator who came along to a practice with a senior coach. Impressed by the students he agreed to help with training on a regular basis. They found money from a variety of funding streams to buy resources and pay for training. Some of the older children underwent Sport's Leadership Training and even came in during exam leave to help coach younger children.

The young English teacher has since acquired a Hockey Coaching qualification herself!

The case study progressed from identifying a need to setting up within a very short space of time, as the practical considerations were few and had already been thought through by the children. However, what moved this club forward was the extra value in the form of resources, staff and pupil training brought about by the teacher who, although she initially knew little about coaching hockey, was fully aware of the benefits of developing partnerships.

Health and safety

Staffing your club with adults other than teachers raises the issue of child protection, health and safety and accountability. It is not possible to go into the complicated area of child protection in this chapter but club leaders should familiarise themselves with and work within school policies and procedures for child protection and be aware of the relevant legislation. It is essential that in all Study Support settings the health and safety of children and adults is not put at risk. There is a wealth of relevant legislation, on topics including health and safety, child protection and food hygiene, which is complex and inter-linked. Policies and procedures already in place within the school will cover most of the provision. You will need to check that these extend to after-hours use of school premises and to your activities in Out-of-

Hours Clubs. The DfEE (2000b) pack *Safe Keeping: A Good Practice Guide for Health and Safety in Study Support* provides comprehensive information and resources.

DO

- Cost out the project in terms of added value.
- Consider your target group carefully.
- Keep numbers manageable – start small.
- Seek out the best venue possible.
- Be innovative.
- Choose tutors with care.
- Check the school's policy for Health and Safety in Out-of-Hours activities.

Monitoring and evaluation

To make a difference, Study Support has to be kept under critical review. Four questions should form an integral part of the monitoring and evaluation process:

- What is going on?
- How well is it working?
- How do we know?
- What can we improve?

The answers to these questions will provide a lot of material to compile a portfolio of evidence about your practice in your Out-of-School Hours Club.

What is going on?

Somewhere there needs to be a simple record of each club or activity, listing the club title, venue, start and end dates, day(s) and time(s), duration, target group(s) and tutors. This should preferably be no more than one page of A4.

For health and safety, as well as monitoring purposes, there will also have to be a register for recording pupil attendance and a way of aggregating these attendances onto a master sheet. You will need to establish what system, if any, exists in your school to collect and manage this data.

How well is it working?

Earlier you will have identified your target group and how many students you can accommodate in your club. Your system should allow you to access information about your target group and the total attendances. Before collecting any data, it is vital to know what it is for, what will be done with it, who will analyse it and how much time it will take.

Basic monitoring should include the number of hours the activity has actually taken place, pupil attendance figures and target group attendance figures. If your system will allow, you may wish to analyse trends such as gender, age group and ethnicity. Collected data will allow schools to compare attendance at Study Support activities with improvement in national tests results.

How do we know?

In addition to quantifiable data, the leader should seek opinions of stakeholders. These can include staff, tutors and outside providers, adults other than a teacher (AOTTs), club members, students and parents. Consider using a variety of methods such as questionnaires, group discussion, School Council, interviews and interactive ICT packages. The Quality in Study Support (QiSS at www.qiss.org.uk) team has developed an excellent interactive CD-ROM which will collect and analyse children's attitudes to Study Support (AtSS).

What can we improve?

In Figure 12.2 some key areas have been identified. Schools may wish to add others as a result of their monitoring and evaluation process or from the various Codes of Practice. After identifying strengths, schools should identify one or two areas at most for improvement and use these to form the basis of an Action Plan.

It is the voluntary participation of children which is the key factor in the effectiveness of study support To encourage and sustain voluntary participation key factors must be present Study Support has most impact when it is embedded within the learning culture of the school	**Consider** • Have you been successful in attracting sufficient numbers of children to attend your activity on a regular basis and do these figures include an acceptable number of targeted children? • Has the club/activity run for the predicted number of sessions and is the venue suitable? • How do the tutors view the experience, would they be willing to run a similar activity again and, if so, what changes would they make? • Have you involved staff, students, parents and other partners in the planning, development and evaluation of Study Support activities? • Are those who run activities suitably trained and qualified and have they been properly vetted and inducted in the ways of the school? • How are the efforts of children and others recognised and rewarded? • Is Study Support part of the School Development plan and is everyone aware of its potential in school improvement and raising standards?
Strengths	
Areas for improvement	

FIGURE 12.2   Evaluating an Out-of-School Hours Club

Final Comments

This chapter is written for the individual such as June who, having identified a need or gap in provision, for a group of children with whom they work, wishes to address that need through developing one or more out-of-hours learning situations within the framework of existing provision in their school. The school may or may not have a tradition of out-of-hours learning within its philosophy and School Development Plan. If there is no tradition of out-of-hours learning in the school, that individual will need to convince the school leaders that additional provision is needed and be clear about the purpose, potential benefits and practical issues. It may be the case that the value of Study Support is not fully recognised, or only in a limited way, and that such out-of-hours activities that do exist are unco-ordinated and *ad hoc*. In this situation, the individual may wish to contribute to the development of a more structured approach to Study Support through the use of audits, pupil questionnaires and raising awareness of the real possibilities that exist of measurable gains in attainment. As we have seen throughout the chapter, research evidence suggests that there are significant improvements in children's school-based attainments through engagement in out-of-school activities. Hopefully, June will be able to realise her ambitions to meet the needs of an identified group of children in order to improve their attendance and performance in school.

Discussion Starters

1 Why is the voluntary nature of Study Support activities to be valued?
2 What are the benefits of having mixed groups of children, i.e. children from the target group and other children who are interested in the club?

Reflecting on Practice

1 Design a means of carrying out an audit of existing provision in your own institution and evaluate its effectiveness.
2 Set up a spreadsheet for collecting and analysing data from an existing Out-of-Hours Club in school. Use it and evaluate the usefulness of the analysis it produces.

Websites

www.educationextra.org.uk/ – Education Extra and Community Education Development Centre (CEDC) merged on 14 October 2003 to form a major community learning called ContinYou.

www.nya.org.uk/ – The National Youth Agency website.

www.princes-trust.org.uk/ – The Prince's Trust website.

www.qiss.org.uk – Quality in Study Support, various documents and advice relating to provision of quality study support activities.

www.standards.dfes.gov.uk/studysupport – advice on Study Support.

www.ufa.org.uk – University of the First Age website with information and links about partnerships, brain-friendly learning and Study Support initiatives.

References

DfEE (1998) *Extending Opportunity: A National Framework for Study Support*, London: DfEE.

DfEE (2000a) *The Study Support Tool Kit: Making it Work in Schools*, London: DfEE.

DfEE (2000b) *Safe Keeping: A Good Practice Guide for Health and Safety in Study Support*, London: DfEE.

DfEE/Prince's Trust (1999) *Prince's Trust Study Support Handbook*, London: DfEE.

DfEE/Schools Plus (2000) *Building Learning Communities: A Report from the Schools Plus Policy Action Team 11*, London: DfEE.

DfES (2002a) *Extended Schools: Providing Opportunities and Services for All*, London: DfES.

DfES (2002b) *The Essential Guide to the Impact of Study Support*, London: DfES.

Education Extra (2003) *Non-Participation in Study Support: Research Study Conducted for the Department of Education and Skills*, London: DfES.

McBeath, J., Kirwan, T., Myers, K. *et al.* (2000) *Study Support: The Scottish Code of Practice*, Glasgow: University of Strathclyde.

McBeath, J., Kirwan, T., Myers, K. *et al.* (2001) *The Impact of Study Support: Research Report RR273*, London: DfES.

13

Investigating Educational Settings: Weaving the Threads

Gavin Fairbairn and Susan A. Fairbairn

Meet Mahnoor

I live in Levenshulme in the South of Manchester. Before I was married I worked in my parent's shop, but now I am a parent helper in the school that my son attends. I am helping because I want to become a teacher so that I can help children to learn. While I have small children it is difficult to take up a full-time university course and so, as a first step, I have enrolled on a part-time course for classroom assistants in a nearby college. One of the things we have to do on the course is to investigate various aspects of our work in school and produce a file of notes and reflections on our findings. My son's head teacher has agreed that I can do it in her school, which is very kind of her. However, I am rather concerned about whether I can manage to fulfil all the things I must achieve. Apparently, I will have to give a short presentation on some of the details of what I have found out about the school. I am expected to investigate it to see what goes on there, so that I can discuss the kinds of things the children and staff do and make some comment about whether I have learned anything from my investigations. I don't know where to start.

Investigating Educational Settings

People investigate educational settings because they want to be able to tell better stories about them, i.e. because they want to be in a better position to inform others as accurately as they can about those settings and what goes on in them. In this chapter, we talk about some approaches to such investigation. Learning a little about these approaches and taking the time to practise them will allow you to develop your ability to harvest information about schools and other educational settings. This, in turn, will allow you to talk in a more informed way about the things that teachers and other staff do in them, and about the educational and social experiences, both planned and unplanned, of their pupils/students.

In introducing these ideas about ways of investigating educational settings, we talk in terms of telling stories about them. Please do not be fooled into thinking that in doing so we are being either simplistic or patronising, since nothing could be further from the truth. We believe that storytelling is central to the whole of human life. Stories allow us to extend the range of our experiences, and they provide a convenient way of remembering ideas, facts and events. Stories form most of our interactions with others. Consider, for example, how you would respond if a friend asked one of these questions:

- How was your holiday?
- Did you have a nice time at the weekend?
- What shall we do if the weather doesn't improve?

Each of these questions invites a story in return, as do many questions that might be asked about what goes on in schools, including:

- Has David settled in better yet?
- Was the new classroom layout helpful in reducing distraction for Mario and Miles?
- How are Aisha's language skills developing?

It is because we recognise the importance of storytelling as a way of sharing information that we believe that whenever you are asked to give your views of a pupil or student, or to report on his or her behaviour or progress, that you should think of what you are doing as telling a story, whatever form that story takes, and however detailed it is. Whether it is focused on a particular aspect, or more general in nature, every report of this kind can be viewed as story-telling and the best, most interesting and most helpful of such stories are those that communicate directly and simply in a way that makes others sit up and pay attention. More than that, we believe that most professional and academic communication could be improved immeasurably if more authors adopted a narrative approach in their writing. That is why, in saying something about academic and professional writing later in this chapter, we emphasise the advantages of such an approach. It is also why we urge you to view the academic writing tasks that you undertake as opportunities for storytelling (e.g. see Fairbairn 2000).

By the time you get to the end of this chapter, we hope you will have some ideas about how you might collect information that will be of interest to a range of audiences. We hope, also, that you will have some understanding about the importance of a storytelling approach to academic and professional writing.

What Kinds of Stories Might You Tell about Educational Settings?

The stories that you tell about educational settings are likely to be different for different audiences and for different purposes, and so the information you will require if you are to tell them in ways that communicate effectively to each audience, and the style in which you will do so, will vary. For example, you would want to tell different stories for teachers and head teachers, local authority officers, parents, governors, a local newspaper, a professional magazine or an academic journal. Although the stories that you tell will be different, it is important to realise that this will not be because the relevant facts differ in each case, but because different audiences will have contrasting areas and degrees of interest – some will want or even need more detail, and some less. For example, inspectors might be interested to hear about the topics covered in the last term and about the ways in which they were taught; parents, on the other hand, are more likely to want more detailed information about their children, e.g. whether they have overcome the difficulties they were having with decimals and about how good they are at estimating answers to money questions.

Of course, the stories that we tell about educational settings need not always focus directly on the activities and attainments of the staff or students/pupils in order to contribute to a useful and accurate picture about it, and might, for example, focus on the resources provided (or not provided) and the nature of the school environment – from the layout of classrooms, to the uses and appearance of the playground or playing field. Indeed, there is no part of a school's business that cannot be investigated and about which stories cannot be told, which can help us to understand it and develop its work. Sometimes these stories will tell us as much about the nature of the school as any examination of the work that pupils carry out or of the teaching strategies adopted.

We can learn a great deal by looking round at the ways a school and its community present themselves to the world. The environment of a school – both inside and outside – can 'speak' for the qualities and values that are to be found or not found there, from the smallest details, e.g. the font used in wall displays, to large physical features such as the type of railings enclosing the playground. For example, one of us once worked for a short time in an inner-city school in which the dead plants on the tables outside some of the classrooms seemed to scream that this was a place that didn't care, in which children need not expect to be treated as important. And when one of our children was in Key Stage 1, we were dismayed at the lack of awareness on the part of the staff, of the fact that although more than 30 per cent of the population was of Pakistani or Indian origin, with perhaps another 10 per cent from African-Caribbean families, there was little evidence of this in the wall displays. Indeed, as far as we can recall, the only gesture at the fact that there are in the world people who are anything other than a pinkish-white colour was a display relating to the amount of money that each class raised for a Third World charity, which showed some pictures of poverty-stricken people in African countries. And the only gesture at the fact that not everyone speaks English as their native language was a large display in the hall which proclaimed in a number of languages 'Happy Christmas', which was charming for a couple of months in the year, but grated on the nerves in June.

To our mind, some stories about educational settings are rather thin and unsatisfying. They include the kinds of stories that are told using tick boxes on charts that list the work that pupils or students have carried out, the things they have been taught and the things they have achieved. Stories of this kind never say enough to allow us to understand what is really going on. Often they are aimed at demonstrating the extent to which performance targets have been reached, and the year-on-year improvements in such performance that are taken as an indicator both that rather than resting on their laurels, successful schools are continually striving to do even better, and that schools that are not yet good enough are at least taking action to address weaknesses.

Unfortunately, some people are fond of such stories, because they can be presented cleanly and give the appearance of scientific and professional rigour, and others who are not fond of them nevertheless expend a great deal of energy in producing them because they are required to do so. Now we would not suggest to anyone that they should avoid carrying out the testing and recording that they are required to carry out in relation to pupils. However, it is worth remembering not only that some kinds of recording and writing about pupils' work make for richer and more interesting stories, but also that such stories are likely to be more instructive and informative – both when they are focused on individual children and when they are focused on whole communities of learners and teachers.

How Might You Investigate Educational Settings?

People investigate schools and other educational settings in a variety of ways, depending partly on the reasons that they are telling their stories, and partly on the audiences they are addressing. For example, during her placement, Mahnoor might develop her understanding of her son's school as a social and educational setting:

- through careful observation, e.g. of lessons, or social situations in the classroom or in the school yard (including both informal observation and the use of observation schedules);
- by maintaining records of the work that the teachers and other adults carry out with pupils;
- by maintaining descriptive and reflective diaries in which she records what she sees and experiences during her placement in the school, including any work that she carries out with children;
- through the compilation and analysis of questionnaires to both parents and teachers, e.g. about homework;
- by using interviews and narrative methods to access the experience of the pupils and the staff in her son's school;
- through documentary analysis, for example, of documents that set out the school's policies and procedures, but also of minutes of meetings, pupils' reports, incident books, records of school trips, etc.

These ways of gathering information about educational settings are the kinds of things that educational researchers do, and that social scientists of all kinds do, when they are trying to understand what goes on in organisations and workplaces. Of course, any investigations that you might carry out as an individual, whether as a student or as a professional, are likely to be different from those carried out as part of a research project, both in terms of the reasons you have for your investigations and in terms of their scale.

For example, whereas much educational research will focus on pupils in settings in which the researcher does not have any personal interest, the investigations you carry out are likely to be in educational settings in which you are working in some way. And whereas the investigations that teachers might carry out in a school in which they are working will usually be undertaken with the intention of directly informing and bringing about improvements in their own practice and in the practice of their colleagues, educational research is most often carried out with the hope in mind of increasing understanding of some aspect of education in a more general way. Finally, whereas much reported educational research has a distant and somewhat formal and scientific flavour about it, the investigations that you carry out in order to develop your practice, or to contribute to school development, are unlikely to produce statistics and scientific-sounding results. Nonetheless, there is a sense in which any investigation that you carry out in order to increase your understanding of an educational setting will be research of a kind. And like all research, it will produce better, more useful results, if it is carefully planned and executed, rather than being carried out in an *ad hoc* way, or planned hurriedly on a piece of scrap paper.

One of the problems with research of any kind is that, however well planned, things never go quite as expected, with the result that it is almost inevitably the case that the strategies for data collection that are planned prove less adequate than they might have been. One way to maximise the likelihood that you will gather worthwhile information from the investigations you undertake is to try out your methods before your main investigation begins – preferably on a different population or group of people. That way, you can locate problems and amend your methods before it matters too much.

Be Aware of Your Prejudices

It is important to select carefully the tools that you intend to use to gather information. Just as there is no point in using a sledgehammer to crack a nut, for example, there is no point in using a research tool that is inappropriate for your purposes. It is also important to be as aware as you can of the personal prejudices and preconceptions that you bring to the study of educational settings. In talking of prejudices, we are not drawing attention to anything so obvious as the kind of prejudice that might arise from deeply felt racial or religious preference, or from an inability to think objectively about difference, although it is undoubtedly important to be aware of such prejudices and the harm they can cause. Rather, we are pointing to the fact that the beliefs and views that we hold about the nature of the world can have an effect on the ways that we view it, and on the ways in which we are inclined to think about the evidence with which we are faced.

We are never neutral observers, no matter what we are observing, but carry expectations as a result of prior experiences. In relation to the investigation of educational environments, the fact that we have all attended school for many years will colour our investigations, because our own experience as pupils will almost inevitably have left traces in our memories about what schools either are or should be like, that will have helped to shape our views of education. Whenever you observe or otherwise investigate what goes on in an educational setting, you should therefore be aware of the effects that your prior experiences might have had on the ways in which you think about the things you see, particularly when those experiences had a strongly positive or negative character.

One way to develop as an objective investigator is to make our prejudices and expectations explicit. In order to do this Mahnoor could find it useful to write the story of one of the schools she attended as a child, focusing on key incidents, particular teachers or aspects of organisation. So could you. You might also find it useful (if you are brave enough) to try writing down a list of your prejudices – with as open a mind as possible, as one of us was asked to do as a student. At that time she wrote that she was prejudiced against men with patterned socks and women with red shoes. What are you prejudiced against or in favour of?

Investigational Tools

We want, now, to say a little more about each of the approaches to the investigation of educational settings that we listed above.

Observation

Observation is a useful way of collecting information, both about the ways in which schools and individual classrooms are organised and structured, and about the performance of individual children, not only in relation to the curriculum, but also in relation to their behaviour and social interactions. Observations can be made informally, simply by remaining aware of what is going on in the classroom; this is how teachers and other educational workers build up their knowledge and understanding of pupils and their ability to address individual needs. However, observations can also be carried out in a more structured way by drawing up a schedule of things to be observed, in which the general focus of the observation is broken down into key sub-areas. Often such schedules are produced in the form of a table on which observers can record what they see in the form of brief notes.

Developing a structured way of making observations can allow you to write more comprehensive reports. For example, if as part of her placement Manhoor decided to observe some lessons, because she was interested in whether teachers used a range of teaching strategies, she could draw up a table of particular areas that she was interested in, say, the extent to which they use oral or written methods for communicating information to pupils. Although drawing up such a table to structure observations would be time-consuming, it would make it more likely that the observations she made would be worthwhile, since it is easy in the heat of lesson to become sidetracked by something interesting that happens which is not relevant to the focus of your observation. Structuring observations can help to prevent such distractions.

Consider, for example, someone who wanted to assess the ways in which children made use of resources in the library corner while they were engaged in a history project. He or she might develop a detailed observation schedule, that allowed an observer to record, not only how many books children consulted and for what purposes, but also how long they spent in the library corner, whether they replaced books accurately, whether they made notes or copied illustrations, and so on. By constructing a detailed schedule, the observer could structure not only what was recorded, but also the ways in which he or she looked and observed what was going on. This would be a useful and worthwhile thing to do. It could provide information that enabled the class teacher to decide what strategies for research had been successfully conveyed to pupils, and which he or she should give more time to in the future.

Maintaining records of work with pupils/students

One of the easiest ways in which you can develop a picture of a school is by maintaining records of the work completed with pupils. However, it is worth remembering that the usefulness of such records as a way of describing some of what goes on will depend upon their structure and nature of the record. We have already made clear our dismay that schools give credibility to tick lists – as if they can demonstrate anything in human terms about the effort that children make and about their achievements as learners, or about the problems that teachers have and their achievements as facilitators of learning. If you decide to make a record of work with children, we suggest that you try to find a more meaningful way of doing so.

One of us has always tried to persuade students in the workplace that it is worthwhile maintaining a small notebook in which, each week, they should aim to record one brief but informative sentence in relation to maths, language, science and one other curriculum area, e.g. history, for each child they teach. The sentence should tell either something that the child has achieved, or something that they want to give some individual attention to, or something with which the child has difficulty. In one way, this seems like a very small amount to record, but if you add it up, you can see that for a class of 28 children, it would involve writing almost 120 sentences per week and nearly 5,000 in a year. In spite of this, it is not only a useful strategy for developing a teacher's ability to remember where he or she is up to with each child in the class, but also a good way to develop a record of the work children have done, and the achievements they have made, and a useful tool for individual planning.

Descriptive and reflective diary keeping

Keeping a diary might not seem an obvious way of collecting information about an educational setting. After all, most often diaries are either a means for remembering what you have to do and when you have to do it, or personal accounts of what you have already done or thought, and experienced, and of where you have been. However, diaries can be both a relatively simple way of recording information and a way of helping you to reflect on your experiences. If Mahnoor made a diary in which on a daily basis she recorded what she saw and experienced in relation to the phenomena, the places, the events and the people that she was investigating, she could usefully think of it as a collection of recollected observations.

The entries she made in such a diary, just as much as live observations that she recorded on the spot, could provide her with important evidence, about many things, e.g. including children's understanding and the ways they participate in the educational process.

Research diaries can be either descriptive or reflective, depending on whether they merely record observations without any evaluation or analysis, or also include the attempt to reflect on and make sense of what is seen or heard or experienced, consciously relating it to earlier experience and knowledge and ways of understanding.

If she chose to use a diary-keeping approach to gathering information during her placement, Mahnoor could sit down at the end of the school day and record her recollections of what had gone on in school that day – what she had witnessed and what she had been involved in. As with observations and interviews, the diary entries could be open-ended and unstructured or semi-structured to address particular questions. For example, she could structure her recollections by deciding before she began what aspects of her experience in the school she would focus on, some details about her most significant interaction that day, say; or her interactions with one particular child or adult over a longer period of time, perhaps a whole week. This might affect what she did in the classroom, by predisposing her to note certain aspects of the interactions between pupils and between the pupils and their teachers. It would certainly focus her diary writing in a way that is similar to the focus that a predetermined observation schedule can give to observations.

Questionnaires

Questionnaires may seem to be an obvious tool to use in investigating educational settings. One reason for this is that we are so familiar with the written questionnaire, because we are forever being asked to complete them by organisations that are undertaking market research. Such questionnaires may contain questions of this kind:

- What newspapers do you read regularly?

- Which holiday destinations do you like best?

- What soap powder do you use and why?

- What do you think about Tony Blair and New Labour?

It is important that familiarity with questionnaires as a respondent does not allow you to think that they are an easy way of gaining information about educational settings, although they are a very good way of doing so. Indeed, in spite of their apparent simplicity, the use of questionnaires needs a great deal of care and planning.

For one thing, it is very important to think carefully about the questions that you ask. For example, you should consider carefully the wording. Questions should be clear and free from ambiguity and you should always check by trying them out on friends, or better still on a pilot group, whether they actually ask what you think you are asking. In addition, you should think carefully about the form of questions. For example, if she used a questionnaire in investigating her placement school, Mahnoor would first have to decide whether she should ask questions that invite what are known as 'free response' answers; questions such as: 'What do you think of the school's approach to bullying?' Questions of this kind are common in the first attempts that people make at constructing a questionnaire. They may be quite off-putting to respondents who are in two minds about whether they can be bothered to complete a questionnaire, which may to them seem like quite a chore, even when to you it seems like the most important thing in the world. The alternative to such questions is to offer respondents the opportunity to choose from a number of options the one that best describes their view. For example, if you wanted to access their views about how successful a school's approach to dealing with the problems of bullying had been, you might ask

Do you think the schools' approach to bullying has been:

Very successful?
Successful?
Neither successful nor unsuccessful?
Unsuccessful?
Counterproductive?
(Please circle your response)

Such a question demands less work from respondents, because they do not have to decide what to write down. However, it is important to notice that it also limits the answers that they give to the ones that are offered by the researcher.

Well-constructed questionnaires offer a convenient way of gathering information from large numbers of respondents in a form that is easy to analyse. However, it is often difficult to persuade people to fill them in. Therefore, in planning a questionnaire, it is always important to think carefully about how you can maximise your response rate (i.e. the number of people who fill it in). A number of things can help with this, including the way in which you arrange to collect completed questionnaires. We are not suggesting that you lock your respondents in a room until they have all handed in their completed question- naires – although this would be an ideal solution! A couple of common alternatives are to give respondents a stamped addressed envelope along with their questionnaires, or to ask them to post them anonymously in a sealed box in, placed, for example, outside the school office.

Finally, as with all other methods of gathering information, it is important to remember that if people think their answers are going to be openly shared with anyone and anybody, they are less likely to be honest. It is therefore always a good idea to assure them that in any use to which their answers are put, they will not be identified.

Interviews and narrative methods

One very good way to develop a general picture of an educational setting is to interview some members of its community. If Mahnoor decided to use interviews in harvesting infor- mation during her placement, it would obviously be crucial for her to target the head, along with a range of teachers. However, if she adopted this strategy to developing her knowledge and understanding, she should also remember to include some non-teaching staff, e.g. including teaching assistants, nursery nurses, caretakers, cooks and lunchtime organisers.

Schools function in many different ways and the view from different places within the organisation can be very different.

Interviews can take different forms, and are usually described as structured, semi-structured or unstructured/free, depending on the amount of freedom that the interviewer gives the interview in determining the content of the talk. The most highly structured interviews are really more like questionnaires that are administered by an interviewer, rather than being left up to the respondent to fill in at his or her leisure. The advantage of this kind of interview over a questionnaire is that face-to-face with a respondent, it is possible to ask further questions when they are hesitant or unsure, and to probe further into responses by asking for the reasons that lie behind them.

Although it is sometimes possible to undertake interviews without the use of a tape-recorder, this is only where the material in question is quite simple and where the interview is highly structured giving the interviewee little room for leeway, otherwise it is important to tape what people say. Of course, before doing so you ask their permission and let them know what you intend to do with their answers and who will have access to them. Most teachers, for example, are unlikely to be critical of school policy or their head, if they think that the governors or head will be made aware of what they have said in a way that identified them as having said it.

Narrative methods are really an extension of interviewing, although the focus is on giving respondents (the people to whom you speak) the opportunity to tell the stories that they want to tell, to share the things that are really important to them. Sometimes it will be possible to get people to share stories using a simple invitation, such as, 'Tell me about a really exciting, or challenging situation you have encountered recently in school.' Sometimes narratives will be easier to harvest if you give respondents the opportunity to tell their stories; for some people, however, it will be best to ask them to write their stories down. Sometimes using both approaches will be worthwhile.

Some people – usually they are people who want to pretend to be real researchers who know about science and that kind of thing – will deny that gathering the stories that people tell can actually tell you anything very much. Usually they do so because they believe that when people tell stories, it is difficult to believe them. Of course, it is always possible that a person might have elaborated or even invented a story that he or she told you about some experience in an educational setting. However, that does not make the story invalid as a source of evidence of views of education. In a similar way, a person could give a false answer to a questionnaire item, or put in a tick in a box, when not really justified in doing so, and this would not make the responses invalid as a source of evidence. Nonetheless, the fact that such deception can go on does point up the need to be careful when thinking about and analysing the evidence that you gather about schools and other educational settings.

Documentary analysis

As an approach to gaining knowledge and understanding, documentary analysis involves critical reading and reflection on relevant documents. In the case of an investigation of a school or other educational establishment, it will involve looking in some detail at, for example, prospectuses, policy statements and procedural guides, and at records of different kinds, including minutes of meetings, pupils' reports, incident books and records of school trips.

All schools produce policy documents and prospectuses in which they outline their aspirations, plans and intentions, and all are bound by other policies produced by the Local Educational Authorities (LEAs) or other bodies that control them. It is therefore important, in getting to know a school, to familiarise yourself with what the governors, the head and the other staff believe in and what they want for their pupils, and one way of doing this is to investigate such documents. However, it is as well to realise that at times such statements of policy can sound a bit grandiose, and that often they are rather vague. This means that it can be quite hard to know what they mean and thus to know what difference they make (or should make) to the ways in which schools operate.

For example, what do you think it means to say that, 'At Smithfield School we nurture our pupils as whole people, body, mind and spirit'? We might guess that it is intended to present in a very general way the benevolent (i.e. kindly) intentions of the governors and staff towards pupils and their recognition of the fact that pupils are complex and that like all human beings of whatever age, they have many needs. However, it is difficult to know precisely what this rather trite declaration means. More importantly, it is difficult to understand how such a generalised benevolent intention might be enacted, i.e. turned into things that people actually do in the school. That is why, alongside their policy statements, all schools will also have a number of procedural documents that outline the ways in which they carry their intentions and aspirations into action.

Perhaps we are being over-pessimistic and over-critical of Smithfield School. After all, every school and educational establishment has an over-arching value statement (sometimes referred to as its 'mission statement') with which it seeks to encapsulate its ethos. The important thing to notice is that we are suggesting that if you really want to know something about a school or other educational setting, simply reading policy statements is never enough. It is always necessary to look also at the way that policy is translated into working procedures, and at how statements of these procedures are played out in practice.

If you decide to try to develop understanding of a school or other educational setting by reading their policy statements and procedural guides, it is important always to read them with a set of key questions in mind. Such questions will depend on the particular focus of your investigation, but examples might be:

- How does the school approach reading development?
- How proactively does the school organise for the inclusion of children with special needs?
- What provision is made for children of faiths other than Christianity during school assemblies?
- How are the problems of bullying addressed?
- What arrangements are made for assessing and minimising risk on school trips?

Can You Be Sure that Evidence You Gather Is Reliable?

It is always best to try to use several sources of data or evidence, because this gives you the opportunity to check these against one another. When independently gathered evidence from several people overlaps, this lends strength to what they have to say. And when, in addition, evidence gathered using several contrasting methods overlaps, this adds strength. Imagine, for example, that you were critically analysing school documents when you discovered that it was a school policy proactively to discourage racial intolerance using a number of measures. The fact that this was a school policy that issued in practice would be supported if you found records in an incident book recording positive steps that had been taken to do so. If in interviewing and gathering stories you came across a number of versions of the same incidents that differed subtly but seemed to share common threads aimed at positively discouraging racial insults in the playground, this would help to support the school's claim to be a place where racial equality was fostered and intolerance was not tolerated. Finally, if in addition these stories came not only from teachers, but also from pupils and parents, you would be justified in having a strong sense that the school was living up to its claims in this area.

Data Is Only as Good as the Tools Used and the Investigator

All of the approaches to carrying out educational investigations that we have outlined above can be viewed as tools. Like all tools, they can be used skilfully, wisely and well, in which case, if the tools selected are appropriate to the task in hand, the information collected will be helpful in constructing a worthwhile story about that setting. On the other hand, each can be used badly, in which case, their usefulness in constructing worthwhile stories about the settings investigated is limited. Consider, for example, someone who decided to use a questionnaire to uncover parental views of work that is planned on the playground. In particular, he or she might be interested in finding out whether they approve of the plan to provide areas for quiet and imaginative play, as well as a five-a-side soccer pitch, somewhat smaller than it used to be. Imagine that the questionnaire included the following:

What do you like best about the changes?

Although it sounds relatively straightforward, this question is flawed because it assumes that the parents' views of the changes are generally positive (it is what is known as a 'leading' question).

Writing Stories about Educational Settings

So far, in this chapter, we have been talking about different ways in which investigating educational settings in a number of different ways can be investigated in order to inform what you write about those settings. We want now to talk briefly about how you might best approach the task of telling such stories in written form.

In our view, academic writing (including both the writing that is done by students and the writing that is done by professional academics like us) should be as simple as possible so that as many people as possible are able to understand what is written. Unfortunately, the style in which many academic authors actually write is often so difficult as to make it impossible for all but the most gymnastic and generous of thinkers to know what they are talking about. This is not really surprising, since many of the journals in which academics must publish if they are to achieve academic success seem to encourage them to write in a way that clouds rather than clarifies meaning. Many academics (in some disciplines, at least) seem to take a pride in making their work difficult to the point at which it seems almost devoid of meaning. They do so by using big words where small ones would do; lots of technical jargon where ordinary words would be just as good (or even better) and lots of references to what other people have written, even when they are not necessary. Unfortunately, many students, under the influence of the kind of stuff they are expected to read for their course try to emulate the work of the academics they read, making their own work more difficult than it need be, often to the point where it becomes literary and, sometimes literally, nonsense. Although before they reach university level, all students, including you, will have had to demonstrate some basic competence in reading, writing and reasoning, all need considerable help in developing these skills further (see Fairbairn and Winch 1996; Fairbairn and Fairbairn 2001).

There is an easy solution to the problems that we have suggested that most students have in writing, along with many and perhaps most professional academics. We want, in ending this chapter, to suggest that you should adopt it, not only when you are preparing reports about investigations into the educational settings that you work in and visit, but also in all of your academic work for your course. The solution to all of your problems as a novice academic author (and incidentally, to the problems faced by most professional authors in all disciplines) is to avoid unnecessary complication and difficulty by thinking of their academic writing in terms of storytelling.

Certain features of successful storytelling are found in the best academic writing, but are notably missing from the worst. For example, a good narrative writer engages the audience and holds their attention by making the plot and its introduction sufficiently interesting to seduce us into reading further, and by ensuring that the characters who inhabit the world he or she is creating are sufficiently believable to motivate us to pursue the narrative to find out what happens to them. Good academic writers do similar things.

All academics have stories to tell. Whatever form their research and scholarship takes – whether it is empirical, documentary or conceptual in nature – the stories they tell will usually involve sharing information about how they came to their conclusions; about their methods and hypotheses; about other writers and researchers whose work relates to their own. Of course, academics of different kinds not only have different areas of interest but different ways of telling their stories.

For example, whereas scientists and social scientists will often employ visual means such as graphs and statistical tables to show what they have found, others – including philosophers, theologians, lawyers and historians – will be more likely to use detailed examples and carefully constructed arguments. The stories you will tell and the stories that Mahnoor will tell about work you have carried out in investigating educational settings may include all of these. For example, it might be appropriate to communicate some information in the form of graphs or tables, say, if you had conducted a study of the ways in which children used the playground and wanted to present your findings about the numbers of children who engaged in different activities. On the other hand, if you wanted in your conclusions to persuade colleagues that it would be worth trying out a new approach to something, you would want to construct a painstaking argument in which you carefully described what you wanted to suggest and gave reasons and evidence to support your view.

If they are to be successful in telling their stories, academics, including novice academics like you, should weave together the various threads that comprise them in coherent, interesting and easily understandable ways, thus, making clear their relationship to the intellectual landscape that they inhabit, and avoiding as far as they can the use of a narrative style that obfuscates rather than communicates. As we have already said, we believe that they should make their tales as easy to understand as possible. They should tell them in ways that engage their audience and hold their attention, rather than expecting of readers that they will be willing to engage in intellectual gymnastics – contorting their minds and exerting themselves beyond comprehension, simply to work out what they are saying.

We invite you to think about the writing you do, about both investigations you carry out in relation to educational settings, and your other college work, as a form of storytelling. To write simply, easily and engagingly, with the intention of communicating with your readers, rather than of impressing them with how clever you are, with what big and complicated words you can use. If you accept our invitation, we think that you will find that your writing becomes more pleasurable, more easy and more successful.

Conclusion

The investigation of educational settings is a large topic and in this chapter we have been able to do little more than invite you to think a little about ways in which you might come to understand the settings in which you either work or undertake placements. In doing so we have not tried to tell you precisely what you should do in order to gather the kind of information that will help you to write better, more interesting and informative stories, because that would take a whole book in itself. Rather, we have tried to say something that will help you to think about what information might be useful, about how you might go about collecting it, and, finally, about how you might best communicate what you have found in ways that even people like us might understand.

Discussion Starters

1 Which of the methods of educational investigation described in this chapter do you think you would find most useful and why?
2 If you were asked to describe a school and what went on in it, what aspects do you think would be most important to focus on?

Reflecting on Practice

1 Keep a diary of everything you do in your workplace for a week. Write it at home in the evenings, and try to make it *purely descriptive*, avoiding analysing and evaluating what you did, why you did and whether or not you did it successfully. Share the story of your week with a colleague who works closely with you. Would his or her story of *your* week be the same?
2 Construct a questionnaire for children to find out what they think about school meals, making sure that none of the questions can be answered using a simple 'Yes' or 'No' and that none of them is unclear. Try it out on a few friends, asking them to imagine how they would answer it as a child.

Websites

www.bera.ac.uk/ – British Educational Research Association.
www.nfer.ac.uk/ – National Foundation for Educational Research, links to information, research reports and conference papers.
www.teachernet.gov.uk/research/ – links to various research reports and publications.

References

Fairbairn, G. (2000) 'Developing academic storytelling', *Education Today*, 50 (2) 32–8.
Fairbairn, G. and Fairbairn, S. (2001) *Reading at University: A Guide for Students*, Buckingham: Open University Press.
Fairbairn, G. and Winch, C. (1996) *Reading, Writing and Reasoning: A Guide for Students*, 2nd edn, Buckingham: Open University Press.

Index

More support for Classroom & Teaching Assistants...

A Handbook for Learning Support Assistants
Teachers and Assistants Working Together

SECOND EDITION

Glenys Fox

From a review of the first edition:
'... a very useful book both for general interest and as a basic reader for those taking further qualifications in the area of classroom support.'

Managing Schools Today

£14.00 • 104 A4 pages • 1-84312-081-X • 2003

Appointing and Managing Learning Support Assistants
A Practical Guide for SENCOs and other Managers

Jennie George and **Margaret Hunt**

Written specially for SENCOs and other managers, this book offers guidance on employing and managing LSAs and all those who support children in mainstream education (LSAs, TAs, SSAs or STAs).

£15.00 • 80 A4 pages • 1-84312-062-3 • 2003

The Essential Guide for Competent Teaching Assistants
Meeting the National Occupational Standards at Level 2

Anne Watkinson

This book is related to the National Occupational Standards at Level 2 for teaching assistants (TAs) and provides the underpinning knowledge for study at a basic level. It can be used to support NVQs or other TA awards, or simply to improve good practice.

£14.00 • 160 A4 pages • 1-84312-008-9 • 2003

The Essential Guide for Experienced Teaching Assistants
Meeting the National Occupational Standards at Level 3

Anne Watkinson

This book provides the underpinning knowledge to support teaching assistants in all phases of schooling when undertaking study at an advanced level.

£15.00 • 224 A4 pages • 1-84312-009-7 • 2003

Supporting Children's Learning in the Early Years
Edited by **Linda Miller** and **Jane Devereux**

PUBLISHED IN ASSOCIATION WITH THE OPEN UNIVERSITY

This book will help you to expand your knowledge and practical skills in the light of recent initiatives.

£15.00 • 256 pages • 1-85346-976-9 • 2003

Working with Children in the Early Years
Edited by **Jane Devereux** and **Linda Miller**

PUBLISHED IN ASSOCIATION WITH THE OPEN UNIVERSITY

By offering practitioners working in a variety of early years settings the opportunity to develop their knowledge, understanding and skills for working with young children, this book builds on the increased government interest in and support for early years provision.

£17.00 • 240 pages • 1-85346-975-0 • November 2002

Understanding Children's Learning
A Text for Teaching Assistants

Edited by **Claire Alfrey**

"A fascinating and essential read for all those employed to support children's learning. At last - in one easy to read yet challenging book - a goldmine of insights into why and how children learn. I am delighted to recommend this book."

Trevor Matthews,
Assistant Director of Education, Newham LEA

£17.00 • 216 pages • 1-84312-069-0 • 2003

Successful Study
Skills for Teaching Assistants

Christine Ritchie and **Paul Thomas**

Specifically written with for teaching / classroom assistants undertaking the foundation degree, this book clearly explains what is expected from study in Higher Education.

Assuming no previous study experience, the easy-to-use approach of this text will be help teaching assistants returning to formal academic training.

£12.99 • 100 pages • 1-84312-106-9 • April 2004

Order today on 020 8996 3610
www.fultonpublishers.co.uk